THE FAILURES OF ETHICS

D1602593

The Failures
of Ethics

*Confronting the Holocaust, Genocide,
and Other Mass Atrocities*

JOHN K. ROTH

OXFORD
UNIVERSITY PRESS

OXFORD
UNIVERSITY PRESS

Great Clarendon Street, Oxford, OX2 6DP,
United Kingdom

Oxford University Press is a department of the University of Oxford.
It furthers the University's objective of excellence in research, scholarship,
and education by publishing worldwide. Oxford is a registered trade mark of
Oxford University Press in the UK and in certain other countries

Published in the United States of America by Oxford University Press
198 Madison Avenue, New York, NY 10016, United States of America

British Library Cataloguing in Publication Data

Data available

Library of Congress Control Number: 2014956629

ISBN 978-0-19-872533-6

Printed and bound by
CPI Group (UK) Ltd, Croydon, CR0 4YY

To

Lyn
Andy and Liz
Sarah, Erik, and Keeley

Love never ends.
—1 Corinthians 13:8

Contents

There you stand in the field
one with all the others
frail tottering headless at a loss

though still with work to be done
to clear away or turn under
mow rake and burn off this failure
if there is to be another crop

—Paul Hunter, "This Failure"

Prologue

The Thread

People wonder about what you are pursuing.

—William Stafford, "The Way It Is"

A few weeks before dying in 1993, the American poet William Stafford recollected a life's work in "The Way It Is," a poem that tracks "a thread you follow." People may "wonder about what you are pursuing," and so, Stafford said, explanation about the thread is important. It is also imperative, he insisted, not to abandon the thread, especially when catastrophes strike and lives are maimed and lost.[1]

Confronting the Holocaust, genocide, and other mass atrocities for more than forty years, I gradually discerned that I have been following a thread that weaves its way through failure. Inescapable and pervasive, failure riddles existence. Following that thread particularly compels me to contend with the failures of ethics. Exposing fault lines in nature and flaws in reality itself, those failures abound in the multiple shortfalls and shortcomings of thought, character, decision, and action that tempt us human beings to betray what is good, right, virtuous, and just, and incite us to inflict incalculable harm.[2] The chapters that follow do not rationalize, let alone justify, such failure. Instead, they support the resistance expressed in the book's governing epigraph: "There you stand in the field / one with all the others / frail tottering headless at a loss / though still with work to be done / to clear away or turn under / mow rake and burn off this failure / if there is to be another crop."[3]

The outlook in Paul Hunter's poem "This Failure" is amplified in "For the Miracle," whose tone voices other moods that thread through these pages.[4] This time Hunter envisions not a barren field but a cluttered workshop. The partners of its grease-stained bench and well-worn but ever-ready vice jaws are old coffee cans filled with assorted nails and screws, mixed bolts and nuts, waiting to be of use. On the floor are broken, shopworn things, odd parts of this and that, stuff in the way that got consigned to this place by someone, sometime, for who knows what. Hunter sees these elements—maybe trash, good for nothing, to some—as basic elements waiting for the caring, imaginative, creative, and even joyful touch that could beneficially salvage and reconfigure them.

My reading of Hunter emphasizes that what is fragmented, what has been ripped apart, let go, broken, heaved, tossed aside, disrespected, and dumped may sometimes have new life and be of use again. But this repairer-of-brokenness should not be misunderstood. Not everything can be fixed and made whole again. Hunter evokes "the muck of history," the sadness, melancholy, and grief that swirl through it.[5] Nevertheless, he advocates doing the best one can to defy the odds that would wear the world out. More than that, he encourages what I call an in-spite-of joy, the deep-down sense of significance and meaning—happiness even—found when what we do protects, preserves, and enhances precious human life. Such action requires protest and resistance; it embraces the contradiction of holding together persistent melancholy and tenacious hope—the latter understood as what the Israeli writer David Grossman calls "the hope of nevertheless," which "does not disregard the many dangers and obstacles, but refuses to see only them and nothing else."[6] Asserted and reasserted in what follows, those qualities are necessities for combating the failures of ethics. They have authoritative standing because the British philosopher G. J. Warnock was right when he said: "That it is a bad thing to be tortured or starved, humiliated or hurt, is not an opinion; it is a fact. That it is better for people to be loved and attended to, rather than hated or neglected, is again a plain fact, not a matter of opinion."[7] No one, Warnock added, should be permitted to bully that truth away. In our lethal world, however, such bullying and worse abound.

Honest ethical efforts to protest and resist those conditions take place on the scarred planks of life's workbenches, and a premium belongs on candid appraisal of the human predicament. That appraisal, which cannot be sound unless it tackles the failures of ethics, must not be general or abstract but needs to bear down with lucidity on historical particularities. Recognizing that life often puts people in dilemmas that involve competing goods, unnerving ambiguities, radical evils, and impossible but inescapable choices, this book explores how ethics in its brokenness may be mended and, at least to that extent, renewed and celebrated.

William Stafford's thread especially connects with mine because he explored decision points where often no option is very good, but where we have to take a stand. In "Traveling through the Dark," arguably his best-known poem, Stafford drew on an episode in his own experience to probe that dilemma and the responsibilities it confers. As he made his way home one night in Oregon, Stafford came across a deer struck to death by a preceding car on the narrow Wilson River road. Realizing the danger that other drivers might encounter, Stafford stopped and dragged the deer to the side, seeing as he did so that her fawn, still alive, was waiting to be born. Stafford hesitated, "thought hard" and then pushed the pregnant doe into the river.[8] Stafford does not say what went through his mind while he hesitated and "thought hard," but it seems unlikely that his thinking turned to salvation for the fawn. He was too realistic for that. More likely, Stafford felt things should not be as they were, but this time—too much of the time—that is how they unfolded. The decision that Stafford made, steeped in regret, sadness, and irony, continued to haunt him, for the poem—it came to him some time after the actual episode—was for the sake of life-saving.

Stafford said that the signals we give should be clear because "the darkness around us is deep."[9] In explorations that concentrate on the Holocaust, genocide, and crimes against humanity that so devastatingly deepen the darkness, the following argument threads its way through this book: Defined by the intention to encourage human action that fits sound understanding about what is *right* and *wrong*, *just* and *unjust*, *good* and *evil*, *virtuous* and *corrupt*, ethics arguably is civilization's keystone.[10] Absent the overriding of moral sensibilities, if not the collapse or collaboration of ethical traditions, the Holocaust, genocide, and other mass atrocities could not take place. Although these catastrophes do not pronounce the death of ethics, they show that ethics is vulnerable, subject to misuse and perversion, and that no simple reaffirmation of ethics, as if nothing disastrous had happened, will do.

Senses of moral and religious authority have been fragmented and weakened by the accumulated ruins of history and the depersonalized advances of civilization that have taken us from a bloody twentieth century into an immensely problematic twenty-first. What, nevertheless, remain essential are spirited commitment and political will that embody the courage not to let go of the ethical but to persist for it *in spite of* humankind's self-inflicted destructiveness. Salvaging the fragmented condition of ethics requires bold summoning of the question, "Are we doing the best we can?" and gutsy backing for every resource that can be found, including: appeals to human rights, calls for renewed religious sensitivity, deepened attention to the dead and to death itself, and especially respect and honor for people who save lives and resist atrocity. *The Failures of Ethics* is grounded in questions raised to keep us awake, tempered by spirits of resistance against despair, and steeped in commitments to mend and repair so that what is broken can yet be of good use. Human existence may turn out to be little more than a fleeting episode in the cosmic scheme of things, but meaning, purpose, and joy remain to be found in combating the failures of ethics. Do we know that efforts in this direction will work? Of course not, but it is vital to try. The thread this book follows never lets go of that conviction.

My writing neared completion during the summer of 2014, a century after World War I began. During that time, my evening reading included John Keegan's history of the Great War. A colossal failure of ethics, that so-called war to end all wars left staggering military losses in its wake: 8.5 million dead, 21 million wounded, 7.7 million "missing"—many of them blown to bits beyond identification by unrelenting artillery fire—or in prisoner of war status. "All that was worst in the century which the First World War had opened," adds Keegan, "had its origins in the chaos it left behind."[11] Pondering that truth, I also recalled the disillusioning observation made by Sigmund Freud in 1915, while the Great War raged but had yet to worsen its dismal losses. "In reality," he said, "our fellow-citizens have not sunk so low as we feared, because they had never risen so high as we believed."[12]

I thought of Freud and studied Keegan by headlamp because near my home in the small town of Winthrop, Washington, lightning strikes on July 14, 2014, ignited wildfire that grew into the largest in the state's recorded history. Its perimeter 200 miles around, the firestorm scorched 390 square miles in the beautiful Methow Valley, left hundreds homeless, and charred 300 miles' worth of transmission lines. Thousands had no electricity for days. The fire was too close for comfort, but my wife and I did not have to evacuate, and our home was not harmed. Many others were less fortunate. The magnitude of what happened in the Methow Valley pales in comparison with what took place in Europe a century ago. But I mention the Carlton Complex Fire, as the gigantic convergence of multiple wildfires came to be called, because it confirmed that human beings can rise higher and be better than we are when the failures of ethics define us. The firestorm brought salvaging help from near and far. Local people shared food, lodging, money, and resources of all kinds with their neighbors. More than three thousand strong in all, firefighters from across the United States—Alaska to Maine and California—joined those from Washington to battle the flames. Lives and homes were saved because people acted ethically in the deepest and most caring ways. The successes as well as the failures of ethics are real. Those achievements can and must grow; they show that the failures of ethics can be curbed, even if not eliminated. Intensified in the fire's darkness, that conviction enlightens what follows.

Part I

Protesting Failures

If ethics is to be a safeguard against its own failures, then people who try to be ethical have to acknowledge the failures, own them when they should, and protest against them. We have to be accountable and take responsibility for the shortcomings that are ours. Among the most discouraging and disheartening failures of ethics are those that have conspired to unleash the Holocaust, genocide, and other mass atrocities. Those failures are widespread because they exist in indifference, silence, bystanding, and complicity as well as in willful perpetration of such carnage.

Acknowledging the failures of ethics as genuine failures and owning our fair share of those failures is a first and necessary step for protesting them, because that accountability reminds and alerts us to the fact that *what is* and *what ought to be* are not identical and very often are profoundly at odds. Protest against the failures of ethics emerges in varied ways, but importantly it grows from within the failures themselves. As the chapters in Part I indicate, the Holocaust, genocide, and other mass atrocities signify immense ethical failure of cosmic proportions, but study of those catastrophes also shows that the Holocaust did not have to happen, nor did any other genocide or mass atrocity crime. Racism, sexual violence, torture, and mass murder continue to ruin human flourishing, but they can spur—often through the voices of their targets, the living and the dead—renewed opposition to such crimes against humanity. Mass atrocities often implicate religion, and certainly they do little to bolster faith, but within the shards of that brokenness are fragments that can be salvaged in ways that provoke needed responses to the failures of ethics.

Lore about the legendary Jewish philosopher Sidney Morgenbesser, who taught for half a century at Columbia University before he died in 2004, includes his pithy distinction between Jewish ethics and the Christian ethics of the German philosopher Immanuel Kant. For Kant, said Morgenbesser, *ought* implies *can*, but in Jewish ethics, *can* implies *don't*.[1] Morgenbesser knew his distinction was oversimplified, but its crisp humor made a necessary point. Good responses to the failures of ethics require both of those outlooks. What ought to be can be enacted, at least to a greater extent that has often been the case. But Morgenbesser saw something equally telling when he underscored that very often human beings should not, must not, do what we can do. We can be indifferent, we can stand by or be complicit while human harm wreaks havoc. We can even perpetrate mass atrocities. But in such cases, *can* must imply *don't*. The chapters ahead argue that saying so and acting that way are key aspects of protesting the failures of ethics.

In 1966, I completed my doctoral dissertation in philosophy at Yale University. It focused on the American philosopher William James. His lifelong conviction held that "philosophical study means the habit of always seeing an alternative, of not taking the usual for granted, of making conventionalities fluid again, of imagining foreign states of mind."[1] I share that outlook; it informs this book.

My dissertation explored James's moral philosophy. Ever since, my work has explored ethical questions: How should I understand ideas such as right and wrong, justice and injustice, good and evil? Why do we human beings—so often, so gravely—intend and unleash harm? What most needs to change, and how could such transformation take place, for individuals and institutions to waste life less and respect each other more? Are we doing the best we can?

In the mid-1960s, although the concept of genocide was relatively new to me, I knew that the Holocaust had happened and that the world had long been full of mass atrocities. My attention, however, did not yet center on those realities. Likewise, although I saw that a huge gap yawned between the way things are and the way they ought to be, my probing had not fully zeroed in on the failures of ethics.

During the 2007–8 academic year, I was the Robert and Carolyn Frederick Distinguished Visiting Professor of Ethics at DePauw University in Greencastle, Indiana. During that year, DePauw opened The Prindle Institute for Ethics. For two years before its opening, I consulted with the University about the development of this institute, which is housed in a magnificent facility generously endowed by alumna Janet Prindle and dedicated to inquiry and discourse about critical issues of our time. To advance that mission, the Institute convened its first annual Undergraduate Ethics Symposium, which brings competitively chosen students to DePauw for intensive work on ethical problems. On April 3, 2008, I delivered the keynote address for that first symposium. The topic I chose and publicly tackled for the first time was "The Failures of Ethics." Now explicit after long weaving its way through my teaching and writing, that thread governs my awareness and takes me where it leads.

1

The Failures of Ethics

Why does this history continue to haunt us . . . ?
—Wendy Lower, *Hitler's Furies*

No obstruction stopped the German machine of destruction.
No moral problem proved insurmountable. . . . The old moral
order did not break through anywhere along the line. This is a
phenomenon of the greatest magnitude.
—Raul Hilberg, *The Destruction of the European Jews*

During the summer of 1992, the historian Wendy Lower traveled to
Ukraine to do archival research. Some of the documents she studied
contained "the names of young German women who were active in
the region as Hitler's empire-builders."[2] That discovery put Lower on
the twenty-year path that led to her deservedly praised *Hitler's Furies:
German Women in the Nazi Killing Fields*, which appeared in 2013.
During that same summer of 1992, I tried to find a publisher for a
book that I was completing with Carol Rittner. Failures seemed to
prevail as rejections accumulated—not because of the book's quality,
the various editors kept saying, but because they doubted there would
be a market for its topic: "women and the Holocaust." Rittner and
I eventually found a publisher, and the book helped to break taboos
about the subject.[3]

Decades later, it is hard to imagine the indifferent and at times
hostile responses that once were commonplace about gender-focused
research on the Holocaust. Lower and *Hitler's Furies* ensure that
confrontations with the Holocaust, genocide, and other mass atrocities *must* have a focus of that kind. That focus, however, raises
difficulties, as Lower acknowledges toward the end of her book
when she wonders why the history of the Holocaust and, in particular, the history of German women in the Nazi killing fields "continue

to haunt us," as they surely do.[4] My contention is that a key reason
why those histories haunt us—indeed why they *must*—has much to
do with the failures of ethics.

THE PROCESS OF BYSTANDING

A three-term taxonomy—perpetrator, victim, bystander—has long
dominated studies of the Holocaust, genocide, and other mass atrocities. In such contexts, those terms are not separable, static, or purely
descriptive. The intentions and actions of perpetrators entail victims,
and victims do not exist without perpetrators. The power of perpetrators and the vulnerability of victims also depend on bystanders.
Importantly, a person is not by nature—born or preordained—to be
one or the other. A person *becomes* a perpetrator, a victim, or a
bystander. Both social circumstances and individual decisions are
parts of that process. In addition, the tone of this three-term taxonomy
is ethical. No person ought to be a perpetrator, a victim, or a bystander
when the intentions and actions of perpetrators victimize others. In
short, it is not good to be a perpetrator, victim, or bystander.

Lower's perpetrator-oriented research shows that while genocide is
committed primarily by men, "genocide is also women's business."[5] If
the German women who became killers in the East numbered "only"
a few thousand, the evidence, says Lower, shows that "at least half a
million women witnessed and contributed to the operations and
terror of a genocidal war in the eastern territories."[6] Driven by
motivations that included ambition and opportunism, patriotism
and a sense of duty, most of these women were not fully fledged
perpetrators of mass murder, but their complicity and partnership
seem to exceed what the bystander category can contain. Of the three
terms—perpetrator, victim, bystander—the last one is the least helpful, partly because it has to cover such a multitude of people and
because it suggests passivity.[7] It is not, however, a category to be
dismissed, at least not completely, for there were women and men in
the Third Reich and even in the Nazi killing fields who can be placed
in what Victoria Barnett calls the far-reaching and complex *process of
bystanding*.[8] That process includes the reality that at key moments, as
Raul Hilberg said, "every individual makes decisions, and . . . every
decision is individual."[9]

A photograph in the extensive collection at the United States Holocaust Memorial Museum illustrates such points by providing a glimpse of what happened in Graz, Austria, on the night of November 9–10, 1938, which is euphemistically known as *Kristallnacht*.[10] Authorized and incited by Nazi leaders when a minor German official died after an assassination attempt by a young Jew named Herschel Grynszpan, the antisemitic riots of *Kristallnacht* (crystal night) targeted Jewish communities throughout Germany and Austria. Sometimes these November pogroms are referred to as the "Night of Broken Glass" because the wreckage included so many smashed windows that the replacement value reached more than $2 million in the cash equivalent at the time. The onslaught, however, was far more devastating than that. A great many Germans, their religious heritage and identity overwhelmingly Christian, were involved and implicated in the widespread carnage. While their friends and neighbors watched, the perpetrators looted and wrecked Jewish homes and businesses, torched hundreds of synagogues while intentionally inactive fire brigades stood by, desecrated cemeteries, killed scores of Jews, and terrorized virtually every Jew in the Third Reich. In the aftermath, some thirty thousand Jewish men were arrested and sent to concentration camps at Dachau, Buchenwald, and Sachsenhausen. The November pogroms of 1938 showed that no Jew could ever expect to live a normal life in Nazi Germany.

Taken during *Kristallnacht*, the Graz photograph depicts local residents watching the burning of the ceremonial hall at the Jewish cemetery in that city. Their backs to the camera, onlookers (men and women; some younger, some older, and probably most of them at least nominally Christian) gazed at the consuming fire. The photographer also saw what happened, but more actively as his or her camera captured the moment and made it motionless. The Graz photo contains no evidence of firefighting or firefighters. Apparently, the ceremonial hall in that Jewish cemetery in Graz was allowed to burn. Nor does the picture identify the onlookers; it tells nothing about what they were doing before they arrived at the scene or what they did after they left it. Although active at the site, the photographer also remains anonymous; the picture says nothing about other photographs he or she went on to take. Nevertheless, despite its anonymity, this photo is part of what Karl Schleunes aptly called "the twisted road to Auschwitz."[11] It has counterparts in the many other genocidal situations that have scarred the earth before, during, and after

Kristallnacht and the Holocaust. Those related photos vary in their focus and detail but all of them would likely capture aspects of what Alexis Herr calls silent witnessing, acquiescent following, and compensated complicity.[12]

The devil, of course, is in the details. As both the Graz photograph and Wendy Lower's book suggest, categories such as *perpetrator*, *victim*, and *bystander* have to be disaggregated and particularized to avoid abstraction. Reflecting on the *bystander* category in regard to the Holocaust, the historian Omer Bartov outlines the magnitude of that problem:

> The majority of the estimated 300 million people under German rule during the Holocaust were neither victims of the camps nor perpetrators. They were bystanders of various degrees and types. Some belonged to Greater Germany, and their kin were either fighting for Hitler or running his camps. Others belonged to Germany's allies, and more likely than not were more supportive of the partnership with the Third Reich in the early phases of the war than toward the end. Others still belonged to the occupied nations, and stood a good chance of becoming victims themselves, especially if they resisted Nazi policies or tried to protect those slated for extermination. But by and large, those who did not carry out genocide and related atrocities, and those who were not subjected to these policies, namely, the vast majority of German-occupied Europe's population, mostly watched in silence or did their best not to see at all.[13]

Paragraphs akin to Bartov's could be written about the Armenian genocide and post-Holocaust genocides in Cambodia, the former Yugoslavia, Rwanda, and Darfur, to mention only a few examples. Bartov's summary, however, does a better job of sketching the magnitude of the bystander phenomenon than it does of describing bystander behavior, at least in the shorthand his paragraph employs. Following Victoria Barnett's lead, one should question whether it is accurate, let alone sufficient, to say that bystanders to the Holocaust and other genocides have "mostly watched in silence or did their best not to see at all." Nor do I think that Bartov gets it entirely right when he says that "genocide cannot take place without a majority of passive bystanders."[14] True, genocide cannot take place without a majority who do not interfere with the hardliners who gain power and use it to target their perceived opposition, but what that "going along" entails is not so much passivity as action that trends in some directions rather than others. For the most part, we human beings are agents and actors; we are *protagonists*. Our decisions may make us stand by; our actions may keep us quiet, out of sight, and averse to difficulty, but action is involved nonetheless. Sometimes we feel the tug of moral responsibility—I should do *this* or I must do *that*—but *I can't* is the response.[15] *Can't*, however, is scarcely passive. Absent the action it entails, *can't* could never have its often decisive significance. As protagonists, we may not be leaders, but even getting along by going along still requires activity, not passivity, at least not primarily.

As used in reflection about the Holocaust, genocide, and other mass atrocities, the bystander category is infused with ethical content. In addition, it embraces a heterogeneous mix, for it can include nations and institutions as well as individuals and groups of people. Importantly, moreover, bystanding is not a static condition but a changeable one that leads *here* or *there* in a spectrum that ranges from becoming a perpetrator to becoming a victim. No single size fits all bystanders, but conditions for inclusion in that category involve knowledge and agency.[16] In particular, the knowing encompasses awareness—sometimes specific, sometimes more general—that people are inflicting or suffering harm, that their lives are threatening or threatened, that they are killing or being killed. The agency entailed by bystanding involves ability to act and intervene in ways, small or large, that could curb the harm and relieve the suffering, contest the threats, or resist the taking of life. Some bystanders seize the benevolent opportunities that their knowledge and agency create, but most do not, and the result is that wrongs multiply and rights diminish. Those who obscure, avoid, or deny the helping and resisting opportunities that their knowledge and agency create only seem, however, to be passive or inactive. For reasons that range from timidity or opportunism, caution or fear, to neutrality, indifference, and resignation—"this problem is not mine and, besides, nothing I can do will make any difference"—bystanders still make decisions and act in particular ways. Unfortunately, their decisions and actions usually do more harm than good, often aiding and abetting the perpetrators of genocide and other mass atrocities.

Not only during the Holocaust but also in other cases of genocide and mass atrocity, the process of bystanding is social and political as well as fluid. Sometimes it turns onlookers into resisters and rescuers, but more often it leads to indirect participation in atrocity through compliance and everyday silence or to direct involvement and culpability as partners, collaborators, accomplices, and perpetrators in a process of destruction. The motivations that take the process of bystanding in those directions typically include job and family responsibilities, professional duties, power aspirations, career objectives, patriotic convictions, peer pressure, greed, jealousy, and revenge. Keeping attention focused for now on persons rather than on nations or institutions, the women studied by Lower were not destined to be accomplices in crimes against humanity, let alone hardliners who harbored and enacted genocidal intentions. They are more accurately described as participants in a process that led them—not by coercion but willingly—to increasingly active roles in the Nazi killing fields. Onlookers before they made choices that led to complicity and collaboration in the Holocaust, they experienced their Holocaust-related circumstances and opportunities in various ways, at different times, and in diverse contexts. Those perspectives informed their decisions and actions, which were individual, as Hilberg emphasizes, but also influenced by friends and families, acquaintances and neighbors, teachers and lovers, co-workers and superiors, political and religious leaders, and by social factors that ranged from economic prospects and national interests to patriotic impulses and partisan ideologies, the latter steeped in antisemitism and racism. Such developments shed light on ethics.

SHEDDING LIGHT ON ETHICS

At its best, ethics emphasizes careful deliberation about the difference between right and wrong, encouragement not to be indifferent toward that difference, cultivation of virtuous character, and action that defends what is right and resists what is wrong. Noting that context and content, observe that Lower's book describes Johanna Altvater as coming from a working-class background and volunteering to serve the German occupation in Ukraine, where she participated in the murder of Jews, including children. Vera Wohlauf, a socialite from Hamburg, married an SS captain, accompanied him to Poland, inflicted cruelties on Jews, and witnessed massacres unleashed against them. Also the spouse of an SS officer, Erna Petri helped to manage an agricultural estate in occupied Ukraine, entertained German perpetrators of genocide, and, on one occasion, contributed to the Holocaust by murdering six starving Jewish children.

What needed to be different to keep women such as Altvater, Wohlauf, and Petri from sustaining the Nazi killing fields?

An adequate answer to that question is as elusive as it is complex, but part of it would have to include not only reflection about bystanding and onlooking and the complicity and collaboration they encourage but also thoughtfulness about the failures of ethics. So, what can be done about those shortfalls and shortcomings? It is too late for Altvater, Wohlauf, and Petri, but what about us? How can we do better at being "upstanders," to use Samantha Power's term? How can we better use our ability to respond in a world besieged by mass atrocities?[17] No one, at least not single-handedly, can stop genocide in its tracks. We may have scant success in preventing mass atrocity crimes. But most of us have some influence, power, and leverage. How might the leverage we possess best be brought to bear on the scourge and aftereffects of crimes against humanity?

When I say *we* or *us* in this book, as in the questions above, I am mindful that life-span variations such as age, health, education, job, and domestic and economic circumstance as well as social, cultural, and political factors—ethnicity, gender, and nationality, for example—affect people's inclinations and abilities to protest and resist crimes against humanity. As far as *we* and *us* are concerned, one size does not fit all when it comes to moral responsibilities and capacities for ethical action. But in confronting the threats and realities of mass atrocities, those relativities and qualifications do not excuse us, at least not completely. The philosopher Albert Camus was right when he held that human beings are not entirely to blame because we did not start history. But, he emphasized, human beings are by no means innocent, because we continue history.[18] No longer can we plead ignorance—"I didn't know what was happening"—as a justification for inaction. Media reports about mass atrocities are too frequent, widespread, and detailed for that rationalization to be credible. As we continue history, whose terrain is drenched in the bloodshed of mass atrocity crimes, we still need to do—within the limitations and possibilities that are ours—what we can to protest and resist crimes against humanity. Indeed, we need to do as much as we can for as long as we can.

Ethics is supposed to guide and inspire us to respond well to such challenges. Considerations of that kind led to observations made by the scholar-journalist Gitta Sereny in her 1974 classic about the Holocaust called *Into that Darkness: An Examination of Conscience.* In 1971, Sereny had the opportunity to interview not a bystander but one of the key perpetrators of the Holocaust, Franz Stangl, who had the dubious distinction of being the commandant of Sobibor and Treblinka, two of the Holocaust's most grisly killing centers. He had been tried and sentenced to life imprisonment by a West German court. In the preface to her book, which is based on the seventy hours of interviews she conducted with Stangl, Sereny took stock of what she had discovered, hoping that her encounters with him might reveal, as she put it, "some new truth which would contribute to the understanding of things that had never yet been understood."[19]

As Sereny probed her findings, she drew the following conclusions, which pertain not only to perpetrators of mass atrocity crimes but also to bystanders and onlookers and to the failures of ethics. Individuals, Sereny emphasized, remain responsible for their action and its consequences, but persons are, and must be, responsible for each other too. What we do as individuals, she underscored, reflects what she called "the fatal interdependence of all human actions."[20] Sereny ended her book as follows:

> Social morality is contingent upon the individual's capacity to make responsible decisions, to make the fundamental choice between right and wrong; this capacity derives from this mysterious core—the very essence of the human person.
>
> This essence, however, cannot come into being or exist in a vacuum. It is deeply vulnerable and profoundly dependent on a climate of life; on freedom in the deepest sense: not license, but freedom to grow: within family, within community, within nations, and within human society as a whole. The fact of its existence therefore—the very fact of our existence as valid individuals—is evidence of our interdependence and of our responsibility for each other.[21]

Our responsibility for each other: ethics succeeds or fails, lives or dies in that neighborhood. So, keeping in mind Sereny's points about "the fatal interdependence of all human actions" and "our responsibility for each other," consider that ethics has had good days and bad.

GOOD DAYS AND BAD

After World War II and the Holocaust, good days for ethics occurred on December 9 and 10, 1948, when the General Assembly of the United Nations adopted the Convention on the Prevention and

Punishment of the Crime of Genocide and the Universal Declaration of Human Rights. The Convention criminalized specific "acts committed with intent to destroy, in whole or in part, a national, ethnical, racial or religious group, as such," which the contracting parties would "undertake to prevent and punish." Proclaiming that "recognition of the inherent dignity and of the equal and inalienable rights of all members of the human family is the foundation of freedom, justice and peace in the world," the Declaration aimed to become a standard for all peoples and nations, securing "universal and effective" respect for "the right to life, liberty and security of person" and rejection of slavery, torture, and other forms of "cruel, inhuman or degrading treatment or punishment."[22] Two good days for ethics in December 1948 called for more of the same, but as far as the Holocaust is concerned, such days—during and after that disaster—have been too few and far between.

Notwithstanding the UN Declaration, the Holocaust had ruptured the notion of universal human rights as the Third Reich's genocidal policies trapped Jews and other victim groups in one "choiceless choice" and lethal dilemma after another.[23] Jean Améry, a Jewish philosopher who endured Nazi torture and survived Auschwitz before eventually taking his own life, experienced and reflected on that breach. The gravest loss produced by the Holocaust, he suggested, was that it destroyed "trust in the world . . . the certainty that by reason of written or unwritten social contracts the other person will spare me—more precisely stated, that he will respect my physical, and with it also my metaphysical, being."[24] Much as he yearned for the right to live, which he equated with dignity itself, Améry found that "it is certainly true that dignity can be bestowed only by society, whether it be the dignity of some office, a professional or, very generally speaking, civil dignity; and the merely individual, subjective claim ('I am a human being and as such I have my dignity, no matter what you may do or say!') is an empty academic game, or madness."[25] Each morning Améry saw the Auschwitz number on his arm, making it impossible to "feel at home in the world" and convincing him that "declarations of human rights, democratic constitutions, the free world and the free press, nothing can again lull me into the slumber of security from which I awoke in 1935."[26] Améry's philosophy is not necessarily a postmortem for human rights, but its assessment tests every affirmation of them.

As the Holocaust unfolded, the most fundamental moral imperative of all—the biblical commandment, "You shall not murder"—was overridden and eclipsed by a "Nazi ethic" whose antisemitic and racist sense of progress depicted the destruction of Jewish life and other "inferior" groups as morally right and good and as a duty that must be fulfilled.[27] While shooting squadrons and gas chambers took their toll, ethical traditions that urged people to aid those in need and to resist injustice proved insufficient to interrupt the power of peer pressure among the German rank and file, inadequate to disrupt the business interests of German corporations that utilized slave labor, and not enough to check the ways of onlookers and opportunists.

After the Holocaust, postwar trials convicted and punished some of the major perpetrators, but justice was scarcely served by the proceedings and the commuted sentences that freed the guilty. Moreover, Wendy Lower points out that barely any of the women she studied were brought to justice. "What happened to them?" she asks. "The short answer is that most got away with murder."[28] Numerous Holocaust perpetrators found safe havens around the world. In the United States, the CIA and FBI enlisted some of them to serve as intelligence agents.[29] As the twentieth century closed, belated efforts to restitute property looted and stolen during the Holocaust were accompanied by initiatives to expand reparations for the survivors of Nazi slave labor and concentration camps. Legal and political wrangling and arguments about property rights, payment distributions, and lawyers' fees left this post-Holocaust chapter bereft of satisfying closure. Meanwhile, Holocaust museums, memorials, and education programs—worthy initiatives all—had proliferated, but the "lessons of the Holocaust" could not prevent a resurgence of antisemitism and Holocaust denial. Nor were such efforts able to forestall mass atrocities—including ethnic and religious cleansing, sexual assault, and genocide—in the Balkans, Rwanda, and Darfur. More recent additions to the dismal list include mayhem in the Central African Republic, genocidal conflict in South Sudan, and assaults by the so-called Islamic State of Iraq and Greater Syria (ISIS) against Christians and Yazidis. Crimes against humanity rampant in them all, these disasters mock the slogan "Never again!"

WRONG—OR NOTHING COULD BE

Nevertheless, a widely shared conviction persists that the Holocaust was *wrong* or nothing could be. An onslaught not only against Jewish life but also against goodness itself, the Holocaust should not have happened, and nothing akin to it should ever happen again. Michael Berenbaum echoes these points when he says that the Holocaust has become a "negative absolute."[30] Even if people remain skeptical that rational agreement can be obtained about what is right, just, and good, the Holocaust seems to reestablish conviction against moral relativism by underscoring that the devastation wreaked by men and women in the Nazi killing fields in Ukraine and Belarus as well as in the Nazi gas chambers on Polish soil at Auschwitz and Treblinka was wrong, unjust, and evil—period. More than that, the scale of the wrongdoing, the magnitude of the injustice, and the devastation of the Holocaust's evil are so radical that humankind can ill afford not to have its ethical sensibilities informed and oriented by them.

Although the masterful Holocaust scholar Raul Hilberg did not consider himself a philosopher, his ethical outlook resonated with Berenbaum's view of the Holocaust as a negative absolute. Hilberg affirmed that ethics is the same today as it was yesterday and even the day before yesterday; it is the same after Auschwitz as it was before and during the lethal operations at that place. Especially with regard to needless and wanton killing, he emphasized, ethics is the same for everyone, everywhere. Hilberg left no unclarity. Such killing is wrong. We know that "in our bones," he said, for such knowledge is the heritage of many years.[31]

Hilberg was a self-identified atheist. If asked about the foundation or grounding for his ethical outlook, he neither would nor could locate them in any divine source. Equally clear, Hilberg was no ethical relativist. He did not think that might makes right. Nor did he follow Friedrich Nietzsche in claiming that the human will alone is the source of values and evaluations. But how should one understand the tantalizing idea that ethical sensibilities like Hilberg's are "in our bones," especially if something such as the heritage of many years, which implies a social or evolutionary formation of ethics, has put them there? In addition, how would that outlook square with the idea that ethics is the same today as it was yesterday and even the day before yesterday?

An outlook such as Hilberg's seems to be grounded in the view that social history or evolution produces a deep-seated ethical consciousness that has universal and, in that sense, timeless qualities. Ethical outlooks do have a history, and they are socially and probably biologically formed. Those elements can fuse to make ethical outlooks, at least some of them, so widely accepted that the appearance of universality, timelessness, and absoluteness attaches to them. Developments of this kind may be at work in making the Holocaust a negative absolute. Thus, the Holocaust's ethical absoluteness, its role in claims that universal moral truth exists, may be a social construction.[32]

The social construction of ethics can be powerful. At the end of the day, such construction may be the best hope for ethics, but with the Holocaust and other genocides and mass atrocities so recent and ongoing, one hardly can take moral comfort in that conclusion. The Holocaust may have deepened conviction that a fundamental, non-relativistic difference exists between right and wrong. Its destruction may have renewed awareness of the importance of ethical standards and conduct. Nevertheless, the Holocaust continues to cast disturbing shadows over basic beliefs concerning right and wrong, human rights, and the hope that human beings will learn from the past. Identification of the Holocaust as a negative absolute that reinstates confidence in moral absolutes is a step that cannot be taken easily, precisely because social construction may be at work in every aspect of such thinking. One may argue, for example, that ethical injunctions against needless and wanton killing obtain normative status because collective experience shows them to have social or evolutionary utility. Such killing is wrong, on this view, because it threatens individual and social well-being and even human existence itself. Over time this lesson may be experienced, taught, and driven home so that the ethical norm becomes embedded "in our bones." Something akin to this development might happen with the Holocaust's becoming a universal moral norm, a negative absolute or something more robust. But what if individuals or groups do not understand wanton and needless killing in the same way?

The SS leader Heinrich Himmler and his associates could agree that wanton and needless killing was wrong, but they did not think that the destruction of the European Jews fitted that description.[33] They can and should be held culpable and accountable for ethical wrongdoing of the most devastating kind, but their deviation from the norm raises suspicion about ethical groundings of the kind that Hilberg seems to have had in mind, let alone appeals that would situate ethical truth confidently in divinity or in universal rationality. None of these "foundations," including appeals to the social or biological construction of morality, deterred the "Final Solution," which did not end until massive Allied violence destroyed the Third Reich. Such realities gnaw at making one of the Holocaust's after-effects the elevation of that disaster as a confidence inspiring absolute. "No obstruction stopped the German machine of destruction," said Hilberg. "No moral problem proved insurmountable.... The old moral order did not break through anywhere along the line. This is a phenomenon of the greatest magnitude."[34]

What Hilberg calls "the old moral order" included questions, such as: Am I doing what is right? Should I go along? Are we doing the best we can? What should we do? To the extent that these questions were asked by those in the processes of bystanding and destruction that produced the Holocaust, they typically were trumped by other questions, anxious and fearful ones such as: How can I take the risk of speaking out and standing against the prevailing powers and policies? Shouldn't I just do my job and carry on as usual? What if I lose my position? What if I am caught and punished? More than that, the answers to these questions might conclude that: "Yes, what I am doing is right, difficult though it may be, because the perceived threats to our cause, our nation, our interests, must not be tolerated, let alone prevail. I cannot afford to lose my position; too much is at stake. Far from speaking out or standing against them, the prevailing powers and policies are the ones I shall serve, any impulses that I have to the contrary notwithstanding." Ethical insight, conviction, and resistance are rather easily overridden.[35] Hilberg was right when he observed that "this is a phenomenon of the greatest magnitude."

A FORLORN CAUSE?

The Holocaust, genocide, and other mass atrocities confirm the singular failure of ethics, which is that ethics has not made us human beings better than we are. What we are, moreover, is often far from being what should make us proud to be human. Human-inflicted abuse of human life and the world that is our home, including inaction and indifference in the face of that abuse, is often so great that shame about our humanity ought to take precedence over our pride in it. One implication is that ethics seems too fragile and weak to do what we hope, at least in our better moments, it can accomplish.

An objection might contend that it is misleading, misguided even, to suggest that the failures should be attributed to ethics itself. The Holocaust, genocide, and other mass atrocities do not signify the failures of ethics but those of men and women, of groups and communities that scarcely follow the light and do not heed the insight that sound ethical reflection provides. But this objection fails, or at least does not succeed completely and convincingly, because it depends upon a distinction between the ethical and the human that cannot pass scrutiny. Ethics is not independent of human existence but is instead an expression, a reflection, of it. Ethics may correspond to or embody transcendent realities that are not entirely human alone, but even then, ethics remains a human project, if not a human projection. Where ethics is concerned, the gap between thought and action, between theory and practice, is about *our* failure, but our *failure* includes failure of the ethical. Repeatedly, the authority and power of ethics, which are neither separable from nor identical with human existence, prove not to be sufficiently convincing or robust enough to deter us from doing immense and irreparable harm. Their appeal is too weak and their footing too fragile; they are trumped and overridden by desires and drives, plans and projects that overwhelm or undermine them. Our reason and freedom, politics, philosophy, and religion have crucial parts to play in establishing ethics. Our reason and freedom, politics, philosophy, and religion also outstrip ethics, which struggles, disastrously often ineffectually and in vain, to keep thought and action under its less than fully persuasive sway. In many ways, then, ethics fails, showing how existence itself is scarred by fault lines and deeply flawed.

The status of ethics after the Holocaust and other genocides is far from settled. One might argue that Nazi Germany's downfall shows that right defeated wrong and that goodness subdued evil, thus revealing that reality has a fundamentally moral underpinning and that there is such a thing as "the right side of history." The Holocaust, however, is far too awesome for such triumphalism. The Nazis did not win, but they came too close for comfort. Even though the Third Reich was destroyed, it is not so easy to say that its defeat was a clear and decisive triumph for goodness, truth, and justice over evil, falsehood, and corruption. Add to those realizations the fact that many Nazis—significant numbers of intellectuals among them—were idealists.[36] They had positive beliefs about right and wrong, good and evil, duty and responsibility. The "Final Solution" was a key part of those outlooks, which were put into practice with a zealous and apocalyptic vengeance.

The eloquent Auschwitz survivor Primo Levi said of philosophy, "no, it's not for me," but as his explorations of "the gray zone" and other Holocaust realities make clear, he had a keen philosophical mind, which he often brought to bear on ethical questions.[37] Levi, who thought that "each of us is a mixture of good and not so good," lacked trust in "the moral instinct of humanity, in mankind as 'naturally' good."[38] In an essay called "News from the Sky," for example, he noted that the German philosopher Immanuel Kant emphasized two wonders in creation: the starry sky above and the moral law within. "I don't know about the moral law," mused Levi, "does it dwell in everyone?...Every passing year augments our doubts."[39] The starry sky seemed to be another matter, but even those considerations gave Levi pause. The stars remain, but the sky—the territory of bombers, hijacked planes, missiles, and drones that can unleash terror and horror capable of annihilating human existence itself—has become an ominous place because of World War II, the Holocaust, and their reverberations.

Levi was not sure that ethics could be salvaged after Auschwitz, but he knew that the failure to try would exact a price higher than humankind could pay. "The universe is strange to us, we are strange in the universe," he wrote, and "the future of humanity is uncertain."[40] Nevertheless, Levi had his hopes. "There are no problems that cannot be solved around a table," he said, "provided there is good will and reciprocal trust—or even reciprocal fear."[41] Probably Levi was too optimistic, for much hinges on his qualification about good will and reciprocal trust. Their scarcity remains one of the Holocaust's most confounding results and one of the most acute failures of ethics.

When asked what his research has taught him about ethics, the Holocaust historian Peter Hayes responded simply but profoundly: "ethical behavior," he said, "is hard."[42] The Holocaust did not have to happen; nor did any other genocide. These disasters have emerged from human choices and decisions, many of them related to standing by and the complicity that goes with that action. Those facts mean that nothing human, natural, or divine guarantees respect for the ethical values and commitments that are most needed in contemporary human existence, but nothing is more important than our commitment to defend them, for they remain as fundamental as they are fragile, as precious as they are endangered. Ethics may not be enough.

It may be what William Stafford called a "forlorn cause."[43] Nevertheless, while existence is shot through with failure, ethics remains and persists. An irreplaceable safeguard, it still possesses the indispensable corrective for its own failures. But ethics meets that test only to the degree that it and we confront mass atrocities, inspire protest and resistance against them, support humanitarian responses to the suffering inflicted by those crimes, and strengthen efforts to prevent their recurrence.

In December 1987, Michael Berenbaum and I began to edit Holocaust: Religious and Philosophical Implications, *a collection of seminal texts about that genocide. Writings by the historian Yehuda Bauer and the political scientist Raul Hilberg were essential. So were reflections by the theologians Emil Fackenheim and Richard Rubenstein. The voices of the Holocaust survivors Primo Levi and Elie Wiesel found their places as well. The significance of those entries, Berenbaum and I agreed, was matched by another essay that had to be included: "Torture," a chapter from Jean Améry's profound 1966 book* Jenseits von Schuld und Sühne (Beyond Guilt and Atonement), *which appeared in English as* At the Mind's Limits: Contemplations by a Survivor of Auschwitz and Its Realities *in 1980. A Jewish philosopher who survived Auschwitz, Améry harbored a deep resentment—unforgiving and unrelenting— against the Holocaust's perpetrators and bystanders, a disposition whose protests against the failures of ethics have had a lasting and growing impact upon me.*

Améry likened torture to rape. That insight gripped me especially as I began to explore with Carol Rittner how rape is a weapon of war and genocide, the topic of the book we published with that title in 2012. In the twentieth century and now in the twenty-first as well, the relationships between torture and rape in circumstances of mass atrocity are as complex and far-reaching as they are brutal and ruinous. The prevalence and persistence of such atrocities testify to the failures of ethics, for if we are not resolutely moved by the fact that torture and rape are wrong, contrary to what is right and good, fundamentally at odds with what ought to be, then far too much is lost. Resentment and protest akin to Améry's are fundamental. Without them, our senses of accountability and responsibility to protect will be perilously diminished.

2

Rape as Torture and the Responsibility to Protect

Somewhere, someone is crying out under torture. Perhaps in this hour, this second.

—Jean Améry, *At the Mind's Limits*

Late in 2014, I put the phrase "rape and torture in Syria" into my computer's Google search engine. Instantly, more than three million "hits" appeared.[1] One of them directed attention to a February 2014 United Nations report, the UN's first about the "unspeakable" suffering inflicted on children engulfed in Syrian violence that has raged since 2011, creating a humanitarian crisis of immense proportions.[2] While holding armed opposition groups accountable, the report, which covers only the period from March 1, 2011, through November 15, 2013, primarily indicted the Syrian dictator Bashar al-Assad and his government forces. They have inflicted on thousands of children "ill treatment and acts tantamount to torture reportedly [including] beatings with metal cables, whips and wooden and metal batons; electric shocks, including to the genitals; the ripping out of fingernails and toenails; sexual violence, including rape or threats of rape; mock executions; cigarette burns; sleep deprivation; solitary confinement; and exposure to the torture of relatives" (para. 19).

Emphasizing that reports about sexual violence in Syria are underreported "owing to fears of reprisals and social stigmatization, combined with the lack of safe and confidential response services," the report went on to note specifically that sexual violence, mostly perpetrated by "members of the Syrian intelligence services and the Syrian Armed Forces . . . was reportedly used to humiliate, harm, force confessions or pressure a relative to surrender" (paras. 34–5). In addition,

"The United Nations also received reports of allegations of rape, including gang rape, and other forms of sexual violence against women and girls, including in the presence of relatives, by Government forces, in particular at checkpoints or during incursions and house searches of families perceived to be pro-opposition" (para. 36).

The United Nations' accounts about the plight of Syria's children, along with others about rape and torture in that devastated country, are telling reminders of the grim accuracy of this chapter's epigraph, a 1966 statement by the Jewish philosopher and Holocaust survivor Jean Améry: "Somewhere, someone is crying out under torture. Perhaps in this hour, this second."[3] As in other places where rape and torture become state policy, many of the victims of those acts in Syria—girls and boys as well as women and men—have been "done to death."[4]

THE DESTRUCTION OF TRUST IN THE WORLD

Adopted by the United Nations General Assembly on December 10, 1984, the Convention against Torture and Other Cruel, Inhuman or Degrading Treatment or Punishment came into force on June 26, 1987, following ratification by the twentieth state party. The Convention defines torture to include:

> any act by which severe pain or suffering, whether physical or mental, is intentionally inflicted on a person for such purposes as obtaining from him or a third person information or a confession, punishing him for an act he or a third person has committed or is suspected of having committed, or intimidating or coercing him or a third person, or for any reason based on discrimination of any kind, when such pain or suffering is inflicted by or at the instigation of or with the consent or acquiescence of a public official or other person acting in an official capacity.[5]

About a decade after the Convention against Torture came into force, specifically in a 1998 judgment against Jean-Paul Akayesu, the first person convicted of the crime of genocide after trial before an international court, the International Criminal Tribunal for Rwanda (ICTR) defined rape as "a physical invasion of a sexual nature, committed on a person under circumstances which are coercive," prefacing the definition as follows:

Like torture, rape is used for such purposes as intimidation, degradation, humiliation, discrimination, punishment, control or destruction of a person. Like torture, rape is a violation of personal dignity, and rape in fact constitutes torture when inflicted by or at the instigation of or with the consent or acquiescence of a public official or other person acting in an official capacity.[6]

Torture denotes more than rape, but those atrocities are closely related and intertwined. In international law, both can be crimes against humanity and acts of genocide. The prevalence of such crimes and their destruction of trust in the world reveal dire failures of ethics.

Prior to his deportation to Auschwitz, Jean Améry was interrogated and tortured in Belgium by his German captors. Torture left marks that went deep down. Likening its first blows to "rape, a sexual act without the consent of one of the two partners," Améry did not say that rape was a method of torture inflicted on him, but he did specify that his torturer was "on me and thereby destroys me," not necessarily by killing but definitely by demolishing what Améry called "trust in the world."[7] It was with similar effects in mind that the ICTR likened rape to torture and stated that, under certain circumstances, rape constitutes torture.

Améry held that "trust in the world" hinges on "the expectation of help, the certainty of help, [which] is indeed one of the fundamental experiences of human beings." Améry added his belief that "the boundaries of my body are also the boundaries of my self. My skin surface shields me against the external world. If I am to have trust, I must feel on it only what I *want* to feel." Thus, the first blows of torture and rape are likely to dash those precious convictions and expectations. As Améry put it, once such violence strikes, "a part of our life ends and it can never again be revived."[8]

No book protesting the failures of ethics can pass muster if it avoids concentrating on the fragility of the human body and its vulnerability to pain and desecration, which is epitomized in rape or in what might better be identified as *rape/torture*, and, in particular, in what I call *rape/torture-as-policy*—intentional and systematic uses of rape/torture as a weapon of war and genocide.[9] So, keeping in mind Améry's claim that "only in torture does the transformation of the person into flesh become complete," note that motivations for rape/torture-as-policy are multiple.[10] They include intentions to humiliate, terrorize, retaliate, control resources, and gain information and to advance ethnic and religious cleansing and genocide. Rape/torture-as-policy, especially in its genocidal forms, involves gender, sex, and tortuous violence but so much more because its wreckage extends beyond the meaning of such terms and the reach of those realities. As the ICTR stated, "the crime of rape cannot be captured in a mechanical description of objects and body parts." In Rwanda, the ICTR went on to say, the genocidal forms of rape-as-policy produced "physical and psychological destruction of Tutsi women, their families and their communities. Sexual violence was an integral part of the process of destruction, specifically targeting Tutsi women and specifically contributing to their destruction and to the destruction of the Tutsi group as a whole."[11] Such acts and outcomes are torture or nothing could be. Sadly, moreover, *Tutsi* is but one of many group names that could be linked to the ICTR's description of the disastrous toll taken by the torture inflicted and encompassed by rape-as-policy.

NEW WORDS

The *New York Times* op-ed writer Nicholas D. Kristof uses his influence and leverage to call attention eloquently and persistently to human rights abuses that affect women and girls.[12] On February 11, 2010, for instance, Kristof published an essay called "The Grotesque Vocabulary in Congo." Beginning with the observation that he had "learned some new words" while in the Democratic Republic of Congo (DRC), Kristof continued his editorial as follows:

> One [of the new words] is "autocannibalism," coined in French but equally appropriate in English. It describes what happens when a militia here in eastern Congo's endless war cuts flesh from living victims and forces them to eat it.
> Another is "re-rape." The need for that term arose because doctors were seeing women and girls raped, re-raped and re-raped again, here in the world capital of murder, rape, and mutilation.[13]

When Kristof identified the DRC as "the world capital of murder, rape, and mutilation," his description may have been hyperbolic, but it made a point nonetheless. "The brutal war here in eastern Congo has not only lasted longer than the Holocaust," Kristof underscored in a *New York Times* editorial dated February 7, 2010, "but also appears to have claimed more lives. A peer-reviewed study put the Congo's war death toll at 5.4 million as of April 2007 and rising at 45,000 a month. That would leave the total today, after a dozen years, at 6.9 million."[14] Although the precise numbers cannot be known, rape, *re*-rape, and the torture they involve have contributed significantly to those millions of deaths.

The new words that Kristof learned relate to paragraphs 138 and 139 of the Outcome Document of the United Nations World Summit, which took place in 2005. Those paragraphs state the following commitments:

138. Each individual State has the responsibility to protect its populations from genocide, war crimes, ethnic cleansing and crimes against humanity. This responsibility entails the prevention of such crimes, including their incitement, through appropriate and necessary means. We accept that responsibility and will act in accordance with it. The international community should, as appropriate, encourage and help States to exercise this responsibility and support the United Nations in establishing an early warning capability.

139. The international community, through the United Nations, also has the responsibility to use appropriate diplomatic, humanitarian and other peaceful means, in accordance with Chapters VI and VIII of the Charter, to help to protect populations from genocide, war crimes, ethnic cleansing and crimes against humanity. In this context, we are prepared to take collective action, in a timely and decisive manner, through the Security Council, in accordance with the Charter, including Chapter VII, on a case-by-case basis and in cooperation with relevant regional organizations as appropriate, should peaceful means be inadequate and national authorities are manifestly failing to protect their populations from genocide, war crimes, ethnic cleansing and crimes against humanity. We stress the need for the General Assembly to continue consideration of the responsibility to protect populations from genocide, war crimes, ethnic cleansing and crimes against humanity and its implications, bearing in mind the principles of the Charter and international law. We also intend to commit ourselves, as necessary and appropriate, to helping States build capacity to protect their populations from genocide, war crimes, ethnic cleansing and crimes against humanity and to assisting those which are under stress before crises and conflicts break out.[15]

The 2005 United Nations World Summit commemorated the UN's founding sixty years earlier. In the wake of World War II, the United

Nations came into existence when its charter was signed in San Francisco on June 26, 1945, and came into force on October 24 of that same year. The charter's preamble affirms that the peoples of the United Nations are determined "to save succeeding generations from the scourge of war, . . . to reaffirm faith in fundamental human rights, in the dignity and worth of the human person, in the equal rights of men and women, and of nations large and small, and . . . to promote social progress and better standards of life in larger freedom." At the same time, the charter stressed that, with the exception of acts of international aggression or actions that threaten or breach international peace, the United Nations is not authorized "to intervene in matters which are essentially within the domestic jurisdiction of any state."[16]

As the latter provisions imply, the United Nations in many ways privileged national sovereignty over human rights, for under the UN charter, massive human rights abuses and even crimes against humanity could take place within a state without those conditions being construed as threats to, or breaches of, international peace, let alone as acts of international aggression. But if paragraphs 138 and 139 of the Outcome Document of the 2005 United Nations World Summit are honored, then for the following reasons national sovereignty does not trump human rights, at least not as much as it could and did before.

First, paragraph 138 affirms that each individual state has the primary responsibility to *protect* its populations from genocide, war crimes, ethnic cleansing, and crimes against humanity. That responsibility also entails that individual states are obliged to *prevent* those crimes from happening to their populations. Second, paragraph 139 indicates that the international community has the responsibility to help populations threatened by genocide, war crimes, ethnic cleansing, and crimes against humanity. Furthermore, if an individual state is unable or unwilling to protect its populations from these mass atrocity crimes, which definitely include torture and rape used as weapons of war and genocide, then the international community has the responsibility to take "collective action, in a timely and decisive manner." If peaceful means are inadequate to provide the needed protection, the international community must take stronger measures, including collective use of force authorized by the Security Council under Chapter VII of the United Nations charter.

A NEW NORM

Gareth Evans, chancellor of the Australian National University, formerly Australia's foreign minister, and from 2000 to 2009 president and chief executive officer of the International Crisis Group, coined the term *responsibility to protect* during his 2000–1 tenure as co-chair of the International Commission on Intervention and State Sovereignty (ICISS). The responsibility to protect (R2P, as it is sometimes abbreviated) concentrates on mass atrocity crimes: genocide, war crimes, crimes against humanity, and ethnic cleansing. It perhaps became more than an idealistic concept in September 2005, when heads of state and government agreed to paragraphs 138 and 139 in the Outcome Document of the United Nations World Summit, an action that gave R2P a foothold in international law.[17]

The political scientist Thomas Weiss has argued that "with the possible exception of the prevention of genocide after World War II, no idea has moved faster or farther in the international normative arena."[18] Arguably, two steps taken by the United Nations might support Weiss's judgment. First, on January 12, 2009, Secretary-General Ban Ki-moon issued *Implementing the Responsibility to Protect*. Noting that the R2P norm is "firmly anchored in well-established principles of international law," this report reaffirmed the key R2P-related provisions of the Outcome Document of the 2005 United Nations World Summit and outlined "a three-pillar strategy" to operationalize that agenda.[19] As summarized by the UN's Office of the Special Adviser on the Prevention of Genocide, the three pillars are as follows:

1. The State carries the primary responsibility for protecting populations from genocide, war crimes, crimes against humanity and ethnic cleansing, and their incitement;
2. The international community has a responsibility to encourage and assist States in fulfilling this responsibility;
3. The international community has a responsibility to use appropriate diplomatic, humanitarian and other means to protect populations from these crimes. If a State is manifestly failing to protect its populations, the international community must be prepared to take collective action to protect populations, in accordance with the Charter of the United Nations.[20]

Second, on April 16, 2014, the United Nations Security Council recognized the twentieth anniversary of the genocide in Rwanda. Part of the commemoration included the Council's unanimous passage of Resolution 2150, which, among other provisions, reaffirmed "paragraphs 138 and 139 of the 2005 World Summit Outcome Document on the responsibility to protect populations from genocide, war crimes, ethnic cleansing and crimes against humanity." This occasion was the first time in which a Security Council resolution included such language about the responsibility to protect.[21] As the latter fact indicates, the potency and status of this new norm are still very much works in progress.[22] The reasons for that uncertainty are multiple and complex. Crucial among them are factors that remain critical more than a decade after the appearance of *The Responsibility to Protect*, the 2001 ICISS report, and its sixth chapter in particular. That report, which was a crucial driving force behind the UN's eventual support for paragraphs 138 and 139 in the 2005 Outcome Document, referred to "conscience-shocking situations crying out for action" (6.36–40, an important section focused on "The Implications of Inaction").[23]

Numerous times the ICISS report refers to rape, including systematic rape, as among those "conscience-shocking situations crying out for action," especially insofar as rape is part of ethnic cleansing and, by implication, genocide. Speaking about "large scale" losses of life and ethnic cleansing, the ICISS report highlights "acts of terror or rape," as indicated in the following propositions:

> Military intervention for human protection purposes is justified in two broad sets of circumstances, namely in order to halt or avert:
>
> - large scale loss of life, actual or apprehended, with genocidal intent or not, which is the product either of deliberate state action, or state neglect or inability to act, or a failed state situation; or
> - large scale "ethnic cleansing," actual or apprehended, whether carried out by killing, forced expulsion, acts of terror or rape.
>
> If either or both of these conditions are satisfied, it is our view that the "just cause" component of the decision to intervene is amply satisfied. (4.19)

As an international norm, R2P is in its infancy. Arguably, if it had existed robustly in, say, 1990, "rape camps" and the torture they involved might not have existed in the former Yugoslavia because there would have been forceful international intervention against ethnic cleansing, and countless Tutsi women might not have been

raped and re-raped because there would have been forceful international intervention against genocide in Rwanda. More recently, if
R2P had existed robustly in, say, 2000, Nicholas Kristof might not
have had to learn new words—*autocannibalism* and *re-rape*—because
there would have been forceful international intervention to protect
Congolese women and girls. Unfortunately, R2P neither existed
robustly then nor does it now, and circumstances, events, and weak-
ness of political will may doom it to be an idea whose time has *not*
come or worse, like the slogan "Never Again," a banal cliché.

Winning the support that R2P needs to be effective may well be a
forlorn cause and one more failure of ethics. But if R2P does gain
traction that can curb if not eliminate rape/torture as a weapon of war
and genocide, work in that direction will have to include what the
eighth chapter of the ICISS report urges: namely, attention to moral
appeals that might prevent, avert, and halt such devastation. Importantly, the report further and aptly notes that "getting a moral motive
to bite means . . . being able to convey a sense of urgency and reality
about the threat to human life in a particular situation" (8.13).

DO THE DEAD CRY OUT FOR ACTION?

Where rape-as-policy and the torture it entails are concerned, how
can "a sense of urgency and reality" about that devastation be bolstered? Could such prospects be enhanced, at least in some significant
ways, by remembering the women and girls and the men and boys
who have been killed after, or as result of, being raped/tortured if not
"done to death" directly and immediately by such atrocities?

Reflection on those questions invites consideration of others, such
as: Can the dead themselves, specifically those whose lives have been
taken by rape/torture, especially in circumstances of rape/torture-as-
policy, ignite and embolden "a sense of urgency and reality" about the
importance of protection and resistance against the sexual torture
that stole life from them? Can those dead "cry out for action" in ways
that the living never can? Could listening to the dead, those "done to
death" by rape/torture-as-policy in war and genocide, improve the
odds that moral motives will bite in the ways we need them to do?

Lest my intentions be misunderstood, some explanation is needed
before proceeding further. When I speak of "the dead," doing so with

specific reference to those whose lives were lost when rape/torture became a weapon of war and genocide, my aim is not to lump individuals together in an anonymous, faceless, genderless, and ultimately disrespectful way. To the contrary, as I think of "the dead," the purpose and point are to underscore that *individual* girls and women, boys and men, have been "done to death" by rape/torture-as-policy. If "the dead" can be said to "speak," their "word" comes from individual persons who compel respect from us, the living, and also from their "chorus," for every individual who has suffered and died through rape/torture-as-policy is one of many. In both forms—as one and as many—the voices of the dead reverberate in awesome ways if we allow them to do so. Listening, trying to hear what these voices—individual and collective—might say to us as they reach a silent but deeply moving crescendo constitutes one of the most respectful and instructive actions we can take.

NO ONE'S DEATH SHOULD COME THAT WAY

If those "done to death" by rape/torture, especially in circumstances of rape/torture-as-policy, can and do speak in and through their silence, what do they say? Here, I believe, a combination of cautious restraint and bold statement must remain in respectful tension. Restraint is needed for two reasons: first, to avoid presumption about speaking for the dead; second, because the bold responses that are right and good are also likely to sound like clichés if they are articulated. Silence followed by action that resists death's waste may be the wisest course. But silence, even when accompanied by action that resists death-dealing rape/torture, may be insufficient and irresponsible.

Those "done to death" by rape/torture, especially through rape-as-policy in war and genocide, can and do cry out for action. Perhaps one way to interpret their cry is not-so-simply to say: Yes, we all are dying and will soon be dead, but no one's death should come *that way*. What *that way* was and means is partly knowable because we have testimony, memoirs, trial records, historical research, and even new words such as autocannibalism and re-rape that state and document the butchery. What *that way* was and means is also unutterable, for one cannot interview the dead. But because the latter realization persists, revealing as it does that, in David Boder's words, "the grimmest stories" are not the ones that are told, responses in word and deed that join with the dead to "see through the gloom" may be found.[24] Such seeing would not dispel the gloom of atrocity. Nothing, not even a robustly normative responsibility to protect can do so, at least not completely. But *seeing through* might suggest a much-needed combination: namely, a linking of seeing through as refusing to forsake those "done to death," however disconsolate that commitment may be, with a seeing through that entails doing as much as you and I can to find ways that make the gloom less than overwhelming. If the responsibility to protect is not one of those ways, what could be? It emanates from atrocity's dead, and fulfilling that responsibility, even if imperfectly, is arguably one of the best ways to hear and respect them.

In concluding his important book, *The Dominion of the Dead*, Robert Pogue Harrison observes that "the dead are our guardians. We give them a future," he says, "so that they may give us a past. We help them live on so that they may help us go forward."[25] That description can fit those "done to death" by rape/torture and our relationship to them. By remembering them, by allowing them to indwell our worlds, by allowing them to speak to and through us, by "giving a voice to the dead," we may yet find ways, including R2P, to curb at least some of the conditions that destroyed them.[26] Such action would not bring back those "done to death" by rape/torture-as-policy, but it would create a present and a future—and even a past—more worth having.

DOING SOMETHING, DOING MORE

Prior to the UN's 2014 report on Syria's children, Secretary-General Ban Ki-moon released his March 14, 2013, study, *Sexual Violence in Conflict*.[27] Focusing on data from December 2011 to December 2012, it interpreted *sexual violence* to include "rape, sexual slavery, forced prostitution, forced pregnancy, enforced sterilization and any other form of sexual violence of comparable gravity perpetrated against women, men or children with a direct or indirect (temporal, geographical or causal) link to a conflict." Implicitly acknowledging the reality of rape/torture as policy, the Secretary-General's account documented the devastation that sexual violence in conflict has wreaked in numerous countries, among them Afghanistan, Bosnia-Herzegovina, Colombia, the DRC, Sierra Leone, Sudan (Darfur), as well as the Syrian Arab Republic.

Neither the countries identified in Ban Ki-moon's report nor even the sexual violence unleashed within them evokes the Holocaust, at least not immediately or primarily. Nevertheless, links exist between current atrocities, including the sexual violence to which Syrian children have been subjected, and those committed in the past. Tracking those connections reveals more about the failures of ethics, but that inquiry entails recognition that *direct* connections between post-Holocaust developments regarding rape/torture as policy and sexual violence during the Holocaust are tenuous. At least two factors support that judgment. First, until a few years ago, sexual violence during the Holocaust, including rape/torture as policy, was little discussed. As Jean Améry's reflections illustrate, survivors did speak about torture, but few survivors or perpetrators spoke openly about rape and, specifically, rape as torture. Postwar trials turned attention elsewhere. Only a few scholars argued that such violence was widespread, and with many taking the opposite position, research about Holocaust-related sexual violence was sidelined, partly because for many years Holocaust studies failed to pay sufficient attention to gender and, in particular, to the sexually specific ways in which Jewish women and girls came under attack by the Germans and their collaborators.[28] Second, attention to rape/torture as policy came to the fore mainly as knowledge grew about the calculated and systematic use of sexual violence in genocidal campaigns in the former Yugoslavia and Rwanda in the mid-1990s and then, more recently, in places such as Darfur, the DRC, the Central African Republic, and Syria. Among other things, this attention led to legal proceedings in which torture was defined to include rape and in which rape was defined in ways that could make it a crime against humanity and an act of genocide. As far as attention to rape/torture as policy is concerned, the lines of connection did not run from the Holocaust to more recent and current events but went the other way instead. Recent awareness and concern about rape/torture as policy, in fact, helped to break down the barriers and to demystify the taboos that blocked testimony and even inquiry about Holocaust-related sexual violence.

Améry believed that "torture was the essence of National Socialism."[29] Without contradicting that judgment, current research indicates that during the Holocaust the infliction of rape/torture was not an officially implemented policy embedded in the Third Reich's genocide against the Jewish people That same research, however, underscores that rape/torture of Jewish women and girls was nevertheless widespread, laws and sanctions against *Rassenschande* (race defilement) notwithstanding. In literally groundbreaking research in Ukraine, Belarus, Russia, and other parts of Nazi-occupied eastern Europe during what he calls "the Holocaust by bullets," Father Patrick Desbois has found that prior to shooting 1.5 million Jews in the killing fields of the East, Germans and their collaborators often raped Jewish girls and women before murdering them.[30] Consistent with Desbois's findings, a key point that emerges from study of what Ban Ki-moon's report calls "sexual violence in conflict" is that wherever genocidal acts are perpetrated, rape/torture—as official policy or not—will likely be among them.

Protests that effectively resist rape/torture, especially in cases where rape/torture is policy, are easier said than done. The responsibility to protect, which includes provisions for humanitarian and even military intervention, offers hope that deserves international support. That support could be enhanced if we learned better to hear those who have had life stolen from them by rape/torture and to listen to the murdered dead, especially those violated by rape/torture. Such hearing and listening has to be part of an educational process, one focused not exclusively but significantly on boys and men. Sexual violence in conflict and rape/torture in particular are perpetrated primarily by males. Men have to be in the vanguard of resistance against these atrocities. Otherwise the chances to curb such acts are greatly reduced.

Related needs came to light on June 24, 2013, not long after Ban Ki-moon released his March 14, 2013, report *Sexual Violence in Conflict*, when the United Nations Security Council unanimously adopted Resolution 2016 (2013).[31] Properly noting that "sexual violence in armed conflict and post-conflict situations disproportionately affects women and girls," Resolution 2016 (2013) gestured toward the impact of such violence on "men and boys and those secondarily traumatized as forced witnesses of sexual violence against family members." More than those gestures are needed because the scope and devastation of rape/torture-as-policy are so far-reaching.

By no means are men and boys victimized only by having to witness sexual violence. Arguably, rape/torture is increasingly inflicted directly on them, a realization necessary to complement the affirmation of Resolution 2016 (2013) that "women's political, social and economic empowerment, gender equality and the enlistment of men and boys in the effort to combat all forms of violence against women are central to long-term efforts to prevent sexual violence in armed conflict and post-conflict situations." Especially important for such prevention is the necessity to combat a culture of impunity that takes sexual violence in conflict to be unavoidable, inevitable, and unpreventable. Education is not sufficient to make that objective achievable, but failure is likely unless sound education advances not only for the young in schools, colleges, and universities but also for adults in government, police forces, and military units, including United Nations peacekeeping forces.

The education entailed by Resolution 2016 (2013) must deepen moral insight and strengthen ethical commitment. In particular, it needs to emphasize honoring the personhood of the other and to stress our responsibility for one another. But what can I do, what can any reader of these words do, to advance those lofty goals, to keep them from being banal abstractions, and to translate them into specific acts in particular circumstances? Fortunately, good responses to that question are so numerous that they can be unending, a prospect that kindles hope even as it confers responsibility.[32] When I think about the conferring of responsibility in regard to deepening moral insight and strengthening ethical commitment, I do not think only, or even primarily, about ethical injunctions, philosophical principles, or religious imperatives that emphasize honoring the personhood of the other and stress our responsibility for one another. Increasingly, my attention is directed to and governed by people whose deeds and words have moved me and challenged me to leverage my best chances to make a contribution, small though it might be, to the protest against rape/torture and, specifically, to the sound education needed to sustain that battle. Some of these people are known to me only through their writings. Jean Améry is one example. After I first read his essay on "Torture," I studied it every year with my students. That work affected my priorities as a teacher and a scholar. Among other things, that path led to my writing this book.

I think, too, of Nicholas Kristof and his *New York Times* columns. Emphasizing testimony he has received, Kristof regularly gives voice to those—including sometimes the dead—who have had life stolen from them by rape/torture. On July 24, 2013, for example, Kristof published "A Policy of Rape Continues," which documents how ten years after genocide began in Darfur, rape/torture continues to be a devastating weapon in the Sudanese government's genocidal policies.[33] His article ends with the testimony of a 17-year-old Salamat girl named Jawahir, raped repeatedly by three men in military uniforms during an 11-hour ordeal.[34] Courageously speaking about her rape/torture and the implications of the cultural dishonor that sexual violation brought upon her, Jawahir told Kristof, "This is something that happened. So people should know. I want to the world to know." Hearing, heeding, and helping to amplify her voice are immensely important for implementing the education entailed by Resolution 2016 (2013).

Jean Améry, Nicholas Kristof, a young Salamat woman named Jawahir—such people, their testimonies and examples, insist that each of us can do something, can do more, to honor the personhood of the other and to stress our responsibility for one another. Successes and failures of ethics hang in the balance of that challenge.

On July 2, 1964, the American president Lyndon Johnson signed the momentous *Civil Rights Act of 1964. An additional landmark followed when his signature put the Voting Rights Act of 1965 into effect on August 6 of that year. A lesser known, but still important, presidential action was taken about seven weeks later on September 29, when Johnson also signed into law the National Foundation on the Arts and Humanities Act, which gave birth to the National Endowment for the Humanities (NEH).*

NEH fellowship and grant funding supported my early scholarship and teaching about the Holocaust and advanced my friendship and writing with Richard Rubenstein. On a much larger scale, NEH resources sustain the humanities councils—fifty-six of them—that enliven inquiry about history and contemporary culture in every American state and territory. Together these councils constitute the Federation of State Humanities Councils. Among many other responsibilities, the Federation, whose national board I chaired in 2011–13, sponsors the National Humanities Conference.

During the autumn of 2013, that conference took place in Birmingham, Alabama. It focused on the pivotal role Birmingham played fifty years earlier in the nation's civil rights struggle against racism and segregation. On April 16, 1963, Martin Luther King, Jr., issued his "Letter from Birmingham Jail," affirming that "injustice anywhere is a threat to justice everywhere." Five months later, on September 15, Birmingham racists dynamited the 16th Street Baptist Church, the city's oldest black church and a center of civil rights advocacy, killing four little girls and wounding twenty church members.

As I participated in a conference session at that church, I remembered my boyhood in southern Indiana, a region where de facto segregation remained well after Brown v. Board of Education, *the 1954 landmark decision by the US Supreme Court, held that de jure racial segregation in public schools violated the Fourteenth Amendment of the US Constitution. At that time, my father Josiah, a Presbyterian minister, worked courageously but unsuccessfully to persuade his congregation's leadership that their church should serve its neighbors, who, in the changing demography of the time, included black families living almost next door.*

Looking back, I discern how formative that family experience has been for me. It gave an early and lasting revelation of what I now call the failures of ethics. No less significant, my coming of age in 1950s America showed me racism's evil—I know not what else to call it.

Later, I came to understand that philosophy, the discipline I love because at its best it pursues truth and justice, was tainted historically insofar as philosophers—including some of the greatest among them— encouraged racism. That awareness coincided with my growing commitment to probe the Holocaust, genocide, and other mass atrocities, which taught me that racism could be much more persistent and destructive than it had been in my Indiana boyhood or even in the Birmingham of 1963. At its core, I came to see, racism tends to be genocidal. Wherever racism rears its ugly but often veiled head—"we are not racists" or "there is no racism here" or "racism is done and gone"—the failures of ethics are not far to find. Protesting those failures requires exposing and protesting every form of racism, including the denial that racism exists.

3

Philosophy and the "Logic" of Racism

My mother's Singer sewing machine, too, vanished in the confusion of war like an orphan...

—Danilo Kiš, *Garden, Ashes*

In the summer of 1880, the French sculptor Auguste Rodin was
commissioned to create a monumental door for an art museum in
Paris. Inspired by Dante's *Divine Comedy*, Rodin called his project
The Gates of Hell. Although the door remained unfinished, its center-
piece, *The Thinker*, became one of the world's best known artworks.

Sarah Waller, a talented Scripps College alumna who studied the
Holocaust with me in the autumn of 1999, created a thought-provoking
interpretation of Rodin's masterpiece. In a simple but striking black-
and-white style, Waller's sketch depicts a thinker—a philosopher—who
is ambiguously situated with regard to lines of barbed wire that front the
figure.[1] The barbed wire suggests the boundaries of a prison, a deportation center, a concentration camp, or some other enclosure whose
ominous presence might be a warning about genocidal threats or a
sign of genocidal intentions. While working on this book, I often thought
of Waller's image.

Philosophy is critical inquiry about reality, knowledge, and ethics.
It explores what is, what can be known, and what ought to be. With
regard to genocide, philosophy's history concerning what ought to
be—the focal point of ethics—shares ambiguities surrounding the
position and perspective of Waller's thinker. Is he or she behind
barbed-wire barricades that have formed hellish places such as concentration camps and killing centers? Has he or she paid a price for
resisting crimes against humanity? Is this thinker, this philosopher,
unjustly imprisoned? Is he or she even waiting to be killed for taking a
bold and courageous stand against genocide? Or is the thinker outside

the barbed wire's constraints but neither innocent nor free because he or she may be "behind" the barbed wire in ways that implicate him or her in wrongdoing.

Waller's thinker invites multiple interpretations of place and posture, but each implies that genocide and human rights abuses ought to provoke philosophical thinking of the most penetrating and ethical kind. They should do so because humankind's capacities—including philosophy—to make plans, pursue goals, and enact decisions not only create injustice and inflict suffering but can also reduce them both. Much depends on how well people think, because thinking well and acting well go hand in hand. For those reasons, much also depends on how philosophers do their work.

PHILOSOPHY IN AN AGE OF GENOCIDE

While the Holocaust raged in the 1940s, Raphael Lemkin, a Jewish lawyer who fled from Poland, coined the term *genocide*, which derives from the Greek word *genos* (race, tribe) and the Latin suffix *-cide* (killing). Initially defining it to mean "the destruction of a nation or of an ethnic group," an emphasis indicating that genocide does not target individuals alone but aims at entire groups, he observed that the term denoted "an old practice in its modern development," for the plight of the Jews under Hitler was not a simple repetition of past historical patterns.[2] Later, Lemkin amplified his initial definition, stressing that genocide involves conspiratorial, criminal intent to "destroy or to cripple permanently a human group"—in particular "national, racial or religious groups."[3] The existence of such groups entails a multiplicity of factors—cultural, political, linguistic, social, and economic as well as those that are physical and biological. In Lemkin's view, assaults against those realities are genocidal insofar as they aim to destroy or permanently cripple a group whose identity and vitality depend upon them.

Debate continues about the degree to which the United Nations' 1948 Convention on the Prevention and Punishment of the Crime of Genocide embodies Lemkin's understanding of genocide, but his insistence and persistence did much to win support for that benchmark, which defines *genocide* in terms of acts, including but not restricted to killing, that are committed "with intent to destroy, in whole or in part, a national, ethnical, racial, or religious group, as such."[4] From the slaughter of Armenians in 1915 and the Holocaust to the genocide in Rwanda in 1994 and what has happened in the Darfur region of Sudan since 2005, genocide's modern development has taken an immense toll on human life and civilization in the twentieth century and now in the twenty-first as well. Despite the existence of the UN's Genocide Convention, it is no exaggeration to say that we live, and philosophy exists, in an age of genocide.

The Holocaust historian Omer Bartov has argued persuasively that the modern development of genocidal catastrophes can neither be understood nor prevented in the future unless one grasps that "scholars have played a prominent role in preparing the mindset, providing the rationale, and supplying the know-how and personnel for the implementation of state-directed mass violence."[5] Philosophers and philosophy are not exempt from Bartov's indictment. Although the history of philosophy shows that philosophers have done much to advance human rights and to defend human equality, the same history shows that genocide has been aided and abetted by philosophies that have advanced racism and antisemitism and by philosophers who have emboldened—inadvertently if not explicitly—political regimes and cultural agendas that turned genocidal.[6] In our post-Holocaust world, nations, businesses, churches, and professions such as medicine and law have been called to account for their complicity or for bystanding while Nazi Germany committed genocide against the European Jews.[7] To some extent philosophers have been held accountable too, but when the history of genocide is taken into account, philosophy and philosophers have not been sufficiently self-critical about their bystanding and complicity.

Generally speaking, philosophy and philosophers have high estimates of themselves. Philosophy depicts itself as occupying high moral ground. Philosophers tend to see themselves—I include myself in these judgments—as extending a tradition that serves free inquiry, truth, goodness, beauty, and justice. But philosophy has darker sides, and philosophers have been less than forthcoming about them, especially with regard to genocide. As the history of the Holocaust shows, and other genocides follow similar patterns, the expertise and cooperation, or at least the indifference, of virtually every professional group within a state and society—teachers, professors, scholars, and philosophers among them—are needed for genocide to take place.

Philosophy and genocide exist in the same world. Unfortunately, their relationship has not always been one of opposition. Although philosophy often highlights characteristics shared by all persons, its history contains theories that have negatively emphasized differences—religious, cultural, national, and racial.[8] Such theories have encouraged senses of hierarchy, superiority, and "us versus them" thinking in which genocidal policies may assert themselves, especially in times of economic instability and political stress. If philosophy is divided between views upholding that all people are equal members of humanity and others stressing differences between groups as fundamental, how can philosophy contribute to stopping or mitigating genocide?

Germany has produced some of the world's most notable philosophers, including Immanuel Kant, G. W. F. Hegel, Friedrich Nietzsche, and Martin Heidegger. Regrettably, neither in Germany nor elsewhere have philosophers done all that they could to protest genocide and other crimes against humanity. On the contrary, as Heidegger's case reveals, philosophy can expedite genocide.[9] Hitler rose to power on January 30, 1933. Three months later Heidegger joined the Nazi Party. On May 27, 1933, he was inaugurated as rector of Freiburg University. Although Nazi book burnings and the dismissal of many so-called non-Aryan academics had taken place a few weeks earlier, Heidegger's inaugural address advocated stepping-into-line with the times, which was at least an implicit embrace of Nazi antisemitism. He also stressed that the Führer's leadership was crucial for Germany's future. In February 1934, Heidegger resigned his rectorship, but he never became an obstacle to the Third Reich's genocidal policies.

Living for more than thirty years after Hitler's defeat in 1945, Heidegger neither explicitly repudiated National Socialism nor said much about the Holocaust. When he did speak about that genocide, his remarks were problematic. Debate continues about his philosophy as well as about the man himself. In *Being and Time* and other major works, Heidegger analyzed human existence, its significance within Being itself, and the need for people to take responsibility within their particular times and places. But arguably, his philosophy includes a fundamental flaw: The abstract, even obscure, quality of its reflection on Being and "authentic" action precludes a clear ethic that speaks explicitly against racism, antisemitism, genocide, and crimes against humanity. Heidegger's example is not the way forward, but, as Bartov argues, it also cannot any longer be credible to philosophize "by applying, as if nothing had happened, the same old humanistic and rational concepts that were so profoundly undermined" by genocidal catastrophes.[10]

Concerns of this kind have led some philosophers to offer new approaches to ethical reflection. The Italian philosopher Giorgio Agamben, for example, concentrates on the *Muselmann*, a concentration camp prisoner irretrievably near death because of exhaustion, starvation, or hopelessness. The Holocaust survivor Primo Levi said of the *Muselmänner* that "one hesitates to call them living: one hesitates to call their death death."[11] The *Muselmann*, contends Agamben, "marks the threshold between the human and the inhuman."[12] In his view, the existence of the *Muselmann* requires not only a fundamental rethinking about what it means to be human—"it is possible to lose dignity and decency beyond imagination . . . there is still life in the most extreme degradation"—but also "a new ethics," one not grounded in ideals such as *dignity, decency, self-respect*, or even *help*, for the *Muselmänner* are "those who are beyond help."[13] Agamben points toward that new path more than he maps it in detail, suggesting that in the vocabulary of ethics it will be important for "certain words to be left behind and others to be understood in a different sense."[14]

Having lost much of his family in the Holocaust, the French philosopher Emmanuel Levinas argued that ethics had failed to concentrate on something as obvious and profound as the human face.[15] By paying close and careful attention to the face of the other person, he affirmed, there could be a reorientation not only of ethics but also of human life itself, for our seeing of the other person's face would drive home how closely human beings are connected and how much the existence of the other person confers responsibility upon us.

Working in a different but related way, and with awareness of the Holocaust and other mass atrocities on his mind if not explicitly referenced in his writing, the American philosopher John Rawls proposed a form of ethical deliberation that could make human life more just. He suggested that we consider ourselves behind what he called a "veil of ignorance." In that position, we would not know our exact status or role in the world, but we could deliberate constructively about the rights and rules that we all would find reasonable to implement. Rawls thought that such deliberation would place a high priority on liberty and equality. Much of his work in *A Theory of Justice* and other influential writings was devoted to considering how those values could best be mutually supportive.[16] Rawls did not conclude that deliberation behind the veil of ignorance would lead reasonable persons to expect that everyone should be treated exactly alike. Inequality of the right kind could be beneficial for everyone, but for that condition to hold, caring attention would always have to be paid to those who are the least well-off.

By no means are Agamben, Levinas, and Rawls the only philosophers who have reconsidered ethics in light of the Holocaust, genocide, and other mass atrocities and with the failures of ethics in mind. Nor is it true that they developed their ideas independently of previous traditions in ethics. Agamben's rejections, including his disagreement with Heidegger, who once was his teacher, depend on his deep immersion in the history of ethical reflection. Levinas took seriously the ancient Jewish teaching that human beings are created in the image of God. The face of the other person, therefore, has at least traces of the divine within it and deserves respect accordingly. Rawls reinvented the idea of the social contract, which thinkers such as Thomas Hobbes and John Locke developed in the seventeenth century. Agamben, Levinas, and Rawls help to show how one can move beyond previous outlooks as they try to encourage humankind to respond to the ethical dilemmas of our time.

RACE AND RACISM

Rodin's thinker embodied protest and resistance at the gates of hell. From inside or outside the barbed wire, philosophy may do so as well by warning that thinking, including its own, can waste lives and by urging that the action inspired by good thinking might save them. Thus, my students often heard me say that if I had the chance to remove one word, one concept, from human consciousness, my first choice, arguably, would be *race*. Few ideas, if any, have been more pernicious and destructive than that one. *Race* has sometimes been used more-or-less benignly as a synonym for *species* (as in "the human race") or as a word that refers neutrally or in some historical sense to physical, cultural, or ethnic differences among people (as in "the black race"). Overwhelmingly, however, the term *race* has done much more harm than good. Embedded in what can be called the "logic" of *racism*, the reasons are not difficult to find.[17]

52   *The Failures of Ethics*

Uses of the term *race* reflect the interests of human groups. Those interests involve power and control. Racial differentiation, usually traceable ultimately to physical differences such as skin color, has typically entailed distinctions between superiority and inferiority. Attempts to justify such distinctions have often appealed to "nature" or to allegedly empirical corroborations, but deeper inquiry into their origins indicates that such appeals have been rationalizations and legitimations for conceptual frameworks that have been constructed to ensure hegemonies of one kind or another.[18] Far from being neutral, far from being grounded in objective and scientific analysis, racial differentiation has promoted division and advanced the interests of those who want to retain prerogatives and privileges that otherwise might not be theirs. The times when racial distinctions have been benign pale in comparison to those when they have fueled abuse, enslavement, injustice, violence, war, and genocide. Whenever the concept of *race* originated, whatever its forms may have been, seeds of destruction were sown with that concept and the schemes that evolved from it. The harvest has been as bloody and lethal as it has been long.

The crops in that harvest include *racism* among the most prominent and fecund. The term *racism* can be variously defined, but in common and minimalist usage it refers to prejudice, discrimination, and institutions, including law, based on beliefs about superiority and inferiority that pertain to groups of people who are thought to share lines of descent ("blood"), physical characteristics (such as skin color), and/or cultural features and identities ("civilization" of one kind or another). Separating groups of people into those that are superior and inferior, splitting groups of people into *us* and *them*, and doing so in ways that find the differences to be *essential* and usually *biological*, racism entails that difference among racially defined groups is threatening. Such threats have often been interpreted in genocidal ways.

These factors remind me that the Serbian novelist Danilo Kiš was the son of a Montenegrin mother and a Jewish father. Subotica, Kiš's Yugoslavian home town, stood near the Hungarian border. When the Germans attacked Yugoslavia in April 1941, Subotica came under Hungary's control. Not until March 1944, when the Germans occupied the territory of their faltering Hungarian allies, did the Jews of Hungary face the Holocaust's full onslaught. When it came, that disaster took Kiš's father to an Auschwitz death.

Narrated from the perspective of a boy named Andi Scham, *Garden, Ashes* is a poignant, semi-autobiographical novel about the

Holocaust. In ways unconventional for that genre, Kiš does not take his readers inside a ghetto, a deportation cattle-car, or a death camp. Instead, as the story's title suggests, one is led to consider the Holocaust as an absence, an unredeemed emptiness and unredeemable ruin—ashes—where once there had been life that flowed and flowered like a rich, green garden. The absence is personified by Andi's Jewish father, Eduard, who was taken away and presumably killed at Auschwitz, although his son was never quite sure of that and kept hoping and looking for his father's return, which never came.

Eccentric, difficult, but in his own ways loving and lovable, Eduard Scham was a writer whose masterpiece remained unfinished. The lack of closure, however, was not due entirely to the murder of its author. Scham's project was to be the third edition of his previously published *Bus, Ship, Rail, and Air Travel Guide.* In its revised and enlarged form, this book became a mystical, metaphysical exploration that included not only "all cities, all land areas and all the seas, all the skies, all climates, all meridians" but also spiraling roads and forking paths that carried him "afield both in depth and in breadth" so that "abbreviations became subchapters, subchapters became chapters" with no end to their multiplying enigmas.[19]

Like Eduard Scham's travel guide, which led in so many directions without arriving at a certain destination, *Garden, Ashes* lacks closure too. One of the reasons involves the Singer sewing machine that belonged to Andi's mother. The novel's early pages describe it; a sketch of the machine in one of the novel's pages adds to the specificity that Kiš conveys. Andi's mother created beauty with that machine, and thus the sewing machine itself was beautiful, for it signified home and a world in which one could be at home. It is even possible that the destination sought by Eduard Scham's travel guide might have been the place where that sewing machine belonged and where it could be found. The sewing machine, however, was not to be found. Apparently it belonged nowhere, for it "vanished in the confusion of war," writes Kiš.[20] The garden it had helped to create was turned to ashes by the Holocaust.

CONSISTENCY AND INCONSISTENCY

For three reasons, I have referred to Kiš's *Garden, Ashes* in these reflections on philosophy, genocide, and the "logic" of racism. First, the detail of Kiš's story is a reminder of the particularity that is often hidden by terms such as *genocide* or *racism*, which are concepts in ways that fathers, gardens, and sewing machines are not. Second, the destruction of such particularities—and many more—is what racism implies, and that implication also means that, at its core, racism tends to be genocidal. Third, whether there will be, even can be, any closure with regard to this connection, particularly in the sense of dissolving the connection and destabilizing the ideas that comprise it, is something that remains to be seen. At least in part, the outcomes depend on what philosophy and philosophers turn out be.

What happened to Eduard Kiš helps to make these points clear. He was deported to Auschwitz because he was a Jew. Antisemitism was at the heart of Nazi ideology. Within that ideology, antisemitism meant that race—specifically the "purity" of German blood and culture—counted for everything. Nothing could be tolerated—least of all a malignant, treacherous, and inferior Jewish race—that would undermine and pollute the racial strength on which the Third Reich depended. In the Third Reich, Jews were a threat that surpassed all others. Germans, the Nazis' persuasive propaganda insisted, could not afford to let Jews remain in their midst.

As the history of Nazi Germany shows, racism's "logic" leads tellingly, if not inevitably, to genocide. For if you take seriously the idea that one race endangers the well-being of another, the only way to remove that menace completely is to do away, once and for all, with everyone and everything that embodies it. Thus, the Holocaust took the lives of approximately 1.5 million Jewish children who were under the age of 15. If most forms of racism shy away from such extreme measures, Nazi Germany's antisemitism was more consistent. It followed the path that racism's "logic" mapped out.

Genocides are never identical, but all of them share features in common. The goals of genocide can be diverse, including acquiring wealth or territory, or advancing a belief or ideology, but all cases of genocide entail one or more targeted groups that the perpetrators seek to eliminate in one way or another. Although not the same in each case, steps to isolate and separate people take place. The means and duration of murder are not uniform, but most genocides, if not all, involve mass killing. The perpetrators are always particular people; so are the victims. Nevertheless, whatever their ethnicity or group identity may be, perpetrators and victims exist in all genocides.

So do accomplices and bystanders. Without them, neither the causes nor the mechanisms of genocide would have their way so easily.

How does racism fit with this pattern of similarity and difference among genocides? In response, two points loom the largest. First, *the "logic" that operates in and between racism and genocide indicates that racism can exist without genocide, and yet racism tends to be genocidal nonetheless.* Racism can exist at lower or higher levels of intensity. It may express itself in various policies and institutions. Racial discrimination need not be as overt or visible as segregation, *de jure* or *de facto*, makes it; racial prejudice need not produce lynchings or pogroms. Nevertheless, insofar as racism is not self-contradictory but true to its fundamental impulses, it has to take seriously the idea that racial difference is fundamentally at odds with what one deeply values. Much racial thinking and racism in particular is self-contradictory. One's racial group is thought to be better than another, but the idea is not taken seriously enough to produce sustained or systematic action based on racial discrimination, perhaps because cultural values make it politically incorrect or impractical to do so. Racism's impulses can be muted, but such pressures do not eliminate the "logic" of racism, which entails that a perceived racial threat to one's own racial group cannot be ignored with impunity. Furthermore, a savvy racism will include the understanding that in the case of racial threats to one's own racial group, many ways exist—sexual, cultural, political, religious—to produce incursions that pollute what is valued and weaken what allegedly should be authoritative. It follows for the "logic" of racism that racial threats to the purity and hegemony of a privileged racial group must be dealt with in a thoroughgoing manner.

Insofar as one harbors racism, whether in full consciousness or only dimly, a person or even a group can be dishonest and inauthentic in failing to acknowledge: (1) that a consistent racism will want to rid itself of the threat that racial difference poses, and (2) that this goal can be achieved fully, once and for all, only through genocide. The "logic" of racism encourages an "honest" racist to be genocidal—not necessarily to agitate for genocide *now* but to be prepared to incite and implement genocide if and when the times for it are opportune. Ironically, such a realization might produce a fortunate step that could reduce racism, for it may be that those who practice racial discrimination (however inadvertently), and are racists to that extent, do not want to be murderous and would even resist pressures in that direction. Nevertheless, it would be unwise to take much comfort from the fact that racism may often be of a lukewarm and inconsistent variety. An inconsistent racism may not be overtly genocidal, but inconsistency does not defang racism, at least not completely. One can be inconsistent today and consistent tomorrow. The history of genocide bears witness to that.

Continuing the exploration about how racism fits within patterns of similarity and difference among genocides, the second point that looms largest goes as follows: *Although genocide can be incited and committed, at least in principle, without explicit appeals to racial difference, superiority and inferiority, few genocides, if any, are devoid of racism in one form or another.* To justify this claim, note, first, that racism involves more than dislike of behavior, disagreement with political or religious views held by others, or even disputes about national identities. Behavior can shift so that the provocation for dislike is removed. A person's or a group's political perspectives or religious beliefs can be altered so that the grounds for disagreement are taken away. Even citizenship is negotiable and changeable; the irritations that activate disputes about differences in those areas can also be dissolved.

With racism, however, more is at stake than behavior, belief, and even citizenship. To have the dubious distinction of being worthy of the name, racism is about *essential* and usually *biological* differences. Racism trades in the allegedly unchangeable. What is taken to be unchangeable may be masked by what is changeable and changing, but claims about what is *essential* remain at the heart of racism nonetheless. The "logic" of these considerations works in two related ways.

First, racism's "logic" encourages one to think that when a racial threat is perceived, something exists that must be preserved and protected against that threat. What is valued, racism's "logic" understands, could be harmed, compromised, polluted, ruined—the unfortunate verbs multiply their invidious distinctions. Racist feeling is often aroused because it is sensed that such polluting actions have taken place and that they have weakened the privileged racial identity that deserves hegemony. The remedy is to restore health to the privileged race and to purge the forces that are contaminating threats. Within this "logic" is the idea that the privileged race is essentially what it is. Even if compromised and contaminated, it remains and requires vindication lest it be lost, which could happen if vigilance diminishes. Such vigilance, if it is thoroughly and consistently focused on the perceived threats, will tend to have genocidal inclinations.

Second, where either genocidal inclinations or actual implementations of genocide are concerned, racism is likely to be an accompanying and energizing factor. At first glance, that claim might seem at odds with the formal definition of genocide, which in the United Nations' formulation speaks of potentially targeted groups—"national, ethnical, racial or religious"—and identifies a variety of acts that can be carried out with intent to destroy such groups "in whole or in part." At second glance, however, far from eliminating racism, those identifications clarify how racism works in genocide and how it is even required for many genocides to take place.

Where the intent is genocidal, the "logic" of that intention means that destruction "in part" is always second-best. The optimal realization of genocidal intent is to destroy a targeted group "in whole." Practical and philosophical reasons back such "logic." The Nazi SS leader Heinrich Himmler captured both dimensions of this "logic" in a speech about the destruction of Jewry that he delivered in occupied Poland to Nazi leaders on October 6, 1943. "We had to answer the question: What about the women and children?" Himmler observed. "Here, too, I had made up my mind.... I did not feel that I had the right to exterminate the men—that is, to murder them, or have them murdered—and then allow their children to grow into avengers, threatening our sons and grandchildren. A fateful decision had to be made: This people had to vanish from the earth."[21]

Destruction of a group "in part" rightly qualifies as an instance of the crime of genocide, but Himmler's reasoning cogently underscores that the "logic" involved here would find it imprudent not to finish the job once the tasks of genocide have begun and the opportunity to continue to the end is available. Most genocides do not go "all the way," but that outcome takes place either because pressure or force from the outside intervenes, which happens mostly too late and too little, or because exhaustion of one kind or another sets in, or because of some combination of the two. But the "logic" of genocide says that the destruction, once started, should continue to the end. Not to achieve that outcome is to come up short.

The UN's Genocide Convention indicates that there can be an intention to commit genocide halfway—"intent to destroy ... in part," as the wording might be read. One need not deny that such intent could be and even has been real, but in those cases a kind of inconsistency has entered into the intentionality. In the case of the Nazis, for instance, it was not understood that 50 percent of the European Jews were a threat or even that only the destruction of the European Jews was the optimal goal to be achieved. Better still and even necessary, as Himmler put it, was action that made the Jewish people disappear from the earth. Nor, according to the Hutu leadership in Rwanda, was it merely 100,000 Tutsi who had to be destroyed. Better still and even necessary, the "logic" of genocide in Rwanda meant that it would be desirable, if possible, for all the Tutsi in Rwanda and, arguably, elsewhere to be eradicated.

An objection to this line of reasoning might invoke the possibility that genocide can simply be instrumental and thus its perpetrators might not want or intend to go "all the way" because doing so would be contrary to their interests. The latter, for example, might involve decimating a population but also sparing some portion of it for enslavement or other forms of exploitation. Such theory and practice can certainly be genocidal, but in such cases one would still have to ask: Why must so many, if not all, of these people be destroyed?

That question brings back into view the fact that genocide does more than envision instrumental opportunities. Its deepest impulse is to remove a threat. The threat, in turn, will scarcely be describable as such unless the targeted population is portrayed as endangering the prerogatives, the hegemony, and superiority of the perpetrator group. From the perspective of the "logic" of genocide, these threats, more-over, are rooted in what are taken to be, at least by implication, characteristics or qualities that cannot be assimilated into the perpet-rator group. If one's group thinks with a genocidal "logic," then that group cannot embrace the national, ethnic, or religious other, even though in principle and over time, all of those identities could change. It cannot embrace them because at the bottom line an essentialist mindset is typically embedded in genocidal "logic," and in the context of genocidal mentalities that essentialist mindset is closely related to racism, if not virtually synonymous with it.

Not all essentialist ways of thinking are racist, but racism is a form of essentialism, and genocidal mentalities typically reflect forms of racist essentialism. At the end of the day, racism and genocide inflame each other. The "logic" of the one often entails the "logic" of the other. If there are exceptions, they prove the rule: Usually genocide includes racism of one kind or another, and racism tends to be genocidal.

Unmistakable genocide that it was, the Holocaust emerged from a deeply racist Nazi ideology. The genocide in Rwanda, arguably the clearest case of post-Holocaust genocide, was also rooted in racism. Thus, Linda Melvern, a discerning scholar of that genocide, underscores the following points:

> The Hutu extremists believed that the Tutsi were a different race and that they had come from elsewhere to invade Rwanda. Hutu Power taught that the Tutsi were different, that they were lazy; that they did not want to work the land, that they were outside human existence—vermin and subhuman. The effect of the Hutu Power radio, with its catchy nationalistic theme tunes and its racist jingles must never be underestimated. The broadcasts of *Radio-Télévision Libre des Mille Collines* (RTLM) were an integral part of the genocide plot and it was thanks to the propaganda that spewed over the airwaves that by April 1994 a large number of people in Rwanda had come to believe that the elimination of the Tutsi, or "cockroaches" as they were called, was a civic duty and that it was necessary work to rid the country of them.[22]

RAISING VOICES IN ABYSSES OF HORROR

In April 1994, the former New Zealand ambassador Colin Keating served as President of the United Nations Security Council. Twenty years later, on April 16, 2014, he spoke during an open Security Council session that commemorated the genocide in Rwanda that began two decades earlier. Although Keating pushed for condemnation of the genocide in 1994 and for UN support to intervene against it, twenty years later in his capacity as former President of the Council, he apologized "for what we failed to do in 1994." While expressing hope that the principle and practice of the responsibility to protect are gaining traction, he lamented "the cascade of tragedy that can occur when there is a failure of political will such as in 1994."[23] Failure of political will of that magnitude is also a failure of ethics or scarcely anything could be.

In late June 1994, while Keating presided over a malfunctioning Security Council as the killing incited by the RTLM was in full cry, Pope John Paul II sent Cardinal Roger Etchegaray as his envoy to Rwanda. Addressing the Rwandan people after his arrival, Etchegaray spoke of "the abyss of horror" created by the mass murder—and, he might have added, by the lack of robust international intervention—that sundered them. Lest his phrase "the abyss of horror" be taken merely as a rhetorical flourish, consider it in more detail.

The word *abyss* has at least three meanings. It denotes, first, a gulf or pit that is bottomless. This meaning suggests that anything or anyone entering an abyss is utterly lost. Second, *abyss* means chaos or even hell; it refers to disorder in which secure existence for anything or anyone would be impossible until order is created or restored. Third, *abyss* has not only spatial, geographical, or cosmological connotations. The term also refers to the ways in which the human mind and spirit as well as its physical condition can be overwhelmed and left bereft by events that apparently elude rational comprehension. In such cases, the human condition itself becomes abysmal.

Events that elude rational comprehension are often riddled with *horror*, another term that should not be spoken or taken lightly. *Horror* refers to intense feelings of a particular kind and to the actions or conditions that cause them. The feelings, which run deep because they are intense and primal, are those of fear, terror, shock, abhorrence, and loathing. Genocide entails *horror*. An *abyss of horror*, then, would be a reality so grim, so devastating, so full of useless pain, suffering, abandonment, death, and despair that it fractures the world—perhaps forever. Genocide opens an *abyss of horror*. Racism is not the only abysmal force in the world, but if racism were absent, it would be possible to have at least a cautious optimism about responses to the question, "Will genocide ever end?"

A genocidal abyss of horror cannot be closed, at least not completely. Nor can the questions that it raises be answered with confidence and finality. What can be done is to recognize that abysses of horror remain and that the questions they raise deserve to be confronted as we human beings assess and take up our responsibility for both—the abysses and our responses to the questions they leave before us. As one pursues those points, it is well to remember that every form of power includes, even depends upon, raising voices. Leaders have to raise their voices to state their principles, express their visions, and rally their supporters. Governments have to raise their voices to define policies, defend interests, and justify decisions. Supporters of leaders and governments have to raise their voices to back visions and policies; otherwise the power of principles and interests declines and even disappears.

To be effective, the "logic" of racism and genocide also depends on raising voices. That "logic" can have little force unless divisions between people are constructed by speech, fears are expressed in ideology and propaganda, and killing is unleashed by voices that proclaim it to be necessary, and even right and good. The "logic" of racism and genocide also depends on "unraising" voices; it counts on the silencing of dissent and on the acquiescence of bystanders. Every voice unraised against that "logic" gives aid and comfort to those who call for and support genocide. That crime can be prevented before it happens, and it can be stopped after it is under way. Neither prevention nor successful intervention, however, can happen without power. Rwanda's genocidal catastrophe resulted from the fact that raising voices against it came too late and too little.

Here an objection may be raised: Raising voices may not count for much, because actions speak louder than words, and attention should focus much more on what people do than on what they say. That point has validity, but it underestimates the relationship between raising voices and taking action. Racism and genocide do not appear out of the blue. Intentions, plans, and many people are necessary to make them operational. Absent raising voices, the coordination of thought and action required by racism and genocide will not and cannot be in place. The same can be said of protest and resistance against the "logic" of racism and genocide.

Philosophy and philosophers have important contributions to make when it comes to raising voices. Where genocide prevention is concerned, one of those contributions can, and should, be the continuing deconstruction of racial thinking. For if such thinking is curtailed, especially in contexts where philosophers equally emphasize the idea and ideals of universal human rights, then racism may be checked. With that outcome, one of the most potent causes of genocide would be kept at bay. Philosophy is by no means the only discipline that emphasizes logical analysis. Nor are philosophers by any means the sole experts in the critical analysis of reasoning. Anyone reading this book, and countless more, has important contributions to make in these regards. But philosophy and philosophers are in the vanguard of those who value and practice thinking that questions assumptions, asks for evidence, and tracks the connections and implications of ideas. They can do much to criticize, expose, and demystify the ways of thinking that lead to genocide, including the powerful inducement that racism has provided for it. Philosophy and philosophers ignore this task at the risk of leaving humankind in further abysses of horror.

These convictions take my reflections on Rwanda back to the Europe of Danilo Kiš and the Holocaust. His novel *Garden, Ashes* ends on somber notes.[24] "We are witnesses to a great breakdown in values," Kiš writes, and Andi Scham observes that his vanished world has left him in a house with a kitchen stove that cannot "generate a real flame: we lacked a real blaze, there was no glow." The novel's last words belong to Andi's mother, who has no husband and no Singer sewing machine: "Lord," she says, "how quickly it gets dark here." The "logic" of racism remains, and with it genocidal shadows darken our twenty-first century world. None of us alone can remove those shadows, but each of us can do something. For philosophers, that responsibility includes raising voices to unmask and deconstruct the "logic" of racism, raising voices to reveal and undermine that logic's murderous, genocidal impulses. High on philosophy's priorities should be the task of diminishing, if not eliminating, the destructively influential parts that the concept of *race* has played in human history and the work of advancing views of universal human rights that can be as persuasive and credible as possible in a world that remains profoundly wounded by and vulnerable to the threats of genocide.

Born in the late Michigan summer of 1940, I have few first-hand recollections of World War II and none of the Holocaust. I can remember the ration books that my musical mother needed to buy sugar and shoes. My father grew vegetables in a "victory garden." I can recall that the family car had a windshield sticker required for gasoline purchases. My mind's eye retains dim visions of strangely clothed men working in the countryside. My father told me they were prisoners of war—probably Germans. A radio broadcast in August 1945 stands out too, because my parents listened to it so intently. It announced the dropping of the atomic bomb on Hiroshima.

At the age of 5, I knew no living Jews or Muslims, but biblical people—Abraham and Moses, Rachel and Ruth, David and Jonathan, Joseph and Mary, Jesus and his followers were vivid in the stories that my parents read to me each wartime night before I fell asleep. I knew about the Ten Commandments and the idea that we should love our neighbors as ourselves long before I had heard of Auschwitz or Rwanda, crimes against humanity and genocide. Those biblical narratives—the people and teachings they contain—made deep and lasting impressions. Their impacts include five persuasions that remain with me still. Although their articulations are nuanced, their meanings textured, in ways that boyhood understanding could neither anticipate nor grasp, these threads are among the most important that I follow:

- Fundamental differences exist between right and wrong.
- The choices that human beings make are decisive, and thus our accountability is as far-reaching as our responsibility is awesome.
- Human beings are finite, fallible, often frail, and prone to error and wrongdoing.
- Human beings can do better and be better than we have been.
- We ought to love our neighbors as ourselves.

With those persuasions informing me, I cannot confront the Holocaust, genocide, and other mass atrocities without reflection on the biblical commandment "You shall not murder." This chapter takes steps in that direction, ones that entail asking how Jews, Christians, and Muslims could do more to correct the failures of ethics.

4

"You Shall Not Murder"

And the Lord said, "What have you done? Listen; your brother's blood is crying out to me from the ground!"

—Genesis 4:10

With World War II and the Holocaust in mind, the French philosopher Albert Camus made a statement as stark as it is bold. "Every action today," he wrote, "leads to murder, direct or indirect. . . . Murder is the problem today."[1] His outlook implies that human beings live in a murderous web of responsibility that implicates us all. The Jewish artist Samuel Bak would understand Camus's perspective, if not accept it completely. In a prolific and magisterial career, Bak has drawn on his experience as a victim and survivor of the Holocaust to assess the damage done by that catastrophe and to weigh how best to live in what he calls "a world that cries out for repair."[2] A moving example of his work is a 1991 painting called "The Number."[3] It depicts two stone tablets tipping and falling into a barren, cemetery-like abyss. The tablets themselves suggest signs of death. In the background, cracked and breaking apart, one of the two is inscribed with Hebrew letters that refer to God. In the foreground, the second tablet bears the number 6. Recalling the sixth injunction of the Decalogue or Ten Commandments—"You shall not murder"—Bak's portrayal makes one wonder: In a post-Holocaust world, what remains of the Sixth Commandment?[4] Has murder silenced God's voice and destroyed the commandment's credibility? The responses that individuals and communities make to those questions are decisive in "a world that cries out for repair," especially because, as Camus said, "murder is the problem today."

A GREAT DEAL OF DIFFERENCE

Some versions of the Ten Commandments substitute *kill* for *murder*. In either case, those key words require definition if the commandment is to make sense, but how much difference does it make if the Sixth Commandment contains one rather than the other? The answer is *a great deal*. That response and the question prompting it make an apt place to engage the failures of ethics that swirl around and through the imperative that is the most necessary, though not sufficient, condition for human civilization.[5]

According to the most reliable biblical scholarship, *murder*, not *kill*, is the best English term to use in translating the Hebrew text. That decision is significant, for the meanings of *murder* and *kill*, although closely related, are not identical. All murder is killing, but not all killing is murder. To kill means to inflict or cause death, which also happens in murder, but distinctions exist because killing acts can be accidental and unintentional. Killing acts of that kind are not murder, which typically requires an intention, often including premeditation and careful planning, to inflict or cause death. In addition, even when enacted dispassionately and coldly, murderous intentions are usually provoked by anger, malice, envy, greed, fear, hate, revenge, or some other violence-inciting emotion. Not all killing actions fit that description, but typically murderous ones do.

Historically, the Sixth Commandment, along with others in the Decalogue, has been understood to be addressed to human beings— to Jews, to Christians, and indeed to all persons and communities— whose distinctiveness includes a capacity for murder that is not found in any other part of the natural world. Various interpretations of its meaning can be found, but they all share and depend upon the understanding that the imperative applies to human beings who are commanded not to do certain things that are within their power. In such cases, *can* implies *don't*. Awareness of these points helps to underscore other crucial differences between *kill* and *murder*.

The Sixth Commandment is unequivocal and absolute. Allowing no exceptions, it does not say, "Murder is wrong in situation X, but it may be permissible in situation Y." Murder, the commandment entails, is wrong—period. Killing, however, is not so easily interpreted that way, unless one stipulates that *killing* means *murder*. In fact, unless killing is qualified in that way, or in some other way that restricts the meaning of that term to forms of killing that are intentional but unjustifiable or inexcusable, a commandment that said "You shall not kill" would be so ambiguous, even nonsensical, that it would be impossible for human beings to obey it no matter how good they might be or how hard they might try.

To see why that situation holds, notice that human life depends on killing. That statement, of course, is as problematic as it is evident, as much in need of qualification as it is unflinching. Therefore, to avoid misunderstanding, clarification is needed. I do not mean, for example, that human life depends on war; it does not, although sometimes war is unavoidable and even necessary to defend human life. Nor do I mean that human civilization depends on capital punishment; it does not, although there may be times and places where justifiable reasons for executions can be found. What I do mean is that human life and civilization cannot exist, let alone thrive, unless people eat, quench their thirst, obtain shelter, raise and educate their young, and, in short, take the actions that are necessary to sustain human life. Unfortunately, those actions cannot be taken without at least some forms of killing. As the philosopher Philip Hallie cogently put the point, "We are in the food web. We are killers, if only of plants."[6]

In addition, if human life, in the biblical words of Genesis, is to be "fruitful and multiply," it unavoidably becomes even more lethal than Hallie said. Human beings are thinkers and doers; we are political, social, and also religious creatures who plan, strive, and build. Scarcely any of humankind's initiatives can be pursued without dislocations and destructions of one kind or another. Even the most environmentally conscious projects that men and women carry out have lethal consequences for living creatures somewhere.

An absolute and unequivocal prohibition against killing is not what the Sixth Commandment can mean if it is coherent. With due qualification, human life depends on killing, but a corollary of that truth is that human existence and especially its *quality* also depend on careful discrimination between killing that is justifiable or excusable and killing that is not. Absent such discrimination, including laws and sanctions to implement the difference socially and politically, it is hard to imagine that human civilization could long endure. Instead, to use Thomas Hobbes's bleak description from 1651, human existence would likely be in "that condition which is called war, and such a war as is of every man against every man. . . . In such condition there is . . . continual fear and danger of violent death; and the life of man solitary, poor, nasty, brutish, and short."[7]

Not even the most thorough, rigorous, and truthful interpretation of the Sixth Commandment, however, may be able to provide a complete analysis of killing that is justifiable or excusable and killing that is not. After acknowledging that some kinds of killing are necessary for the basic sustenance of human life, the category of killing may still remain larger than the category of murder. At least in many cases, if not ordinarily, murder is not the category into which one places killing in self-defense, for example, or killing to prevent the murder of another person or to combat warring aggression. Even when unjust war unleashes killing that is met with armed resistance, a gray zone of moral classification may exist, and it will be debatable whether all the killing done by the warring aggressor, wrong though it surely is, should be called murder. In short, there remain cases of killing, justifiable or unjustifiable, that are not necessarily cases of murder, or at least not clearly so. That realization, however, does not cut slack for killing; at least it should not, because most killing can and should be found wrong and condemned without inevitably and always being classified as murder.

MAKING SENSE

Much killing, but not all, is murder, but now two more questions must be addressed for the Sixth Commandment to make sense: When is killing murder? What constitutes murder? My response to those questions emerges from the perspectives that inform my thinking about the Sixth Commandment. Those perspectives sometimes involve biblical narratives and, in particular, the story in Genesis 4 that depicts Cain's slaying of his brother Abel, the murder that the Hebrew Bible identifies as the first.

According to that account, when God favored Abel's offering but "had no regard" for Cain's, the latter's anger got the best of him. "Let us go out to the field," Cain said to the apparently unsuspecting Abel. "And when they were in the field," the biblical text continues, "Cain rose up against his brother Abel, and killed him." The story reports that God responded: "What have you done? Listen; your brother's blood is crying out to me from the ground!" Cain's killing made him "a fugitive and a wanderer on the earth," one who "went away from the presence of the Lord," but God spared Cain's life, marking him "so that no one who came upon him would kill him."

At rock bottom, murder takes place when one person kills another intentionally, deliberately, and unjustifiably. (Much hinges on the latter term in particular, a point to which we will return in due course.) Cain's killing of Abel was murder—*homicide*—or nothing could be. Moreover, like the Sixth Commandment itself, the Genesis narrative leaves no doubt that murder is wrong. That same account, however, raises as many questions as it answers. For instance, was Cain's killing of Abel clearly premeditated? Genesis does not say so explicitly, although far from being excluded, the text definitely invites such an inference. Furthermore, when Cain "rose up against his brother," was that action murderous from the outset? Again, the text allows for the possibility that it might not have been that way, although Cain's "rising up" resulted in killing that was unlikely to have been accidental. Otherwise, Cain probably would not have tried to fend off God's question—"Where is your brother Abel?"—by denial and evasion: "I do not know; am I my brother's keeper?"

The ambiguities do not end there. When Cain questioned whether he should be held accountable as his brother's keeper, was he implying that creation did not yet have a moral structure that condemned murder as the Sixth Commandment would do explicitly later on? Cain's defense might have been that he unfairly received an ex post facto judgment from God. Who says, and where and when was it said, Cain might have protested, that I am to be Abel's keeper? However, if Cain made a legalistic move of this kind, Genesis shows that God had none of it. Prior to Cain's murdering Abel, the biblical account in Genesis brims with language about what is good, about the knowledge of good and evil, about obedience and disobedience. The Genesis tradition, moreover, makes clear not only that God "created humankind in his image, in the image of God he created them; male and female he created them" but also that "God blessed them." Could it make any good sense for God to create human beings in God's image, bless them, and then permit them with impunity to slaughter one another intentionally? At the end of the day, ambiguity notwithstanding, no credible reading could interpret Genesis as doing less than defining murder quintessentially or as doing anything other than finding murder wrong—period.

The biblical affirmation is that God created human life in God's image. In God's sight, and usually in ours, that act was good. It was also awesome, even sacred, for in the ultimate sense, no human being has the power to create human life—not even the wonders of twenty-first century science contest that fact—and murder destroys human life in ways that are beyond our repair and recovery. God may or may not resurrect the dead, but human beings utterly lack the power to do so. The result is that no human act rivals murder in defying, disrespecting, and denying God. The Christian philosopher Stephen Davis succinctly sums up the biblical outlook on this point: "Murder, then, is a crime both against the victim and his family and friends, and also (and most importantly) against God."[8]

TWO EPISODES

The biblical narrative combines the introduction of murder into the world with injunctions against such wasting of life. History shows the fragilities and the failures of the injunctions whenever they are eclipsed, as so often they are, by the murderous wasting of life that has bloodied and scarred the world almost beyond belief. Linked to Cain's murder of Abel, even though they are millennia removed from that act, two episodes drive home that point.

Richard Rhodes's *Masters of Death: The SS-Einsatzgruppen and the Invention of the Holocaust* details how Nazi Germany's mobile killing units murdered 1.5 million Jews in eastern Europe during World War II. "Maps in Jewish museums from Riga to Odessa," writes Rhodes, "confirm that almost every village and town in the entire sweep of the Eastern territories has a killing site nearby."[9] Gratuitous and sadistic violence accompanied the slaughter. Rhodes describes one instance as follows: "A woman in a small town near Minsk saw a young German soldier walking down the street with a year-old baby impaled on his bayonet. 'The baby was still crying weakly,' she would remember. 'And the young German was singing. He was so engrossed in what he was doing that he did not notice me.'"[10]

Although such brutal murder should rightly leave one speechless, there are many things that ought to be said about it. One of them is that if such action is not an example of unjustifiable killing, what could be? Of course, the young German and his Nazi superiors, Adolf

Hitler and SS leader Heinrich Himmler first and foremost among them, would have argued differently. In their Nazi eyes, the mass killing of Jews was not only justifiable but also morally right and imperative. To them, Jews were such an unrelenting, pestilential threat to the "superior" German *Volk* that Jewish life—including, significantly, the Jewish tradition that emphasized the Sixth Commandment—must be eradicated root and branch. Arguably Hitler and Himmler did not advocate gratuitous and sadistic violence. They likely would have disapproved of young Germans who found joy in impaling infants on their bayonets. They wanted "decent" killers instead.

Hitler, Himmler, and the young German soldier in Rhodes's account were neither insane nor completely irrational. They had a worldview that made sense to them, and they acted on it.[11] Nevertheless, rational and ethical scrutiny far better and deeper than theirs underscores how much the Nazis' reasoning, planning, and acting were misguided and immoral. For no matter how sincerely Hitler and his followers held their beliefs or how valid they took them to be, those convictions and the mass murder that flowed from them were based on error and terror, on deceit and delusion, on theft and tyranny, on falsehood and aggression, on disrespect and hate for human life other than their own. That catalog does not exhaust the criteria that brand killing unjustifiable, but no killing arising from those conditions, dispositions, or motivations can reasonably be justified.

Unjustified and unjustifiable, so much of the killing done by Nazi Germany and its collaborators was not only murder but also *mass murder*. Mass murder kills individuals; it may even have to target them one by one. But mass murder also destroys groups of people, and when that intention governs the killing, mass murder becomes genocidal. Cain committed homicide and fratricide but not genocide. The United Nations' definition indicates that genocide—the intended destruction, "in whole or in part [of] a national, ethnical, racial, or religious group, as such"—can take place without direct murder, but typically genocide is no less an occasion for murder than is the case with homicide and fratricide. Granting some genocidal exceptions, all three are instances of murder; all three involve the intended, deliberate but unjustifiable taking of individual lives. In genocide, however, the murderous aim is immensely escalated, and a person's life is at risk not for anything in particular that he or she has done but simply because one exists at all as a member of a targeted group. The fact that the group is targeted is crucial, because all human individuals are fundamentally defined by factors of group identity of one kind or another. Indeed, there can be no individual human life without such identities. Unfortunately, not even genocide is the end of the matter where mass murder is concerned, and thus we come to a second episode, one involving calculations of time and distance.

In 1994, the political scientist R. J. Rummel, a demographer of what he calls *democide*, published an important book called *Death by Government*. Writing before he could have taken account of the late twentieth-century genocidal atrocities in Bosnia, Rwanda, and Kosovo, or the twenty-first century genocide in the Darfur region of Sudan, Rummel estimated that "the human cost of war and democide"— he defined *democide* as "the murder of any person or people by a government, including genocide, politicide, and mass murder"—is more than "203 million people in [the twentieth] century."[12] (What the precise figure would be today, God only knows.)

"If one were to sit at a table," Rummel went on to say, "and have this many people come in one door, walk at three miles per hour across the room with three feet between them (assume generously that each person is also one foot thick, navel to spine), and exit an opposite door, it would take over *five years and nine months* for them all to pass, twenty-four hours a day, 365 days a year. If all these dead were laid out head to toe, assuming each to be an average of 5 feet tall, they would reach from Honolulu, Hawaii, across the vast Pacific and then the huge continental United States to Washington, D.C. on the East coast, *and then back again almost twenty times*."[13]

While Rummel may have thought that such calculations would make the abstraction of huge numbers more concrete, it is not clear that he even convinced himself, for he placed an endnote number at his calculation's conclusion. Note 14 reads as follows: "Back and forth, over 4,838 miles one way, near twenty times? This is so incredible that I would not believe the calculation and had to redo it several times."[14] The Sixth Commandment has neither functioned nor fared nearly as well as God and humankind should desire. Things could always be worse, even to the point of *omnicide*, the total extinction of life, which may now be within the willful killing and murderous prowess of human beings, but humanity's murderous ways lend all too much credence to the point made by Elie Wiesel when he said, "At Auschwitz, not only man died, but also the idea of man. . . . It was its own heart the world incinerated at Auschwitz."[15]

KNOW BEFORE WHOM YOU STAND

Desecrated but not destroyed completely in the November 1938 Nazi pogroms collectively called *Kristallnacht*, a Torah ark from the synagogue in the German town of Nentershausen is honored in the permanent exhibition at the United States Holocaust Memorial Museum (USHMM) in Washington, DC. Such respect is more than appropriate because the *Aron ha-Kodesh* (the Holy Ark), as it is called in Hebrew, occupies a special, sacred space in every synagogue. It does so because the ark houses scrolls, precious possessions for each and every Jewish community, that contain inscriptions of the Pentateuch, the Five Books of Moses—Genesis, Exodus, Leviticus, Numbers, and Deuteronomy—the most important parts of the Hebrew Bible (*Tanakh*).

Visitors to USHMM are not told what happened to the Torah scrolls that were once safely kept in the ark of the Nentershausen synagogue. It is not far-fetched, however, to think that those scrolls, like so many others during the years of the Holocaust, were mutilated and burned. So, as one stands before the Torah ark from Nentershausen, an absence can be felt. The disrespect and defacing inflicted on the scarred and empty Torah ark would silence—if it could—scripture that proclaims one God to be the creator of the world and human life (Genesis 1–2), tells the story of Abraham, whose faith gave birth to Judaism, Christianity, and Islam (Genesis 11–25), and affirms that "you shall love your neighbor as yourself" (Leviticus 19:18).

In *A World without Jews*, an astute book by Alon Confino, the author rightly argues that too little attention has been paid to the torching of synagogues and, even more importantly, the burning of Torah scrolls—destruction of the Bible—during *Kristallnacht*. That night was not the only time when scripture was destroyed in Nazi Germany, but on the night of November 9–10, 1938, thousands of Torah scrolls in hundreds of communities, small and large, were put to flames. These transgressions were public events; children as well as adults participated in them. Sometimes Jews were forced to rip the Torah scrolls apart and ignite them.[16]

The scripture burning was more than antisemitic mayhem. It was more than a prelude to genocide against Jews alive at the time. Destruction of Hebrew scripture meant freedom from old morality that inhibited the racist new world order envisioned by Nazi ideology. A decisive failure of ethics, the destruction of Torah scrolls signified unbounded rejection of Jewish tradition, a "cleansing" of the Ten Commandments and their injunction against murder. A dissenting German pastor, Helmut Gollwitzer, active in the Protestant Confessing Church, which opposed Nazi intervention in church affairs, understood this implication. A few days after *Kristallnacht*, on November 16, he preached in the Berlin suburb of Dahlem during the annual Day of Prayer and Repentance service, beginning his sermon by asking, "What should one preach today? . . . Can we do anything else today but be silent?" Later that day, he noted: "According to the old Prussian liturgy of the Day I read the Ten Commandments. In the dead silence of the shocked community they sounded like hammer blows."[17] Most Germans, however, neither heard nor felt things that way. The testimony of a pro-Nazi German Christian leader, Siegfried Leffler, fitted their outlook better. Earlier, at a theological meeting in February 1936, he said:

> As a Christian, I can, I must, and I ought always to have or to find a bridge to the Jew in my heart. But as a Christian, I also have to follow the laws of my nation [Volk], which are often presented in a very cruel way, so that again I am brought into the harshest of conflicts with the Jew. Even if I know "thou shalt not kill" is a commandment of God or "thou shall love the Jew" because he too is a child of the eternal father, I am able to know as well that I have to kill him, I have to shoot him, and I can only do that if I am permitted to say: Christ.

For Leffler to say "Christ" entailed that Jesus and Germany had to be severed and cleansed from everything Jewish. From that point of view, the destruction of synagogues, the burning of Torah scrolls, the obliteration of "Jewish" ethics, and a world without Jews and Judaism were not shocking but morally right and imperative.[18]

Absence and silence can be intensified as one stands before the Nentershausen Torah ark at USHMM because, while the Torah scrolls from the Nentershausen ark are missing, Hebrew writing on its lintel, a supporting beam or mantel above the ark's doors, is not. Like many Torah arks, the one at Nentershausen had an inscription taken from the Talmud (Berachot 28b), the authoritative rabbinical commentary on the Torah: *Da lifnei mi attah omed*—Know before Whom you stand. These words, which call one to attention and accountability, to reverence and awe before God, the source and sustainer of life, did not escape the notice of those who plundered the Nentershausen synagogue in November 1938, for an unknown assailant attacked them in a violent attempt to silence their voice, erase their authority, and eradicate their credibility. Their scarred condition bears witness to shameless arrogance even as the wounded words provide a fragile and poignant, if not forlorn, judgment against the hubris and hatred that divide humankind.

One of my encounters with the Nentershausen Torah ark at USHMM took place in October 2007 during a Jewish-Christian-Muslim "trialogue," that explored how confronting the Holocaust might affect interreligious understanding.[19] When the participants reconvened after exploring USHMM's permanent exhibition, discussion concentrated on the Torah ark. We came to feel that the ark had addressed us through the words on its lintel: Know before Whom you stand. Differences in our religious traditions meant that our experiences were not identical during and after the time when we faced those words, but all of us agreed that the encounter with the desecrated Torah ark and its scarred inscription made us deeply aware of concerns we shared. Whether our identities were Jewish, Christian, or Muslim, we all could feel the loss, including the denial of freedom to practice one's religion that would be ours if places and writings sacred in our own traditions were so horrifically disrespected and profaned with such impunity. We could also feel abhorrence for any person or community identified with our own tradition who would stoop to such atrocity, an experience that made us mindful of our accountability and responsibility for the traditions that are ours.

As we took stock at USHMM, focusing our attention and trialogue on renewed and deepened awareness that we stand responsible before God, our co-religionists, and those who profess faiths related to but different from our own, we were well aware that our work was taking place in a post-9/11 world, one in which the al-Qaeda attacks on New York's World Trade Center and the Pentagon in Washington, DC, had exacerbated suspicion about Islam and hostility toward Muslims. We scarcely could have anticipated, however, the upsurge of such suspicion and hostility that erupted in the summer and autumn of 2010, when plans for the construction of an Islamic cultural center and mosque near "Ground Zero" in New York City became so highly charged and volatile that the answer to the question "Is America Islamophobic?"—the cover of *Time* magazine raised it explicitly on August 30, 2010—arguably was yes.

If genuine trialogue among Jews, Christians, and Muslims was not conspicuous by its absence during the summer and autumn of 2010, too often its place was replaced by strident, intolerant, religiously and politically partisan, and belligerent voices, which were epitomized by that of Terry Jones, an obscure Christian pastor from Gainesville, Florida. His "Burn a Koran Day" campaign was thwarted only after American political and military leaders intervened with warnings that Jones's plans would seriously inflame much of the Muslim world and endanger Americans in places such as Afghanistan. Even that intervention, however, was insufficient to deter Jones completely. On March 20, 2011, he publicly burned the Qur'an. Within days, news of that provocation swept through Afghanistan, leading to demonstrations and violence that left more than twenty people dead, including several United Nations employees, and about 150 wounded.

More recently, further tests for interreligious understanding and trialogue in the United States loomed large. One involved two pressure cooker bombs that exploded near the finish line of the Boston Marathon on April 15, 2013. Murdering three persons, including an 8-year-old boy, and seriously wounding 140 others, the bombing was carried out by Tamerlan Tsarnaev, 26, and his brother Dzhokhar Tsarnaev, 19, whose links to militant Islam complicated, among other factors, already difficult issues about American immigration policy. Then, in September–October 2014, the murderous ISIS regime beheaded American freelance journalists James Foley and Steven Sotloff, British aid worker Alan Henning, and Peter Kassig, an American medical aid in Syria. Subsequently, in January 2015, Islamist militants terrorized Paris, murdering journalists at the offices of the satirical weekly *Charlie Hebdo* and taking hostages at a kosher supermarket, killing four of them. Meanwhile, Nigeria's militant Islamist group Boko Haram continued the bombings, assassinations, and abductions that have slaughtered thousands in that region. The likelihood that ISIS and other jihadists will murder more and more in the name of Islam and Allah drives home all the more the frail but imperative status of the Sixth Commandment: You shall not murder.

NO ETHICAL INJUNCTION IS MORE IMPORTANT

No ethical injunction is more important than "You shall not murder." Human civilization depends on it. So does the value of religion, including Judaism, Christianity, and Islam, the traditions that, in one way or another, trace their origins back to the biblical patriarch Abraham. Christianity, my religious tradition, emphasizes the Ten Commandments, especially as they are stated in Exodus 20 within the Hebrew Bible. Yet, Christians—individually and collectively— have often disobeyed the Sixth Commandment. Indeed, Christians have even incited and committed murder in God's name. Jews and Muslims have been victims of that crime. When it comes to murder, there is much need for Christian repentance and atonement.

The facts stated above have many implications for me. How, for example, can I best respond to Christianity's staggering violations of the commandment against murder? Where does Christianity's sometimes murderous history allow me—require me—to stand when it comes to dialogue with Jews and Muslims? In addition to Christianity, how do Judaism and Islam fare in relation to the Sixth Commandment? What if all three of the Abrahamic traditions, in their own particular, distinctive, and non-equivalent ways, are implicated in violations of the Sixth Commandment? How can and should "trialogue" go forward in response to the possibility that murder must be faced in multifaceted ways by all three of these traditions—again, in their own particular, distinctive, and non-equivalent ways? Honesty requires accuracy and accountability concerning the ways in which the Abrahamic traditions are—and are not—complicit in murder and in which they and their adherents have been its targets. Can such assessments avoid the failures of ethics that will result if the outcome is irreconcilable differences about who has done the most harm or suffered the greatest loss? Instead, can reflection about the Sixth Commandment be a touchstone for trialogue that can benefit Judaism, Christianity, and Islam individually, in relation to each other, and in ways that might bring about changes that make it at least less necessary to speak of ours as an age of genocide?

According to the biblical scholar David Flusser, the Christian New Testament "does not use the term 'Ten Commandments' even once," but the injunction against murder is emphasized in multiple instances, and especially by Jesus in ways that are thoroughly consistent with the Jewish tradition that was his.[20] In Matthew 19:16–22, Mark 10:17–22, and Luke 18:18–23, for example, Jesus stresses the importance of obeying God's commandments and explicitly condemns murder. Paul does the same in Romans 13:9, adding that the

Sixth Commandment, along with those prohibiting adultery and theft, "are summed up in this word, 'Love your neighbor as yourself.'" Flusser's observation about the Christian New Testament arguably may be appropriate for the Qur'an as well. If the latter does not cite the biblical "Ten Commandments," it prohibits murder both explicitly and implicitly. Representative passages such as the following bear witness to that claim: (1) "Whoever kill[s] a human being, except as a punishment for murder or other villainy in the land, shall be looked upon as though he had killed all mankind . . ." (5:32). (2) "You shall not kill—for that is forbidden by God—except for a just cause" (6:151). (3) "Do not kill except for a just cause (manslaughter is forbidden by Him)" (25:68).[21] These texts use *kill* more than *murder*. If qualifications such as "except for a just cause" surround the former, as they often do in Jewish and Christian interpretations as well, at least an implied imperative against murder exists in these passages. That imperative is without qualification—unless, of course, one argues that an instance of murder is really an instance of justifiable killing and thus not murder at all. All three of the traditions have dubiously employed such reasoning and discourse when it suited them, a fact that complicates, but by no means invalidates, the injunction against murder. It is in this fraught area that some of the most crucial aspects of contemporary Jewish-Christian-Muslim trialogue are to be found, particularly as violence rages in the Middle East, the Central African Republic, and elsewhere, improvised explosive devices (IEDs) and suicide bombers deal death, drones strike, and problematic claims about the "justice" of what are murderous actions are sounded on all sides of conflicts in which Jews, Christians, and Muslims are deeply affected, embedded, and implicated.

Here it is important to underscore that interreligious discussion focused on the Sixth Commandment will be complicated by the fact that in specific times and places, one tradition and its members may be deeply and distinctively implicated in murder, while others have such responsibility to a lesser extent or not at all. Both within and among the Abrahamic traditions, these differences must be identified and acknowledged, their meanings probed and their reverberations assessed. During the Holocaust and in the Rwandan genocide, for example, Christianity and Christians had immense involvement in and distinctive responsibility for the devastation. More recently, the *Washington Post* editorialist Michael Gerson rightly criticized Mahmoud Ahmadinejad and other Iranian Muslims for inciting genocide with their deadly rhetoric that repeatedly insisted that Israel must be "wiped off the map."[22] Just as Christians struggle to be accountable for Christianity's complicity in genocide, Muslims need to intervene against the murderous violence currently advocated or unleashed from within that tradition, currently but not only in Syria and Iraq, and Jews should keep testing Israeli governmental and military policies in light of the Sixth Commandment as well.[23] The necessary soul-searching requires self-study and self-criticism from within each tradition, but when such inquiry is carried on interreligiously—in contexts where the soul-searching is mutually encouraged and supported—inquiry may go deeper, honesty may be more profound, and openness to constructive change may be increased. The possibilities and prospects for such work are themselves matters that need discussion within and among the Abrahamic traditions. To the extent that multifaceted soul-searching can develop, chances remain to salvage the Sixth Commandment from the fate that "The Number," Samuel Bak's painting referenced at the outset, foresees and fears even in its resistance against that oblivion.

On October 11, 2014, Bak opened an exhibition featuring what he calls his H.O.P.E. paintings, which explore the prospects for hope in a world that so often crushes them. In these paintings, Bak explains, "the H.O.P.E. letters appear in various stages of visibility, half hidden, broken, unbelievably large or miniscule. And the beholder is asked to make a corresponding effort, for the issue of visibility is related to the problem we all share in searching for Hope when it is so difficult to find."[24] One painting in the exhibition is called "Helping Hands." In a devastated landscape, the large letters H.O.P.E. are battered, bruised, and disordered, but creaking wheels make them movable. Three figures are visible. One holds and guides the letter H. Another does the same with the letter E. The third may be giving directions about what to do with the letters. What will happen next, however, remains in suspense. Are the letters being moved to create H.O.P.E. or to dash and trash it? Will H.O.P.E. become more visible or less so? Is the title of Bak's painting—"Helping Hands"—ironic, despairing, resisting, encouraging, or some mixture of those moods? Bak says that he practices "the art of asking questions." This particular painting asks: Whose "helping hands" does it depict, and what kind are they? Do our hands, especially those of Jews, Christians, and Muslims salvage hope or dispel it? As Bak's art suggests, prospects for such salvage and for the interreligious trialogue that could help to promote it must remain guarded. To some extent the Sixth Commandment has had a braking effect on humankind's propensity for violence. Unfortunately, a frank historical appraisal leads to the conclusion that the most distinctive quality about the Sixth Commandment is not the hope it contains but the extent to which it has been violated—disregarded, dismissed, and disrespected. Coupled with those characteristics, one must add that the Sixth Commandment has never been backed sufficiently by credible sanctions, divine or human, that would ensure full respect for and obedience to it.[25]

An injunction that is not heeded lacks credibility. When Nazi Germany, supported by many German Christians, unleashed the Holocaust, the force of the imperative "You shall not murder" was impugned and ethics failed to such a degree that millions of Jews were slaughtered. It took the violence of a massive world war, which left tens of millions more corpses in its wake, before the Third Reich was crushed and the Holocaust's genocidal killing ended. The Sixth Commandment will continue to be the imperative that is the most necessary, although not sufficient, condition for human civilization. No less clear is the fact that this commandment will continue to be violated, often immensely, and with a large measure of impunity. Furthermore, the God who prohibits murder is also the One who apparently will do relatively little, if anything, to stop human beings from committing homicide or genocide. Nevertheless, the commandment against murder remains, disrespected and impotent though it often is. If that injunction is not at the heart of ethics in all three of the Abrahamic traditions, their moral stature is bereft and suspect.

To my mind, the point of Jewish-Christian-Muslim trialogue is much more ethical than theological. Granted, ethical and theological perspectives are often related and even inseparable, but they are not identical. Ethical relationships, characterized by caring for one another, are what trialogue most needs to achieve. At the core of those relationships stands the commandment and commitment not to murder one another. I doubt that trialogical discussion about God, important though it can be, is likely to advance this cause much beyond a basic agreement that murder is wrong.

What may be more helpful, but only by a little, I expect, is discussion that clarifies what is included or excluded in the concept of murder. The problem here is that the human propensity for rationalization and self-righteousness will try to justify killing as non-murder, thus explaining murder away, while at the same time indicting opponents as murderers when their actions attack one's own people. If agreement that murder is wrong can serve as a basis for Jewish-Christian-Muslim trialogue, then that agreement will need to get beyond rationalization, self-righteousness, and every other impulse that finds "them" murderous but never "us."

As noted earlier, killing acts can be accidental and unintentional. Killing acts of that kind are not murder, nor are those carried out in self-defense or to protect others from life-threatening violence. But those qualifications still leave murder taking an immense toll, not only in individual homicidal acts but also in terrorist attacks, war crimes, crimes against humanity, and genocide. Typically, murderous actions require an intention, often including premeditation and careful planning, to inflict or cause death. Importantly, intent ought not to be construed too narrowly lest murderous acts are falsely denied and swept away by the defining strokes of self-serving pens. Where murder is concerned, particularly the mass murder associated with terrorist attacks, war crimes, crimes against humanity, and genocide, intent should not be restricted to premeditation and careful planning. Room should also be left for indictments based on considered judgments that there are good reasons to think that the actions a person or group has carried out or is undertaking were, or are likely, to inflict death in ways that exceed reasonable understandings of self-defense or the protection of others against life-threatening violence. No one-size-fits-all rationale exists to decide these cases, or even to define the terms that are unavoidably in play within such judgments. For that reason, I suggest a different approach that might make the injunction against murder a more credible and fruitful basis for Jewish-Christian-Muslim trialogue. This approach concentrates neither on God nor on concepts but on the dead.

So many of the dead are dead not because they lived to a ripe old age or even because disease, untimely though it may have been, ended their lives. So many of the dead are dead—children and women as well as men, the young and the old—because they were murdered. If most of the murdered do not have their lives stolen by what we typically mean by homicide, neither are the murdered ones killed as enemy combatants in warfare nor are they the unfortunate civilian casualties of euphemistic "collateral damage" during military operations, a category that unethically washes murder away.[26] The murdered ones include the innocent—a real and valid category, notwithstanding ideologies that make all victims "guilty"—especially in recent times, the innocent slaughtered in rocket attacks, drone launches, and air strikes, wiped out by suicide bombings and IEDs, annihilated in mass shootings, starved to death, beheaded and butchered in hundreds of lethal ways.

Those unjustly robbed of life by human decisions and human actions are the ones we need especially to see and to heed. But if we settle for calling these dead *victims*, we misplace where key aspects of the emphasis need to be placed. By speaking of victims, we rightly call attention to the victimizers, to the murderers. By speaking only of victims, however, we obscure the faces of the dead and the humanity of the murdered. If we see the dead, if we listen—carefully, thoughtfully—for what they "say," the humanity of their mutilated bodies, the screams that cry out in silence, demand "You shall not murder." How could they not? No voice divine or human can speak with more authority, more passion and urgency, than that. Neither the figurative face of God nor the face of the actual living other can exceed what the faces of the murdered ones tell us about the fragile preciousness of the gift of human life. If we cannot heed what the murdered ones say, Jewish-Christian-Muslim trialogue will fall short of its potential for good.

CARRY ON, CARRY ON

The legendary Irish musician Tommy Sands has shown for decades that seemingly fragile and powerless realities—for example, his guitar and voice singing songs he recalls from the past or writes for the present and future—can be resilient sources of encouragement and strength, protesting against the failures of ethics and inspiring commitment to deepen understanding, cultivate respect, and heal discord. Two hallmarks of his music, which played important parts in the peace process that calmed the violent "troubles" long separating Protestants and Catholics in Northern Ireland, are persistence and inclusion.

"Carry on," says one of Sands's famous songs, "carry on, / You can hear the people singing, / Carry on, carry on, / Till peace will come again."[27] Traditional Irish music, and Sands's versions of it are no exception, is scarcely triumphal. It assumes no guarantees that what is right and good will prevail. Seeing and remembering the murdered dead, lamenting the wounding and loss of life, yearning for conditions that preserve and sustain the existence and good that people share, this music carries on by summoning resistance, encouraging the hope of nevertheless against the joy-robbing afflictions produced by disrespect for and exclusion of the other. Absent persistence that refuses to stop combating the causes of injustice and suffering, what Sands calls "the lonely years of sorrow" are likely to go on and on, leaving immense waste and no peace in their wake.[28]

Signs of Sands's persistence were visible during the summer of 2010, when he and his multi-talented musical family accepted Leonard Grob's invitation to visit the Stephen S. Weinstein Holocaust Symposium, the eighth in a biennial series at Wroxton College in England. Some of the participants in the aforementioned USHMM trialogue are members of this symposium, which was the source from which that particular Jewish-Christian-Muslim interaction evolved. Sands and his family had recently returned to the United Kingdom after bringing their music and testimony to embattled Israelis and Palestinians, whose prospects for peaceful coexistence remain so fraught that even a Tommy Sands might have been deterred from trying to improve them. Far from being deterred, however, Sands and his family took their fragile instruments, their seemingly powerless music, and carried on by offering visions of alternatives that invited Israelis and Palestinians to join him in song and in creative politics too.

As Sands made clear, the alternatives he envisions emphasize inclusiveness, and his understanding of inclusiveness places a premium on hospitality, on welcoming the stranger, indeed, on turning strangers into friends. "Let the circle be wide round the fireside," Sands sings, "And we'll soon make room for you / Let your heart have no fear / There are no strangers here / Just friends that you never knew."[29]

Are such sentiments more than feel-good wishful thinking? Perhaps not, and yet when Sands and his family sing this song, skepticism and cynicism can be laid to rest, if only momentarily. It is worth noting, too, that the participants in the USHMM trialogue were once just that—strangers who came from religious traditions that have harbored and often intensified fear of each other. Some of us—Jews and Christians—were strangers when we first met at the Wroxton symposia initially organized by Leonard Grob and Henry Knight in 1996. Friendship grew, and its circle expanded to include the Muslim participants in the USHMM discussions—some of them strangers to each other as well as to their Jewish and Christian partners before they accepted the risky invitation to engage in trialogue and found friendship in that process. This small but expanding circle confirmed that Sands's vision—"There are no strangers here / Just friends that you never knew"—could be more than sentimental, feel-good, wishful thinking.

As the trialogue unfolded, it became increasingly clear that the goal for our small circle and for the interreligious understanding needed so much in our twenty-first century world is one and the same. In Sands's words, that goal is to "make room for you," to meet and treat each other well. Translated into the terms of interreligious relations, this goal means that Jews, Christians, and Muslims need to show hospitality to one another, and nothing is more fundamental to that hospitality than pluralism, which at its core entails that religious differences are more than "tolerated" or even "respected" but are welcomed. Even that way of putting the point, however, remains too abstract, for the key is that religiously different persons and communities need to welcome one another. For that to happen people and communities often have to change internally as well as in relation to each other. Such work is easier said than done. It requires setting aside the exclusive and all-too-often violence-prone conviction that my way is right and yours is not; it entails embracing Tommy Sands's precarious but truthful insight that closing "our eyes to the other side" makes us "just half of what we could be."[30]

No one-size-fits-all grasps what the hospitality of pluralism entails. For the three Abrahamic traditions, for the individuals and communities in which those traditions live, the hospitality of religious pluralism always must be attentive to needs, responsibilities, and opportunities that reflect the particularity and specificity of time and circumstance. Yet in those details, the shared, persistent, and inclusive goal of the hospitality of pluralism is to create and sustain welcoming conditions so that "There are no strangers here / Just friends that you never knew." Hospitality extended to the other, what Tommy Sands calls making "room for you," is at the heart of ethics in the Abrahamic faiths. The hospitality of religious pluralism entails a profound and humane humility that can help to turn strangers into friends. Jews, Christians, and Muslims can and should care deeply about their traditions and about how to make them the best that they can be. They can even say that for them it would not really be thinkable to embrace another tradition as one's own. But at the same time, the hospitality of pluralism requires recognition that neither *my* way nor *your* way is *the* way.

All religious traditions—individually and even collectively—are incomplete, fallible, in need of correction and revision as they encounter one another, probe themselves, and expand their horizons. To cite Tommy Sands once more, the Abrahamic traditions, each and all, need to see that if they close their eyes to the other side, they are just half of what they could be. But if these traditions open themselves in hospitality to one another, they will come closer to what shows itself to be right, good, and truly awesome—the "beyond," the divine, that each seeks and can find, at least in part, even while its fullness eludes our human grasp, as it must. Camus remains correct: Murder is the problem today. But if the right interreligious responsibilities become more pronounced and widespread, the fragile commandment "You shall not murder" may still be heard and obeyed enough so that it is not destined to be the shattered and abandoned number 6 in Samuel Bak's poignant painting. Instead, the Sixth Commandment may enlist Jews, Christians, and Muslims to provide the helping hands needed to salvage hope from the failures of ethics.

In 1976–7, I was a fellow at the National Humanities Institute at Yale University, an initiative underwritten by the National Endowment for the Humanities. During that year, I wrote a book called A Consuming Fire: Encounters with Elie Wiesel and the Holocaust. *With particular reference to my Christian tradition, it probed the challenge posed by the epigraph from Wiesel with which this chapter begins: the enigma of God's action—or lack of it—in history.*

My thinking was enriched, my writing complicated, by a growing friendship with Richard Rubenstein, who was also one of the twenty fellows at the Institute. A year earlier, he had published The Cunning of History: The Holocaust and the American Future. *Its visibility boosted when the American novelist William Styron discussed the book in* The New York Review of Books *in 1978, and then referenced it at some length in his award-winning* Sophie's Choice *a year later.* The Cunning of History *concluded that we live in a "functionally godless" world.*

Almost every day during lunch at the Institute, Rubenstein and I talked about such matters, which he had put on my mind ten years earlier with the 1966 publication of After Auschwitz. *Appearing as I completed my doctoral dissertation at Yale, Rubenstein's book anticipated themes in* The Cunning of History *by arguing that the Holocaust had "permanently impaired" long-held beliefs and assumptions about God, humanity, and ethics. A chief casualty was the idea that God acts providentially in history.*

Friends usually do not agree completely. So it has been with Rubenstein and me, but along with Wiesel's influence on my thinking, Rubenstein's impact has been immense. I am not convinced that we live in a functionally godless world, but if we do not, then quarreling with God's failures—something that Elie Wiesel helped me to discern as an ethical act in its own right—looms large as a factor in protesting against the failures of ethics. Such concerns are among the threads I follow as I try to find my way through aftershocks of the Holocaust, genocide, and other mass atrocities.

5

God's Failures

> You will sooner or later be confronted with the enigma of God's action in history.
>
> —Elie Wiesel, *One Generation After*

Religion was not a sufficient condition for the Holocaust, but it was a necessary one. What happened in the Nazi killing fields and at Treblinka and Auschwitz, including the failures of ethics that occurred in such places, is inconceivable without beliefs about God first held by Jews and then by Christians. Holocaust and genocide scholars have explored the similarities and differences between the Holocaust and other genocides. Although the field of comparative genocide does not often make the point, one aspect of the Holocaust that is qualitatively different from other schemes of extermination and mass destruction in the modern period can be stated as follows: No example of mass murder exceeds the Holocaust in raising so directly or so insistently the question of how, or even whether, such catastrophe can be reconciled with God's providential involvement in history. More than any other disaster in modern times, the Holocaust resonates and collides with the theological and ethical traditions of biblical religion. The tension raises the question: Do human failures implicate God—and to such an extent that the nineteenth-century French writer Stendhal (Marie-Henri Beyle) hit the mark when he said, "The only excuse for God is that he does not exist"?[1]

BREAKING SILENCE

Steeped in silence, which it also broke, Elie Wiesel's memoir, *Night*, abridged from the Yiddish version (*Un di velt hot geshvign [And the*

World Remained Silent], 1956), appeared in French (1958) and then
in English (1960).[2] One of its recollections focuses on the observance
of Rosh Hashanah at Auschwitz in 1944. Amidst the congregation's
sighs and tears, Wiesel heard the leader's voice, powerful yet broken:
"All the earth and the Universe are God's!"[3] As the words came forth,
Wiesel recalls that they seemed to choke in the speaker's throat, "as
though he lacked the strength to uncover the meaning beneath the
text."[4] *Night* does not explain that meaning, silently leaving readers to
wonder about it.

Almost thirty years after that Rosh Hashanah observance in
Auschwitz, another Holocaust survivor, the philosopher Sarah Kofman, also wrestled with silence when she spoke about smothered and
knotted words that "stick in your throat and cause you to suffocate, to
lose your breath"; they "asphyxiate you, taking away the possibility of
even beginning."[5] Expressing the dilemma she felt as a survivor trying
to communicate with others, Kofman went on to ask, "How is it
possible to speak, when you feel . . . a strange *double bind*: an infinite
claim to speak, *a duty to speak infinitely*, imposing itself with irre-
pressible force, and at the same time, an almost physical impossibility
to speak, a *choking* feeling"?[6]

Wiesel and Kofman help to show that *silence*—the word and
reality—is fraught with meanings. They can include a lack of interest,
even indifference about events and ideas. Silence may reflect ignorance,
humility, or shame; it may be a response to awesome beauty or
immense destruction. It may signify, with special intensity and emotion, that even when one speaks, it is still possible to be speechless, for
one may not know what to say or cannot find words that are appropriate, meaningful, and credible in relation to what is present, remembered, or yet to be faced. The failures of ethics can have effects like those.

It is one thing to remember that the Holocaust happened, to
memorialize that disaster, to find ways to incorporate memory and
memorialization into religious ritual, and to do so with reverence and
love.[7] It may be something else, however, to deal with the philosophical, religious, and ethical questions that continue to jar consciousness
and conscience as those actions take place. Whatever silences—
mythical or otherwise—may have surrounded the Holocaust during
and after that disaster, questions about God, justice, evil, and meaning
reverberated in that chasm and continue to do so.[8] Theologians and
philosophers have a long history of attempts to respond to versions of
those dilemmas, but what responses did they make—and when did

they make them—as awareness of the Holocaust first grew? In what ways did their encounters with that catastrophe make theologians and philosophers grapple with metaphysical and moral silences that still leave their traditions shattered and even reduced to silence when the Shoah penetrates them deeply? As post-Holocaust theology and philosophy attempt to salvage fragments of meaning from the Holocaust's devastation, the credibility of those efforts depends on reckoning with silences that remain even when they are broken.

Forty years after World War II, the Jewish philosopher and theologian Emil Fackenheim made an exaggerated but still valid point when he asserted that "philosophers have all but ignored the Holocaust."[9] Fackenheim prominent among them, notable exceptions to that judgment could be found in the relatively early postwar years.[10] Nevertheless, the Holocaust has never attracted as much philosophical and specifically ethical inquiry as might be expected after an event of such devastating proportions. Perhaps philosophy's reluctance to break the silence about the Holocaust is an expression of humility, a profound puzzlement about what to say, but a stronger case can be made that much of philosophy in the second half of the twentieth century and into the twenty-first has simply not attended to history as much as it might have done. Meantime, while the impact of the Holocaust on religious thought and practice—within Jewish and Christian traditions in particular—was felt to a greater extent, and earlier too, it remains to be seen how deeply the Holocaust's reverberations have penetrated and to what lasting effect.

Especially among Orthodox Jews, whose eastern European communities were devastated by the Shoah, a great deal of theological reflection took place—as circumstances permitted—in German-occupied areas, ghettos, and camps or in places of refuge to which Jews had escaped while the Holocaust raged. Many of those who produced these wartime *Responsa* did not survive the Holocaust. According to Gershon Greenberg, a leading scholar on this *Responsa* literature, during the first two postwar decades, the wartime theological reflections, whether their authors survived or not, were "overlooked by the historians, even denied."[11]

In the anguished wartime reflections of those who wrestled with God and the catastrophe engulfing them, one finds versions of the themes and quandaries that remain key parts of post-Holocaust religious thought, except that the wartime *Responsa* are particularly poignant because they were made in the midst of the destruction.

Some of the major issues include the following: (1) How is the traditional covenant between God and the Jewish people to be understood in the light of that people's decimation? Will there be a saving remnant, and, if so, what is its destiny? (2) How, if at all, is God involved in the devastation? Is the destruction part of a redemptive plan? Does it signify the birth pangs of the Messiah? (3) Is something new and unprecedented taking place, or does the destruction fit within traditional interpretations of the tribulations that have befallen the Jewish people in the past? (4) How should God be identified in such crushing circumstances? As omnipotent? Hidden? Suffering? Silent? Beyond understanding? (5) What responses to God are appropriate? Rejection? Protest? Faithful waiting? Repentance? Martyrdom? Justification of God's ways—theodicy? Silence?

During and after the Holocaust—whether in the first two decades or those that followed—versions of these issues have remained central in post-Holocaust religious thought, and their ethical implications are enormous. As those post-Holocaust efforts explore events and the meanings beneath words and texts, versions of Kofman's "double bind" are detectable. The Holocaust may make one feel a duty to speak, an obligation to state how the Shoah relates to religious traditions, but such work can produce a choking feeling, a sense that too much harm has been done for a good recovery to be made, a suspicion that religious convictions may be overwhelmed by the challenges they face. The bind is double because any attempts to overcome these difficulties remain hopelessly optimistic and naive unless they grapple with the despair that encounters with the Holocaust are bound to produce. To be touched by that despair, however, scarcely encourages religious commitment and belief. Hasia Diner's study of postwar American Jewish life, for example, shows that the Holocaust produced a resurgence of Jewish identification in the United States, but she aptly cites Albert Gordon, rabbi and anthropologist, whose 1959 study concluded that although the suburban Jew "believes that there must be a God who created this world, he cannot understand [God's] continuing association with the Jews or, for that matter, with mankind. He has seen so much misery and wretchedness.... The fate that recently overtook six million Jews in Europe has shaken what little faith was left in him."[12] In the twenty-first century, the relevance of that judgment and its challenges still hold.

Whatever the silences produced by the Holocaust, they were not absolute. In the English-speaking world, important Jewish thinkers such as Martin Buber, Abraham Joshua Heschel, and Chaim Grade early on raised anguished questions about how traditional beliefs about God could be sustained in a world shadowed by the Holocaust. On the Christian side, the work done before, during, and after the Holocaust by the British scholar James Parkes forcefully documented the Christian roots of antisemitism and persistently made important contributions to postwar Christian-Jewish relations.[13] In the Anglo-American context, however, the most widely discussed and long-term influential theological writings by individual thinkers who focused explicitly and persistently on the Holocaust did not appear primarily in the late 1940s, the 1950s, or even the early 1960s. A longer gestation period seems to have been required, as writers struggled to figure out what most needed to be said and then sought the words to break difficult silences. The results were more challenging than comforting, a point that can be illustrated by attention to four significant thinkers— three Jews and one Christian—who have done much to sustain attention on issues that deserve to remain prominent in post-Holocaust religious thought and specifically in relation to the failures of ethics.

THE GOD OF HISTORY

In the summer of 1961, the young rabbi Richard Rubenstein planned to begin a research trip to West Germany on Sunday, August 13. That same day, the East Germans created a major Cold War crisis by hastily building a wall between East and West Berlin. Postponing his trip for two days, Rubenstein arrived in Bonn, the West German capital, and accepted an invitation from his hosts, the Bundespressamt (Press and Information Office) of the Federal Republic to fly to Berlin to see the unfolding crisis. In an atmosphere charged with fear that nuclear war might erupt, Rubenstein took the opportunity to interview Heinrich Grüber, a prominent German Christian leader who had resisted the Nazis, rescued Jews, and suffered imprisonment in Sachsenhausen.[14] Earlier in 1961, Grüber had been the only German to testify for the prosecution at the Jerusalem trial of Adolf Eichmann, a leading perpetrator of the Holocaust.

With American tanks rumbling through the streets of Dahlem, the West Berlin suburb where Grüber lived, Rubenstein interviewed him in the late afternoon of August 17. When their conversation turned to the Holocaust, this meeting became a turning point in Rubenstein's personal and intellectual life. Grüber affirmed a biblical faith in the God-who-acts-in-history. More than that, he held that the Jews were God's chosen people; therefore, he believed, nothing could happen to them apart from God's will. When Rubenstein asked Grüber whether God had intended for Hitler to attempt the destruction of the European Jews, Grüber's response was, yes. However difficult it might be to understand the reason, he told Rubenstein, the Holocaust was part of God's plan.

Rubenstein was impressed that Grüber took so seriously the belief that God acts providentially in history, a central tenet of traditional Judaism and Christianity. To Grüber, that belief meant specifically that God was ultimately responsible for the Holocaust. Although Grüber's testimony struck him as abhorrent, Rubenstein appreciated the consistency of Grüber's theology, and the American Jewish thinker came away convinced that he must persistently confront the issue of God and the Holocaust. The eventual result was Rubenstein's first and immensely important book, *After Auschwitz: Radical Theology and Contemporary Judaism*, which appeared in 1966. A second edition of *After Auschwitz*, so extensively enlarged and revised as to be virtually a new book, was published in 1992 with a different subtitle: *History, Theology, and Contemporary Judaism*.

After Auschwitz was among the first books to probe unrelentingly the significance of Auschwitz for post-Holocaust religious life. Rubenstein's analysis sparked ongoing debate because it challenged a belief that many people have long held dear. After Auschwitz, Rubenstein contended, belief in a redeeming God—one who is active in history and who will bring a fulfilling end to the upheavals in the human condition—is no longer credible.

In the late 1960s, the stir caused by *After Auschwitz* linked Rubenstein to a group of young American Protestant thinkers— Thomas Altizer, William Hamilton, and Paul van Buren among them—who were dubbed "death of God" theologians. The popular media picked up the story. *Time* magazine's cover article on April 8, 1966, featured the topic, and the movement ignited public discussion for some time.[15] Although the spotlight eventually moved on, these thinkers' contributions—especially Rubenstein's—did not fade. Their outlooks posed questions and their testimonies raised issues too fundamental to disappear. Yet neither the labeling nor the clustering of these thinkers was entirely accurate. None was atheistic in any simple sense. Nor were their perspectives, methods, and moods identical. What they loosely shared was the feeling that talk about God did not—indeed could not—mean what it had apparently meant in the past. In that respect, the term "radical theology" described their work better than the more sensationalistic phrase "death of God." Creating breaks with the past and intensifying discontinuities within traditions, they ventured to talk about experiences that were widely shared even though most people lacked the words or the encouragement to say so in public. Unlike his Protestant brothers, however, Rubenstein put the Holocaust at the center of his contributions to radical theology in the 1960s. *After Auschwitz* provoked Holocaust-related searches that continue to this day.

THE 614TH COMMANDMENT

Emil Fackenheim fled his native Germany in 1939 after imprisonment in the Nazi concentration camp at Sachsenhausen, taught for many years at the University of Toronto, and then emigrated from Canada to Israel, where he died in 2003. In 1968, he delivered the Charles F. Deems Lectures at New York University, which were published two years later as *God's Presence in History: Jewish Affirmations and Philosophical Reflections*.[16] This brief and often reprinted book contains one of the most powerful of the relatively early religious responses to the Holocaust. According to Fackenheim, the Holocaust was the most radically disorienting "epoch-making" event in all of Jewish history.[17] In contrast to Rubenstein, Fackenheim argued that the Jewish people must respond to this shattering challenge with a reaffirmation of God's presence in history. Fackenheim acknowledged that it is impossible to affirm God's saving presence at Auschwitz, but he did insist that while no "redeeming Voice" was heard at Auschwitz, a "commanding Voice" was heard, and it enunciated a "614th commandment" to supplement the 613 commandments of traditional Judaism. The new commandment was said to be that "the authentic Jew of today is forbidden to hand Hitler yet another, posthumous victory." Fackenheim spelled out the 614th commandment, which he first articulated in 1967, as follows:

> We are, first, commanded to survive as Jews, lest the Jewish people perish. We are commanded, second, to remember in our very guts and

bones the martyrs of the Holocaust, lest their memory perish. We are forbidden, thirdly, to deny or despair of God, however much we may have to contend with Him or with belief in Him, lest Judaism perish. We are forbidden, finally, to despair of the world as the place which is to become the kingdom of God, lest we help make it a meaningless place in which God is dead or irrelevant and everything is permitted. To abandon any of these imperatives, in response to Hitler's victory at Auschwitz, would be to hand him yet other, posthumous victories.[18]

Few, if any, post-Holocaust religious statements by a Jewish thinker have become better known.[19] For some time, Fackenheim's 614th commandment struck a deep chord in Jews of every social level and religious commitment. Much, but by no means all, of Fackenheim's writing was on a philosophic and theological level beyond the competence of the ordinary layperson. Not so this passage, which is largely responsible for the fact that Fackenheim's interpretation of the Holocaust arguably became for a time the most influential within the Jewish community. A people that has endured catastrophic defeat is likely to see the survival of their community and its traditions as a supreme imperative. By referring to a divine commandment, Fackenheim gave potent expression to this aspiration. Instead of questioning whether the traditional Jewish understanding of God could be maintained after Auschwitz, he implied that those who questioned God's presence to Israel were accomplices of the worst destroyer the Jews have ever known.

The passion and the psychological power of Fackenheim's position are undeniable. Nevertheless, his position could have unfortunate consequences. Not only were those Jews "who denied or despaired" of the scriptural God seemingly cast in the role of Hitler's accomplices, a serious and controversial allegation indeed. In addition, Fackenheim went so far as to suggest that those who did not hear the "commanding Voice" from Auschwitz were *willfully* rejecting God: "In my view," he wrote, "nothing less will do than to say that a commanding Voice speaks from Auschwitz, and that there are Jews who hear it and Jews who *stop their ears*."[20] To stop one's ears is a voluntary act. Apparently, Fackenheim excluded or ignored the possibility that some Jews might honestly be unable to believe that God was in any way present in Auschwitz, no matter how metaphorically the idea was presented. Furthermore, in spite of its power, Fackenheim's position was not without difficulty even for the tradition he sought to defend. Given his conviction that revelation was inseparable from interpretation, it was not clear whether the commanding Voice was to be taken as real or metaphorical.

Subsequently, there was reason to believe that Fackenheim would reject both alternatives and hold that the commandment would have been unreal without an affirmative Jewish response. Taken literally, there does not appear to be any credible evidence that anybody heard the 614th commandment, as indeed Fackenheim's later description of how he came to write the passage indicates. In his 1982 book *To Mend the World*, Fackenheim told his readers that after he had come to the conclusion that the Holocaust was a radical challenge to Jewish faith, "my first response was to formulate a '614th commandment.'"[21] Clearly, as understood in traditional Judaism, one does not formulate a commandment. It derives from a divine source. In any event, whatever the psychological power of the 614th commandment, its status as commandment remains ambiguous.

Fackenheim's critics also found considerable difficulty with his assertion that the commanding Voice enjoined Jews to "survive as Jews." In the case of traditional Jews, no such commandment was necessary. They have always believed that Jewish religious survival was a divine imperative. They had no need of an Auschwitz to receive such an injunction. In the case of secularized Jews, the commandment appeared perhaps to be a case of pedagogic overkill. It hardly seemed likely that even a jealous God would require the annihilation of six million Jews as the occasion for a commandment forbidding Jews to permit the demise of their tradition.

Perhaps the most important aspect of the 614th commandment was the injunction not to deny or despair of God lest Hitler be given "yet other, posthumous victories." Here Fackenheim confronted the fundamental issue of Holocaust-related theology. He told his readers what God has commanded, but did that mean that Fackenheim perpetrated a fiction in order to maintain the theological integrity of his reading of Judaism? Given Fackenheim's faith in some sense of a Divine Presence, it was hardly likely that he could have thought of God as absent from Auschwitz. As Fackenheim came to realize that the real difficulty lay in formulating a view of God that took the Holocaust into account, he understood that one could no longer speak of a *saving* presence at Auschwitz. Yet, utter defeat and annihilation could not be the last word. A way out of the ashes had to be found. The 614th commandment expressed what most religious Jews regard as their sacred obligation in response to the Holocaust. In the language of Jewish faith, that response could most appropriately be communicated in the imagery of the commandments. Fackenheim's 614th commandment is religiously and existentially problematic. That outcome, however, may remain beside the point. It is perhaps best to see Fackenheim's 614th commandment as a cry of the heart, transmuted into the language of the sacred. That would at least help to explain why it has touched so many Jews—and sometimes Christians too—so deeply.[22]

A CREDIBILITY CRISIS

Along with interest in Wiesel's *Night* and his essays and fiction, the writings of Rubenstein and Fackenheim influenced numerous Christians as well as Jews.[23] One of them was Franklin Littell. On July 23, 1998, his friend Yehuda Bauer interviewed Littell at Yad Vashem in Jerusalem, where the two scholars frequently led seminars on the Holocaust. The interview provides an overview of Littell's primary concerns and concludes with remarks that succinctly capture his character, outlook, and aspirations. Underscoring that his motivation in writing and teaching about the Holocaust was above all to prevent "premature closure," Littell ended the 1998 interview by declaring his intent "to keep this thing [the memory of the Holocaust] irritating— you know, be the harpoon that the fish can't escape."[24] Those who knew Littell may hear his voice in those words—a voice that was earthy and earnest, intense and impassioned, edged at times with laughter and humor, but one that cut to the chase as he expressed his conviction that the unredeemable atrocities of the Holocaust and of all genocides must ignite protest and provoke resistance against the injustice and indifference that produce them.

The United States Library of Congress catalogs more than thirty books authored or edited by Littell. The earliest titles, from the 1950s, suggest that this ordained Methodist minister, who held a doctorate in theology and religious studies, might have had a conventional professorial career. During this early period, he concentrated on church history in the United States, with an emphasis on Protestant Christianity and church–state relationships. However, much more was gestating. A visit to Nazi Germany in 1939 made an indelible impression on Littell—one that was deepened and intensified by his work in postwar Germany, where he served as the chief Protestant advisor for the US occupation forces. These experiences honed the harpoon that Littell would thrust at multiple targets, including, first and foremost, his own Christian tradition.

Two books loom largest in Littell's body of works. Christian scholars James Parkes and Edward Flannery preceded Littell in documenting their tradition's culpability for antisemitism, but Littell's 1975 monograph *The Crucifixion of the Jews* was nonetheless ground-breaking in that it drove home Christian responsibility for, and complicity in, the Holocaust. Written in the aftermath of the military attacks on the State of Israel in 1967 and 1973, Littell's book also staunchly defended "the right of the Jewish people to self-identity and self-definition."[25]

Littell often referred to the Holocaust as an "alpine event," his way of identifying its watershed significance. In his view, the Holocaust constituted the most severe "credibility crisis"—another of his favorite terms—to afflict the Christian tradition. That tradition's "teaching of contempt" about Judaism and Jews had contributed mightily to genocide against the Jewish people, he believed. Only profound contrition and reform, including fundamental theological revision that tackled the New Testament's anti-Judaic themes, could restore integrity to post-Holocaust Christianity.

Littell's belief that Christianity faced a monumental credibility crisis was not based solely on his knowledge of the centuries-old history of Christian hostility toward Judaism and Jews. More immediately, his postwar experiences in Germany made him painfully aware of the failures of ethics. He saw that most German churches had embraced Adolf Hitler and Nazism. He recognized the complicity of German churches in the Holocaust, as well as the widespread indifference of the churches outside Germany when it came to the plight of Jews under the swastika. Yet, he understood that some Christians and churches in Germany had resisted Nazism and, at least to some extent, assisted Jews. Thus, even before Littell published *The Crucifixion of the Jews*, his pioneering work resulted in the other entry that looms largest among his works, the 1974 volume *The German Church Struggle and the Holocaust* (co-edited with his friend Hubert G. Locke).

Important in its own right—among other things it contains a memorable exchange between Richard Rubenstein and Elie Wiesel— this volume signaled the pivotal role that Littell played as an organizer and leader in both Holocaust studies and Christian-Jewish relations.

The German Church Struggle and the Holocaust emerged from a conference that Littell and Locke convened at Wayne State University in 1970. Focused on Christians in Nazi Germany, their support for and resistance against Hitler's regime, and that conflict's implications for the future of Christianity and its relationship to Jews and Judaism, the meeting was the first in a series of conferences that would become the Annual Scholars' Conference on the Holocaust and the Churches. This interfaith, interdisciplinary, and international gathering of scholars, educators, clergy, and community leaders remains the longest continuously running initiative of its kind. The conference's work, including many publications, has significantly influenced and advanced the field of Holocaust and genocide studies, and stands as a tribute to Littell's influence and his persistent thrusting of a "harpoon that the fish can't escape."

NO MORE THEODICY

Influential contributions to post-Holocaust religious thought were also made relatively early by the Jewish philosopher Emmanuel Levinas. By the 1960s and 1970s, he was developing an important post-Holocaust ethical perspective, which drew extensively, if not always explicitly, on his Jewish heritage by arguing that previous ethical theory had failed to concentrate on something as obvious and profound as the human face.[26] Close attention to the face of the other person, Levinas affirmed, could produce a reorientation not only of ethics but also of human life itself, for our deepest seeing of the other person's face drives home how closely human beings are connected and how much another person's existence places responsibility upon us.[27]

Levinas did not write explicitly about the Holocaust very often, but traces of that catastrophe appear, and the overt emphases of his thought make plain that the Shoah is a powerful point of reference between the lines, in the silence—the void even—that shadows his philosophy. On some occasions, however, the Holocaust comes to the fore in Levinas's writing. One example is found in his brief but highly significant essay called "Useless Suffering," which did not appear until 1982. In that article, Levinas explicitly states a conviction that permeated his thought early and late. "The Holocaust of the Jewish people under the reign of Hitler," said Levinas, "seems to me the paradigm of gratuitous human suffering, in which evil appears in its diabolical horror."[28]

As a French prisoner of war, Levinas did forced labor under the Nazis, and almost all of his Lithuanian family perished in the Holocaust. It made a profound impact upon him. Calling the twentieth century one of "unutterable suffering," he emphasized that suffering of the kind that the Nazis and their collaborators inflicted on Europe's Jews was and is "for nothing." To try to justify such suffering religiously, ethically, or politically was what Levinas called "the source of all immorality."[29]

When Levinas said that the useless suffering inflicted during the Holocaust was "for nothing," he did not overlook Nazi "logic" and what it meant. To the contrary, he took National Socialism to be about arrogant destruction, its grandiose rhetoric about a thousand-year Reich notwithstanding. The chief element in National Socialism's arrogance was that regime's remorseless determination to deface the human face. The Nazis did this not in some abstract way, but by useless suffering visited upon Jewish women, children, and men that made its antisemitic prerogatives dominant until overwhelming force stopped them.

Levinas believed that "all evil relates back to suffering," which is not confined to "persistent or obstinate" bodily pain but includes "helplessness, abandonment and solitude," an abjection intensified when "a moan, a cry, a groan or a sigh" bring no relief but are swallowed up by silence. He distinguished between "*suffering in the other*" and what he called "suffering *in me*." The latter's uselessness could have meaning insofar as it was "a suffering for the suffering (inexorable though it may be) of someone else." As for the uselessness of the suffering of the other, Levinas thought that striving to relieve it and to resist the forces that created it should be "raised to the level of supreme ethical principle—the only one it is impossible to question—shaping the hopes and commanding the practical discipline of vast human groups."[30]

No sooner did Levinas write those words than he issued a caution about them. In no way should they be construed as a justification for suffering, as a mitigation of suffering's uselessness because such suffering could become the means to the good and the virtue of relieving it. Observing that its temptations should not be underestimated, Levinas rejected all forms of *theodicy*, the attempt to make suffering "comprehensible," to find "in a suffering that is essentially gratuitous and absurd, and apparently arbitrary, a meaning and an order." Noting that "Nietzsche's saying about the death of God" had taken on "the meaning of a quasi-empirical fact" in the Shoah and that Fackenheim's allusion to the commanding voice at Auschwitz, which entails "a revelation from the very God who nevertheless was silent at Auschwitz," was inescapably paradoxical, Levinas nevertheless affirmed that Fackenheim saw something of seminal importance not only for Jews but for humanity itself. Levinas put his point in the form of an extended question: "Must not humanity now, in a faith more difficult than before, in a faith without theodicy, continue to live out Sacred History; a history that now demands even more from the resources of the *I* in each one of us, and from its suffering inspired by the suffering of the other, from its compassion which is a non-useless suffering (or love), which is no longer suffering 'for nothing,' and immediately has meaning?"[31] Levinas could not answer this question, at least not simply, because the response to it depends on how humanity breaks the silence that follows his asking.

AND YET...AND YET

Attempts to maintain traditional understandings of God's presence in history, analyses denying the credibility of providential divinity, searches that affirm the more-important-than-ever status of ethics and religion in times when traditions are in crisis and in contexts of atrocity and suffering that make every theodicy problematic—all of these perspectives and more emerged during the Holocaust and in its relatively early aftershocks. If it took time for some of these developments to unfold, if it is still taking time for them to find expression, then that outcome should not be surprising. What would be lamentable is failure to keep asking and pursuing the questions that the Holocaust raises—sometimes in words, sometimes in silences.

The Holocaust's place in history was not fixed at the time of its happening or in its short-term aftermath. The philosophical and religious quandaries evoked during and after the Shoah continue to resist closure. Responses made at one time will not suffice for all times, and no response should ever settle what deserves to remain unsettled and unsettling. The Holocaust's place, its presence, is still in the making, with aftershocks that will continue to require the recognition and reconsideration of silence, the contesting and breaking of it, particularly with regard to God's death, reality, power, and relationship to history.

Such considerations, however, scarcely refute the judgment that God's failures combine with human shortcomings to create a glut and a void of useless suffering. If God is dead or non-existent, God may have the excuse that Stendhal identified, but then the idea or ideal of God is a failure. If God is real, then God's power fails, either because it is powerless to curb the excesses of human freedom, or because it lacks the will to intervene against those excesses and thus abandons the responsibility to protect, choosing instead indifference or complicity when crimes against humanity are committed. As a result, history is so marred by unutterable suffering that the failures of ethics seem to put God's relationship to history beyond redemption.

"And yet . . . and yet," Elie Wiesel has said, "this is the key expression in my work."[32] That outlook should also be a key response to the failures of ethics, including God's failures, because life persists, history continues, and they embody so much that is good and precious, so much that must not be abandoned—perhaps even God?—lest failure is compounded to the point of no return. What is good and precious includes the people who—sometimes for religious reasons but often without such motivations—have resisted genocide and other mass atrocities and have rescued, often at the risk of their own lives, and helped to heal at least some of those targeted by mass atrocities. Not to stand in solidarity with the resisters and rescuers, not to emulate them as best one can, only contributes to the failures of ethics. Although confrontations with the Holocaust, genocide, and other mass atrocities invite aftershocks of despair, the face of the other is still present, conferring responsibility upon us. If Wiesel was correct when he said, "everything to do with Auschwitz must, in the end, lead into darkness," his "and yet . . . and yet" remains to protest against premature closure and to insist on asking, "What is the next step?"[33] The next step cannot put the failures of ethics to rest permanently and forever—that task is more than human energy can accomplish. Probably Albert Camus was right when he said that even by its greatest effort humanity "can only propose to diminish arithmetically the sufferings of the world." But he was also right when he added that "the injustice and the suffering of the world . . . will not cease to be an outrage."[34] Striving in that spirit against the failures of ethics—God's among them—is a step that cannot be shirked with impunity.

Part II

Resisting Failures

Sooner or later, anyone who confronts the failures of ethics that lead to genocide and other mass atrocities must deal with a fundamental question: Do the perpetrators and their accomplices know that they are inflicting untold suffering and death on human beings? As the philosopher Henry Theriault points out: "It has become an article of faith that a condition necessary for genocide is the dehumanization of the victims in the minds of perpetrators."[1] Such faith has two crucial implications. It suggests, first, that those who are doing their worst do not think of their targets as human beings. Second, it may mean that if the perpetrators and their accomplices recognized their targets' humanity, that recognition might curb dehumanization and diminish, if not eliminate, mass atrocities. Such an account would indicate, in turn, that the key to resisting the failures of ethics is to persuade everyone to see the "other" as human, to do to others as we would have them do to us, and, in particular, not to do to others what is patently despicable if done to us.

Wisdom abides in such outlooks, but it is not sufficient to deal with all of the failures of ethics. The reason is that the perpetrators of genocide and other mass atrocities do target human beings and, most of the time, do so knowingly. As Theriault aptly puts the point, "recognized humanity" drives the destructive processes that intend to destroy the other.[2] Otherwise, the destructive acts, including the immense cruelty, anguish, and suffering that are part and parcel of them, cannot have the significance that the perpetrators impute to them, which may include "protecting" a culture from a lethal menace, advancing economic interests, or even exercising the "right" to dominate others, and to justify that "right" by showing how "inferior," "undesirable" and "unwanted" the other turns out to be.

Resisting the failures of ethics must grapple with the fact that the perpetrators and accomplices who have unleashed the Holocaust, genocide, and other mass atrocities did so with the knowledge that the targeted ones—girls and boys, women and men—were human beings. Dehumanization definitely took place, but it required and began with "recognized humanity," which perpetrators and their accomplices degraded and defaced. Deep-down recognition of the other as human is a necessary condition for correcting the failures of ethics, and every available resource needs to be directed to that end. But resisting those failures also requires determination to stop human beings whose vision of the future entails what George Orwell called "a boot stamping on a human face—forever."[3]

Such resistance implies exercising political power or exerting armed force. This book's second part neither underestimates nor downplays the crucial and even irreplaceable roles that such initiatives play if there is to be effective prevention and intervention where mass atrocity crimes—threatened or unleashed—are at hand. The themes threading through these chapters, however, move in different but related directions. As they show, all resistance involves power, but the ways in which it does so take different forms and involve varied strategies. Absent key *ideas*, for example, resistance cannot make sense. Without sound *scholarship*, resistance will not be well informed. Apart from *testimony*, resistance lacks clarity about what to oppose and defend. Unless held to account by *teaching*, resistance ducks criticism, stirs self-righteousness, and risks overreaching. Lacking *deep confrontation with death itself*, resistance loses meaning. Resisting the failures of ethics entails the steadfast holding of many threads, including those focused in the chapters that follow.

Elie Wiesel's mood turned somber during one of my visits with him. He wondered whether his work had changed the world very much, whether it had made a substantive difference. "Well," I replied, "you definitely changed me." I spoke those words as a Christian whose understanding of Judaism, and much more, has been significantly and positively changed by Wiesel's life and work.

Regularly, people ask how I became interested in the Holocaust and its reverberations. Sometimes they assume that I am Jewish, perhaps because Roth is often a surname that belongs to Jews. In fact, Richard Rubenstein's After Auschwitz *led to my first published writing about the Holocaust. In* The American Religious Experience, *co-authored with Frederick Sontag in 1972, I reflected on Rubenstein's place in the so-called Death of God movement that attracted much attention in the United States at the time. That effort to connect American culture and reflection on the Holocaust anticipated concerns that became major threads in my work. I had not yet experienced fully, however, the Holocaust turn that would reorient my professional and personal life. It took tears for that to happen.*

Following Sontag's suggestion, I began serious reading of Wiesel's writings in the summer of 1972. In what now seems more like destiny than the chance it involved at the time, my study of Wiesel was under way when my second child, Sarah, was born on the Fourth of July. The collision I experienced then between my good fortune—fatherhood, a promising academic career—and the destruction of family and hope explored in Wiesel's Holocaust reflections left lasting marks upon me.

My reading of Wiesel led me to respond in writing of my own, which I have done frequently over the years. It has been more than four decades since I wrote about Wiesel for the first time. That piece was called "Tears and Elie Wiesel." "Lately something has been puzzling me," it began. "I do not think of myself as an emotional person, so why do I sometimes find myself about to weep? Nobody notices, but why is it that especially in church on Sunday mornings tears well up in my eyes?"[1] From time to time, that experience continues.

In writing that initial article, I began to understand that my tears were partly a response to the Holocaust and to Wiesel in particular, an awareness that has become even more meaningful with the passing of time. Not long after it appeared, Wiesel read my early essay. He sent me an encouraging note, and I wrote back. Soon we met, and even though we live on opposite sides of the United States and both of us are aging, we continue to keep in contact. Thanks to tears and Elie Wiesel, my life and work took the Holocaust turn that led to confrontations with the failures of ethics, including those threading through Christian relations with Jews and Judaism.

6

The Holocaust's Impact on
Christian-Jewish Relations

Where are we going? Tell me. Do you know?
—Elie Wiesel, *A Jew Today*

The best of Elie Wiesel's versatile writing includes the brief Holocaust-related dialogues that appear in his books from time to time.
Spare and lean, they often consist of a few hundred words or less.
These dialogues are distinctive not only for their minimalist quality
but also because their apparent simplicity, their unidentified settings,
unnamed characters, abrupt and open beginnings and endings raise
fundamental questions in moving ways. In Wiesel's *A Jew Today* one
of these dialogues comes from "A Mother and Her Daughter."
"Where are we going?" it begins. "Tell me. Do you know?" The
mother tells her daughter, "I don't know," but then when the child
asks again, "Where are we going?" her mother says, "To the end of the
world, little girl. We are going to the end of the world."[2] The failures
of ethics in its shadows, this dialogue is as ominous and dark as it is
personal and poignant. For those reasons, it makes a good point of
departure for a chapter about the Holocaust's impact on Christian-
Jewish relations, primarily but not only as those relations have developed in the United States.

Christian understandings—better identified as *misunderstandings*—of Judaism have produced immense suffering and sorrow.
They contributed mightily to the end of the world that took place
on the ramp at Auschwitz when a family was separated. Elie Wiesel
never saw his mother and little sister again but was left to imagine
what they, and hundreds of thousands like them, might have said to
each other as life and love were taken away. It is an understatement to

say that Christian understandings of Judaism are important. The Holocaust bears witness to that. Although they have come too late and may be too little, post-Holocaust Christian understandings of Judaism, fortunately, are much better than they were before and during the Shoah. Wiesel has decisively influenced *some* of those developments. I put the accent on *some* because it is one thing to say that his life and work have deeply affected individual Christians but quite another to assess how much Wiesel has changed Christians' and Christianity's understanding of Judaism overall.

Numerous Christians probably know six things about Wiesel. He is: (1) a Jew, (2) a survivor of the Holocaust, (3) the recipient of the Nobel Peace Prize, (4) a defender of human rights, (5) a founder of the United States Holocaust Memorial Museum, and (6) perhaps most important of all, the author of the widely read Holocaust memoir called *Night*. If that depiction is valid, it means that most Christians do not think of Wiesel primarily as a novelist or as a post-Holocaust interpreter of Judaism, although his fiction and his writings on Jewish religious traditions and themes are among his most sustained and significant accomplishments. Only for a relatively small number of Christians, moreover, does Wiesel loom large as a thinker and writer who has changed—and is changing still—Christian understanding of, and appreciation for, Judaism.[3] Nevertheless, his influence is significant, and it deserves to be long-lasting.

QUESTIONING CONVENTIONAL WISDOM

In two primary ways Wiesel has definitively changed some Christian understandings of Judaism. First, he calls into question Christianity's conventional wisdom about Judaism. While Christians know and interact with Jews, their understanding of Judaism too often remains stuck in a New Testament interpretation that sees Judaism as eclipsed and replaced—superseded—by Christian "truth." Contesting that view, Wiesel shows that Judaism is a vibrant, rich, and living religion whose continuity and development, though ruptured at times, have persisted in immensely difficult circumstances, including dispersion, persecution, genocide, and post-Holocaust conflict in the Middle East. Wiesel helps Christians to understand not only that Judaism has autonomy, authenticity, and appeal that are independent of

Christianity but also that Judaism tests and challenges Christians and Christianity, particularly by making us Christians consider profoundly what we ought to teach and how we ought to act. The first of Wiesel's major contributions to a revised and renewing Christian understanding of Judaism is that he can help us Christians to be better Christians by confronting Judaism's ongoing challenge to Christianity.

To the extent that they are good, all religious traditions should celebrate their own existence. On that basis, we Christians have reasons to rejoice—but not too much. We can begin to become rightfully, painfully, aware of the "not too much" by considering another moment in Wiesel's *A Jew Today*. That book begins by reflecting on his awareness of Christianity as a boy growing up in Sighet, Romania, where a Holocaust education center now exists in his childhood home. Early on, he understood that his Jewishness made him a minority in such a way that "everything alien frightened me."[4] In his circumstances, Wiesel emphasizes, *alien* was synonymous with *Christian*. Thus, for this young Jew—and he speaks for millions before and after—Christmas and Easter were not holidays. To the contrary, "they imposed a climate of terror upon our frightened community."[5]

As Wiesel recounts these early relationships with Christianity, the account becomes even more telling. It does so because he underscores that their effect was not to breed within him curiosity about Christianity or even animosity toward it. "We seemed to intrigue them," he observes, "but they left me indifferent."[6] Powerful though Christians might be, dependent on them though the Jews surely were, the effect that Christianity had on the young Wiesel was to render that tradition so utterly incredible that it was not to be taken seriously as a religious faith.

Importantly, Wiesel came to a different appraisal of some Christians and of some aspects of the Christian tradition. If we Christians are to find ourselves within that affirmation, however, we need to start with Wiesel's boyhood impression, which was empirically grounded in his experience with Christians and churches. That impression convinced him that Jews should be wary of Christian power, but by virtue of the same fact this tradition showed itself to contain little if anything that was worth spiritual inquiry.

For anyone like me who has lived within the Christian tradition and often found it rich and meaningful, Wiesel's challenge is nothing less than shocking. The shock, it must be emphasized, is *not* that of receiving an undeserved affront—it is far from and much deeper than that. Rather, the shock is one of recognition. Rooted in historical awareness, such recognition produces understanding that Wiesel's boyhood appraisal of Christianity was precisely what it should have been—not in the sense that his appraisal is what Christians ought to desire but, to the contrary, in the sense that his appraisal is what Jewish honesty could rightly produce, given the relations Christians have too often and too long sustained with Jews.

Wiesel's boyhood appraisal of Christianity existed before the Holocaust. With good reason, it intensified after Auschwitz, as a further statement from *A Jew Today* testifies: "For we had been struck by a harsh truth: in Auschwitz all the Jews were victims, all the killers were Christian. . . . It is a painful statement to make, but we cannot ignore it: as surely as the victims are a problem for the Jews, the killers are a problem for the Christians."[7] Wiesel has long opposed theories of collective guilt, and, one must stress, his intent is not to heap guilt on contemporary Christians. He does want, however, to encourage Christian responsibility. Thus, he would be the first to distinguish between Christians who are genuinely faithful and Christians who are not. For Christians, however, an acute problem remains because it took the Holocaust to drive home much of what that distinction entails.

After the Holocaust, Wiesel helps us Christians to see—and to see through a challenging re-understanding of Judaism—that the genuine Christian must give priority to mending the world and Christian-Jewish relations in particular. Before and during the Holocaust that same priority should have existed. The fact that it did not goes far toward explaining how and why Auschwitz scars the earth. Those who destroyed the European Jews, and also those who stood by while the process of destruction occurred, were products of, and even baptized within, a Western civilization that remains indelibly Christian even in a so-called post-Christian age. If the perpetrators and bystanders did not practice their Christianity as they should have done, that fact is a problem for Christians. If they practiced genocide instead, or observed it without protest, that is a problem for Christians even more so. At least it must be for those of us who are persuaded that Christianity—in spite of its shortcomings—still has valuable contributions to make.

Elie Wiesel's challenges to Christianity and his contributions to a renewed and renewing Christian understanding of Judaism emerge not only from a profound sense of the injustice that the Christian tradition has done to his. They emerge even more from a yearning based on the hope of friendship. The friendship Wiesel has in mind accents honesty, deplores domination, and encourages mutual trust and esteem. Such friendship is what he contemplates when he writes, again in *A Jew Today*, "I believe that no religion, people or nation is inferior or superior to another; I dislike facile triumphalism, for us and for others. I dislike self-righteousness. And I feel closer to certain Christians—as long as they do not try to convert me to their faith—than to certain Jews. . . . I have more in common with an authentic and tolerant Christian than with a Jew who is neither authentic nor tolerant."[8]

Suggestions about what Wiesel can admire as authentic and tolerant in Christianity appear throughout his writings. Wiesel has not forgotten, for example, a Christian boy name Pishta, who was different from so many others in Sighet. He helped Wiesel after the Germans established the ghetto in Sighet before deporting its Jews to Auschwitz in May 1944.[9] Wiesel recalls, too, that Maria, his family's housekeeper, was "part of the family." As the Nazi threat came closer, she offered safety in her family's mountain cabin. She slipped through ghetto barricades to bring food and friendship to the family she served. Wiesel massively understates the case when he says, "Dear Maria. If other Christians had acted like her, the trains rolling toward the unknown would have been less crowded. . . . It was a simple and devout Christian woman," Wiesel adds, "who saved her town's honor."[10] Maybe Maria saved some of Christianity's honor too.

Perhaps in honor of Sighet's Maria, Christian women with that iconic name appear more than once in Wiesel's writings. In the drama *The Trial of God*, for example, Maria works for Berish, a Jewish innkeeper, who was forced to watch his daughter Hanna raped and tortured on her wedding day during a murderous pogrom in Shamgorod in 1648. Ever loyal to Berish and Hanna, who survived the onslaught, Maria does what she can to thwart the renewed pogrom that erupts a year later. In Wiesel's novel *The Gates of the Forest*, another Maria protects a Jewish refugee at her own risk. Another novel, *The Fifth Son*, includes "some good honest people" who are willing to hide a Jewish child from the Angel of Death in Hitler's Europe.[11] The examples could be multiplied. They even include a recollection in *Night* of a Hungarian police inspector who had promised to alert the Wiesel family about Nazi danger in Sighet. After the war, Wiesel learned that the policeman had acted on his promise by trying to give them a warning.[12] The policeman did not succeed, nor did the honest people in *The Fifth Son* who tried to save a Jewish child. Nonetheless, the fact that they tried, when so many others did not, gives them a special place in Wiesel's memory. Often these caring non-Jews are not specifically identified as Christians in Wiesel's writings. Whether they were or not, they provide examples that we Christians need.

WORK TO DO

Wiesel's contributions to a Christian understanding of Judaism supply other things that Christians need, among them elements of spirituality and theological insight that can enrich Christian traditions. Thus, a second major way in which Wiesel has contributed to a Christian understanding of Judaism involves biblical themes in his writing.[13] They nurture a specifically Jewish spirit, which involves quarrelsome interrogation of texts and God alike.

The Bible abounds with allusions to faces.[14] One of the most moving and poignant examples is found in a benediction that plays important parts in both the Jewish and the Christian traditions: "The Lord bless you and keep you; the Lord make his face to shine upon you, and be gracious to you; the Lord lift up his countenance upon you, and give you peace" (Numbers 6:24–6). Can contemporary men and women still receive and extend that ancient benediction—even after the Holocaust, genocide in Rwanda and Darfur, and other mass atrocities in the Democratic Republic of Congo, the Central African Republic, Syria, and Iraq? Wiesel explores such questions. In the process, he contributes to a sound Christian understanding of Judaism and thereby of Christianity too. To elaborate these themes, and particularly the motifs of *protest* and *resistance*, which I find especially compelling in Wiesel's Judaism, consider Moses and Job, two of the biblical figures depicted in his writing.

A question for Wiesel: what is work to you? Answer: "Justification. I have to justify every second of my life."[15] Intensified by his deep sense of responsibility as a survivor of the Shoah, that ethical theme governs Wiesel's *Messengers of God*, a series of biblical portraits and legends that deal with work, with justification, with every second of our lives and God's. Adam and Eve, Cain and Abel, Abraham and Isaac, Jacob, Joseph, Moses, and Job—the Third Reich sought to burn stories about them and to eradicate the moral accountability emphasized in those narratives. The protesting and resisting task that Wiesel sets for himself in *Messengers* is to tell and retell the stories of those biblical people.

According to *Messengers of God*, the tasks set for us are monumental: "It is given to man to transform divine injustice into human justice and compassion."[16] Moses did such work. "After him," says Wiesel, "nothing was the same again."[17] Life without Moses? Think of it. No Torah. Nothing to distinguish Jews from other human groups. No Christianity, no antisemitism (belief or behavior hostile toward Jews just because they are Jewish), and no Holocaust. None of us Jews or Christians—not even God, at least as those traditions have understood God. But there is Moses standing before his homeless people, setting before them life and death, urging them to choose well. Moses set so much of history's course.

Moses knew God as One who sets people free. He also knew God as a consuming fire, and even as One who "tried to kill him" (Exodus 4:24). It was not Moses's first choice, but "he filled two equally difficult roles: he was God's emissary to Israel and Israel's to God."[18] More than one writer contends that the God of history, not to mention God's covenants with human creatures, went up in smoke from Nazi ovens. That conclusion is hard to resist, if we see the faces of God only in terms of traditional notions of full omnipotence and total goodness, but Wiesel's Moses never had such illusions. He recognized the sovereignty of God and knew that to confront God was to stand on ground that was holy but not simply good. Thus, he came to understand that to enter self-consciously into relation with God is to find oneself in a struggle for liberty that requires people to contend with God as well as with themselves and each other.

Moses discovered that the God of history encountering him was problematic. What Moses found is that the One sustaining and dealing with humanity is a God who cares, but who does so largely by leaving people to sort out a gift of freedom that is at once incredibly vast and wonderful and yet immensely destructive. Directives are given and pacts are established as part of the bargain, but they increase the tension more than they release it. Amazing, then, that

Moses did not find God a cosmic sadist, a hollow mask of indifference broken only by mocking laughter.

Reasons why? First, Moses saw that people are forgetful, foolish, cowardly—and even worse that they are deceitful, calculating, treacherous, and ready to sell souls for almost any price. And yet the counterpoint was that people could be different—not perfectible but surely less imperfect. Second, an irreplaceable source of courage to struggle for good against evil could come through a sense of covenant with God, so long as it was understood that human service for God required one to be against God too. Moses is so often pictured as the obedient leader who constantly had to deal with a people stubborn in their rebelliousness, yet that Moses was actually the most profoundly rebellious of all in his refusal to accept that realities cannot be better than they are. Without God, Moses could be nothing. With God, Moses saw ways to bring people to places from which they could at least catch glimpses of a promised land. One religious task, Wiesel's Moses suggests, is to explore whether we can see not the face of a God of history who pulls the strings of events, nor even who uses people as instruments of God's own judgment, but rather One whose covenant with a world of freedom requires our moral rebellion if that world's goodness is to flourish.

Job experienced and understood these relationships too. Wiesel gives him a voice this way: "Job spoke his outrage, his grief; he told God what He should have known for a long time, perhaps since always, that something was amiss in His universe. The just were punished for no reason, the criminal rewarded for no reason. The just and the wicked were subjected to the same fate—God having turned His back on them, on everyone. God had lost interest in His creation; He was absent."[19]

If Wiesel's Job, a just man, were here today in our post-Holocaust world where atrocity and genocide rage on and on, what would he have to say? Maybe: "I would speak to the Almighty, and I desire to argue my case with God. . . . See, he will kill me; I have no hope; but I will defend my ways to his face" (Job 13:3, 15). Would he say, "I know that my Redeemer lives, and that at the last he will stand upon the earth; and after my skin has been thus destroyed, then in my flesh I shall see God, whom I shall see on my side, and my eyes shall behold, and not another" (Job 19:25–7)? After God "answers" him out of the whirlwind—"Where were you when I laid the foundation of the earth" (Job 38:4)?—would Job say, "Now, having seen you with my own eyes, I retract all I have said, and in dust and ashes I repent" (Job 42:5-6)?[20]

The last passage is especially troubling because it suggests, at the end of the day, a simple resignation. Or is more going on than meets the eye at first glance? Wiesel suggests that, far from resignation, Job's answer is resistance and rebellion instead, masked and expressed in hasty abdication. Ultimately, God cannot be defeated. That fact may be both Job's and our hope and despair, Job's and our cause for lamentation and thanksgiving. But in confessing—when God, with greater reason to do so, did not—Job, says Wiesel, "continued to interrogate God."[21]

Where are we going? In that dialogue between a mother and a daughter with which these reflections began, the little girl tells her mother that she is "really tired. Is it wrong, tell me, is it wrong to be so tired?" Her mother answers: "Everybody is tired, my little girl." A question in response: "Even God?" And this reply, tinged with defiance and protest in the face of death: "I don't know. You will ask Him yourself."[22] The Lord bless you and keep you? The Lord make his face to shine upon you, and be gracious to you? The Lord lift up his countenance upon you, and give you peace? The Holocaust and its reverberations ... The failures of ethics ... Elie Wiesel and his pro-testing reading of scripture ... atrocity and genocide that rage on and on ... God ... you, me, us ... face-to-face confrontations with all of these realities challenge creation and its Creator to make that bene-diction work.

NO CHRISTIANITY = NO HOLOCAUST

In some circles, constructive Christian-Jewish dialogue preceded the Holocaust, and respectful postwar Christian-Jewish relationships have often been motivated by desires to improve communal cooper-ation and to extend interreligious understanding that are unrelated to, or at least not focused explicitly on, the Shoah.[23] Nevertheless, as Elie Wiesel's outlook makes clear, no event haunts Christian-Jewish relations more than Nazi Germany's genocide against the Jews, for that mass atrocity cannot be separated from the centuries of anti-Jewish hostility that have been deeply rooted in Christian thought and practice. Neither Christianity nor any single person, institution, or motivation—from the power of Adolf Hitler and the SS, for example, to the widespread racist antisemitism embraced by millions of ordinary Germans during the Nazi period—was *sufficient* by itself to make the Holocaust happen. But Christianity was a *necessary* condition for the Holocaust. No Christianity = No Holocaust.[24]

As a Protestant American Christian, one deeply influenced by Wiesel, I think that the Holocaust's most important impact on Christian-Jewish relations has been, first, to make at least some of us Christians deeply aware of the Holocaust itself. With that awareness has come recognition of both our tradition's complicity in that genocide and our responsibility to challenge and correct what took Christianity in that direction. Hand in hand with those factors, at least some of us Christians try to keep learning about Judaism and Jewish traditions and to seek and welcome friendship that respects Jewish particularity and its differences from Christian ways. We also support the State of Israel's need to find just and lasting peace in a turbulent and dangerous Middle East. Steps in these directions, especially when they involve, as they often do, reciprocity from Jews toward Christians, help to confirm that Christian-Jewish relations in the United States, rocky though they sometimes remain, are probably as good as they have ever been.

A specific event exemplifies and undergirds the impact I have described. Virtually every day since its doors first opened in April 1993, the United States Holocaust Memorial Museum (USHMM) in Washington, DC, helps to make Americans aware of the Holocaust and Christianity's involvement in it. According to USHMM data, as of late 2014, more than 37 million people have visited the museum. An estimated 90 percent of them are not Jewish, which means that a very large, if unspecified, number would be Americans who, in one way or another, identify themselves as Christians. Arguably, no other event in the United States does more to exemplify the Holocaust's impact on Christian-Jewish relations, which must begin, after all, with deepened awareness of the Holocaust itself, than the daily opening of the doors at USHMM.

As the twenty-first century further unfolds, however, what is the Holocaust's impact on Christian-Jewish relations in the United States likely to be? Will that impact grow or diminish? Will it improve or disrupt those relations? As indicated by the Holocaust Memorial Museum's presence in the heart of the nation's capital, remembrance and study of the Holocaust have been extensively institutionalized in American life. Yom Hashoah observances, for instance, take place annually in American synagogues and on many college and university campuses. Christian communities often participate in these observances or acknowledge the Holocaust in other ways. By now, such practices are so widespread as to approach routine. In some places and primarily among individuals, attention to the Holocaust continues to produce deep wrestling with basic issues that Judaism and Christianity encounter about God, scripture, the identity of Jesus, forgiveness, and much more. But the sense that the Holocaust creates ongoing upheaval, unfinished business and even crisis, for these traditions and their relations may have crested. Outlooks within and between Judaism and Christianity have been changed by the Holocaust, but it is dubious that the depth and influence of the changes are growing and intensifying. Instead, as the Holocaust recedes further into the past and the survivor generation passes away, urgency about attending to it diminishes, an outlook accompanied and driven by feelings that enough, even too much, attention has been paid to that event—"Holocaust fatigue"—and that there are current disasters that deserve attention instead. In short, in the United States and elsewhere too, the Holocaust seems not to jar Jews and Christians so much anymore, but the calm can be deceptive and disrupted as events unfold. Two dilemmas illustrate that point.

The first one pivots around unresolved tensions concerning the papacy and religious pluralism. Access to it can begin with the fact that no Christian is more visible, more emblematic of the Christian tradition, than the person who is the pope at any given time. Currently, Pope Francis, the fourth post-Holocaust pope to visit Israel, more than fits that description. Almost from the moment that the College of Cardinals elected the Argentinian Jorge Mario Bergoglio to the papacy on March 13, 2013, he has enjoyed warm relations with Jews worldwide. Notable in this regard is his long-standing friendship with the Argentinian rabbi, Abraham Skorka. Written prior to Bergoglio's elevation, their bestselling book, *On Heaven and Earth*, includes significant dialogue about the Holocaust. Dealing with a sore spot in Catholic-Jewish relations, Bergoglio emphasized that the Vatican archives relating to the Holocaust should be opened to clarify what did—and did not—happen with regard to Church policy toward Jews during World War II. "The objective," said Bergoglio, "has to be the truth."[25]

On April 27, 2014, when Francis declared the sainthood of his predecessors, Pope John XXIII and Pope John Paul II, two pontiffs who responded courageously to the Holocaust and its aftermath, those steps, followed by his May 2014 visit to Israel, also bolstered the improving Catholic-Jewish relations that hearken back to the Second Vatican Council (1962–5) and specifically to the October 28, 1965, proclamation by Pope Paul VI of *Nostra Aetate* (In our age), a "Declaration on the Relation of the Church to Non-Christian Religions."[26] A turning-point document in Christian-Jewish relations, one significantly advanced by US Catholic leaders such as Cardinal Richard Cushing and Cardinal Francis Spellman, *Nostra Aetate* did not explicitly mention the Holocaust, but it did reject key elements of what the French Jewish historian Jules Isaac called the Church's "teaching of contempt" toward Jews and Judaism.[27] Insisting that "the Jews should not be presented as rejected or accursed by God," *Nostra Aetate* decried "hatred, persecutions, displays of anti-Semitism, directed against Jews at any time and by anyone." In addition, it rejected a pernicious deicide charge by proclaiming that the crucifixion of Jesus Christ "cannot be charged against all the Jews, without distinction, then alive, nor against the Jews of today." Furthermore, emphasizing the Jewish origins of Christianity, *Nostra Aetate* affirmed that "God holds the Jews most dear."[28]

Looking back, *Nostra Aetate*, which arrived twenty years after Nazi Germany had nearly destroyed European Jewish life, may seem scarcely more than too little, too late, but it was groundbreaking for Christians and Jews at the time, and it opened doors for further steps in its direction. In retrospect, it can also be said—tentatively perhaps, but said nonetheless—that if *Nostra Aetate*'s teachings had been in place and taken to heart earlier on, the Holocaust might not have happened. That judgment, however, must remain as tentative as it is speculative, because *Nostra Aetate* did not do enough to call into question the assumption that Christianity is still superior to Judaism, one of the presumptions that led Christianity to become a necessary condition for the Holocaust.

An intriguing variation on that theme surfaced in March 2011, when headlines in the announcement of the publication of the second volume of Pope Benedict XVI's book *Jesus of Nazareth* emphasized Benedict's view that the Jewish people cannot be held responsible for the death of Jesus Christ.[29] Having been stated in *Nostra Aetate* forty-five years earlier, this proposition was not new, but in some Jewish quarters it was hailed almost as though it were. Observing that "Holocaust survivors know only too well how the centuries-long charge of 'Christ-killer' against the Jews created a poisonous climate of hate that was the foundation of anti-Semitic persecution whose ultimate expression was realized in the Holocaust," Elan Steinberg of the American Gathering of Holocaust Survivors and Their Descendants added that the pope's new book "seals it [refutation of the deicide charge] for a new generation of Catholics."[30] Abraham Foxman of the Anti-Defamation League called the book's release "an important and historic moment for Catholic-Jewish relations," one that would take the teaching of *Nostra Aetate* "down to the pews."[31] The statements by Steinberg and Foxman indicated that *Nostra Aetate* and what followed in the decades since 1965 did not lay to rest Jewish suspicion that Christianity still harbors supersessionist inclinations, which are never removed from Christian awareness that Jews do not regard Jesus as the Messiah, let alone as God incarnate.

Meanwhile, Pope Francis emphasizes listening to others, engaging in open and honest dialogue, and serving the poor and needy—qualities that thus far have endeared him even to many who reject religion. But deep down a question lurks: Given his role responsibilities as pope, how far can Francis take his commitment to pluralism and fallibility? No matter how much he accents dialogue that is civil, open, and sincere, insists that respect must be shown for the equality and dignity of dialogue partners, and holds that "God makes Himself felt in the heart of each person," Pope Francis, ultimately, may not be able to avoid the reality that his papal responsibilities entail thinking and acting upon the conviction that his tradition fundamentally embodies the Truth in ways that trump Judaism.[32]

Evidence pointing in this direction exists in *Dialogue in Truth and Charity: Pastoral Orientations for Interreligious Dialogue*, which was issued in Rome by the Pontifical Council for Interreligious Dialogue on May 19, 2014.[33] Emphasizing the importance of interreligious dialogue, the document encourages Catholics engaged in such discussions to build on its "recommendations" (55). The document, however, does much more than offer optional guidelines; instead it emphasizes "essential elements" that will keep Catholic dialogue partners "properly guided by faith" and ensure that dialogue does not "generate a kind of relativism" (6). Respect for the equality of dialogue partners is essential, but the equality does not mean that the doctrines held by non-Catholic partners are equivalent in truth to those of Catholic authority. Nor are the founders of other religions to be seen as equivalent to Jesus Christ (13–14). Furthermore, although "interreligious dialogue, in itself, does not aim at conversion, ... dialogue neither takes the place of, nor excludes, *evangelization*" (4–5, 11). Meanwhile, the purpose of interreligious dialogue goes beyond identifying common values. Its aim is to probe their ultimate foundation and to discern truth, which entails grasping, in the words of Pope Benedict XVI, "the essential relationship between the world and God" (12). The truth about that relationship, it turns out, is found in the Church's "basic theological foundations," which include not only that "God is the creator of all human beings" but also that "the focal point of the universal plan of salvation is Jesus Christ, the Incarnate Word of God, fully divine and fully human. In Him, God entered history, assuming human nature in order to redeem it from within. The mystery of man is clarified only in Him" (14–15).

Commitment to the truth of such "basic theological foundations" appears to be non-negotiable as far as properly oriented Catholic partners in interreligious dialogue are concerned. Some commentators have suggested that *Dialogue in Truth and Charity* much more reflects the thought of Pope Benedict XVI than the disposition of Pope Francis, but the current pontiff is not likely to disagree, at least not openly, with its direction. If he were to say otherwise and put Christianity and Judaism on truly equal footings with regard to their truth status, the result would be earth shaking. That step would also be a significant correction for the failures of ethics, which have a long history of breeding in Christianity's claiming—implicitly if not explicitly—that it is more truthful than Judaism, a tradition that continues with *Dialogue in Truth and Charity* despite its embrace of interreligious dialogue.

A related landmine in Catholic-Jewish relations adds to the tensions swirling around religious pluralism and the papacy. Indeed, it has implications for Christian-Jewish relations generally. For decades, few if any Holocaust-related controversies have been more fraught than the ones churned by the conduct of Pope Pius XII during and toward the Holocaust, a matter exacerbated by the delay in the opening of the Vatican's archives pertinent to his reign (1939–58). On December 19, 2009, Pope Francis's immediate successor, Benedict

XVI, currently Pope emeritus, confirmed the 2007 findings of a Vatican committee that attributed "heroic virtues" to the controversial Holocaust-era pontiff, significantly moving him forward in a vetting process that can culminate in Roman Catholic sainthood.[34] Normally, Pius XII could be beatified when a miracle attributed to his intercession is officially certified, and the recognition of a second miracle would set the stage for canonization. Although Pope Francis advanced John XXIII's canonization without those formalities, he has indicated that he would not do so with regard to Pius XII. The elevation of Pius XII, however, may still be waiting in the wings. Reasons for thinking so can be found in Pope Francis's interview, dated June 13, 2014, in the Spanish-language magazine *La Vanguardia*. Referring to "poor Pius XII," Francis urged that the actions of the wartime pope need to be seen "in the context of the time. For example, was it better for him not to speak so that more Jews would not be killed or for him to speak?" As far as resistance against the Holocaust is concerned, lamented Francis, "everyone takes it out against the Church and Pius XII." But before World War II, Francis claimed, Pius XII was seen as "the great defender of Jews," and during the war, the pontiff "hid many [Jews] in convents in Rome and in other Italian cities, and also in the residence of Castel Gandolfo."[35]

Just as Pope Francis's historical judgments about Pius XII are debatable, it is not certain, at least at the time of this writing, what Francis's ultimate position toward Pius XII will be. No one, moreover, can be certain what the reverberations, one way or the other, will be if the Vatican ever declares Pius XII a saint. But his canonization is unlikely to help Christian-Jewish relations in the United States or anywhere else because no matter how many miracles may be attributed to Pius XII, his papacy is so encumbered by Holocaust-related ambiguity that the proclamation of his sainthood will always be awkward. Probably the Catholic Church and Christianity generally can never get beyond damage control where Pius XII is concerned. That problem pertains not only to ambiguities surrounding his wartime papacy but also to his posture about the Holocaust and the Jewish people in the aftermath of World War II.[36] Virtually every Jew and countless Christians, including most Roman Catholics, would breathe a sigh of relief if plans to canonize Pius XII were shelved and put to rest forever.

THE PALESTINIAN–ISRAELI CONFLICT

Turning to the second major dilemma confronting Christian-Jewish relations, while debates continue about links between the Holocaust and the establishment of the State of Israel in 1948, reverberations of the Holocaust affect the Middle East generally and the Palestinian-Israeli conflict in particular. In turn, Christian-Jewish relations in the United States and elsewhere are deeply affected by the Palestinian-Israeli conflict, and the Holocaust's part in that impact is considerable, if frequently understated.[37]

Following yet another collapse of Israeli-Palestinian peace talks in late April 2014, Shmuel Rosner persuasively argued that the failure of those negotiations succeeded in showing that while Israelis and Palestinians overwhelming prefer to live without violence, "they also want many other things, some of which they want more passionately than peace." More important than "peace and calm," contended Rosner, are "things like national pride, sacred traditions, symbols and land."[38] Such an analysis is not optimistic as far as peace prospects are concerned, but it has frank realism in its favor. Including the Hamas–Israel war that erupted in early July after the 2014 peace talks broke down, three Israeli teens were murdered by Palestinian extremists, and revenge was taken by Israeli extremists who tortured and murdered a young Palestinian, the complex effects of the Palestinian–Israeli conflict on Christian-Jewish relations are too complicated to permit adequate treatment of them in this chapter. It must suffice to say that American Christians are scarcely of one mind about the Palestinian–Israeli struggle. With San Antonio, Texas, pastor John Hagee, founder of Christians United for Israel (CUFI), a pro-Israel group established in 2006, often in the vanguard, Christian Zionists have strongly supported Israeli security initiatives, including Jewish settlements in the West Bank and military intervention in Gaza, and are much less inclined to have sympathy for Palestinian interests than is the case for American denominations who have close ties to Palestinian Christians.[39] My former denomination, the Presbyterian Church (USA) (PCUSA), whose members number about 1.8 million, provides a rancorous example.

For a decade, the PCUSA debated but rejected, albeit by narrow margins, divestment in companies that supply Israel with equipment and products used to dominate Palestinian territory.[40] In a contentious episode on June 20, 2014, however, the church's General Assembly voted 310 to 303 to sell church holdings in Caterpillar, Hewlett-Packard, and Motorola Solutions—worth about $21 million—because those corporations aid and profit from Israeli policies deemed hostile to Palestinian rights. The PCUSA contended that its action on divestment was not "an alignment with or endorsement of the global BDS (Boycott, Divest and Sanctions) movement"—its goals range from boycotting Israeli companies and institutions to rolling back Israeli settlements in the West Bank and east Jerusalem. The divestment measure included reaffirmation of "Israel's right to exist as a sovereign nation within secure and internationally recognized borders in accordance with the United Nations resolutions." But the denomination also established a study task force whose charge includes exploring "whether the General Assembly should continue to call for a two-state solution in Israel Palestine, or take a neutral stance that seeks not to determine for Israelis and Palestinians what the right 'solution' should be." Commenting on the crucial divestment vote immediately after it was taken, Heath Rada, the General Assembly's moderator, claimed that the outcome did not reflect "lack of love for our Jewish brothers and sisters." A few days later, on June 26, 2014, the denomination issued "An Open Letter of the Presbyterian Church (U.S.A.) to Our American Jewish Interfaith Partners." It asserted that "we are committed more than ever to sitting at the table and living in community with you."[41]

Although debate about these measures was eclipsed by the Hamas–Israel war in Gaza, which provoked antisemitic protests and even allegations of genocide that distorted Israel's actions and trivialized the Holocaust, most Jews found the official Presbyterian rhetoric about the divestment vote unconvincing and misleading. Tragic and hostile, sad and shameful, hurtful and devastating, disgraceful and outrageous—those words, also voiced by Presbyterians who disagreed with the church's divestment decision, were frequently pronounced in Jewish reactions, which included predictions of rupture with the PCUSA. Underscoring that the divestment move "is an affront to the Jewish community," Rabbi Gary M. Bretton-Granatoor, a vice president of the World Union for Progressive Judaism, alleged that the PCUSA's recent posture toward Israel indicates that Presbyterians "have not . . . developed a language of understanding and respect upon which to respectfully engage with Jews on political questions."[42] Jane Eisner, editor of the *Jewish Daily*

Forward, put a sharper edge on that outlook when she said that Presbyterian divestment felt antisemitic. "When Jewish treatment of Palestinians is judged worse than the way any other dominant group treats a minority, when it is deemed worthy of unique sanction, when other horrors around the world are ignored," said Eisner, "how can I believe that this isn't about the Jews? And that, my Presbyterian friends, is anti-Semitism."[43] By no means did such views belong to those two commentators alone. Rabbi Noam Marans, director of interreligious relations at the American Jewish Committee, also struck a shared note when he stressed that the PCUSA decision would be "celebrated by those who believe they are one step closer to a Jew-free Middle East."[44]

The Holocaust was not at the center of the PCUSA's 2014 General Assembly. Nevertheless, it still shadowed the church's divestment decision because the PCUSA includes pro-Palestinian outlooks, which sometimes stress that the largely Christian West sought to make amends for the Shoah by establishing a Jewish homeland in Palestine. "Kairos Palestine," a 2009 statement issued by a group of Christian Palestinians and widely circulated by the Israel/Palestine Mission Network (IPMN) of the PCUSA, put this point as follows: "The West sought to make amends for what Jews had endured in the countries of Europe, but it made amends on our account and in our land. They tried to correct an injustice and the result was a new injustice."[45] Controversy about such claims intensified in 2014 when the IPMN issued "Zionism Unsettled: A Congregational Study Guide," which questioned the legitimacy of the State of Israel. As Chris Leighton, executive director of the Institute for Christian & Jewish Studies (ICJS) and an ordained Presbyterian minister, aptly evaluated this problematic document: "It portrays Zionism as inexorably leading to 'ethnic cleansing' and 'cultural genocide.' The condemnation of Zionism, in all its forms, is not merely simplistic and misleading; the result of this polemic is the theological delegitimization of a central concern of the Jewish people."[46] With anger about this publication reaching a crescendo in the days following the Presbyterian vote on divestment, the PCUSA announced on June 27, 2014, that "Zionism Unsettled" would no longer be for sale through its website.

Provocative variations on the claims contained in the 2009 and 2014 IPMN documents have been articulated by Mark Braverman, an American Jew, in his hard-hitting book called *Fatal Embrace:*

Christians, Jews, and the Search for Peace in the Holy Land. Braverman argues that Christian attempts to atone for the Holocaust and Christianity's complicity in that disaster, appropriate though they are, have also had the unfortunate consequence of reinforcing Jewish exceptionalism and chosenness in ways that make many Christians complicit in crimes that Braverman believes the State of Israel is committing against Palestinians. Even well-intentioned Christian-Jewish dialogue, he suggests, has contributed to these unfortunate outcomes, because it can intensify Christian guilt in ways that play into the hands of a problematic pro-Israel orientation. Theologically speaking, for example, Braverman contends that "attempts to correct for Christian supersessionism by preserving or incorporating God's election of Israel ultimately replace Christian supersessionism with Jewish exceptionalism. And if Christian triumphalism as expressed in supersessionism led to the ovens of Auschwitz, then Jewish triumphalism as expressed in political Zionism has led to the ethnic cleansing of Palestine."[47] Put more bluntly, Braverman suggests that "out of repentance for the Holocaust, 'sensitivity' to the feelings of Jews, and fear of being labeled anti-Semitic," many Christians have "sold out the Palestinian people."[48]

Such allegations were at least in the background of the PCUSA's divestment stance in June 2014. They strike many Jews and Christians, including many Presbyterians, as inaccurate and outrageous, not least because they are likely to inflame antisemitism, adding to the distressing findings of "ADL Global 100: An Index of Anti-Semitism," the Anti-Defamation League's largest-ever global survey about anti-semitism, conducted in 2014. Polling more than 53,000 people in 102 countries and territories, it found that 26 percent of them—representing about 1.1 billion adults worldwide—"harbor anti-Semitic attitudes." The most problematic areas were in the Middle East and North Africa, where 74 percent have antisemitic views. In the Palestinian territories of the West Bank and Gaza, the figure rises to 93 percent, a number that likely rose as a result of the 2014 Hamas–Israel war. Furthermore, the report stated, "thirty-five percent of those surveyed had never heard of the Holocaust. Of those who have, roughly one-third believe the Holocaust is either a myth or greatly exaggerated."[49]

The report further indicates that smaller percentages of Europeans—34 percent in Eastern Europe and 24 percent in Western Europe—hold "deeply anti-Semitic views," but arguably those numbers do not sufficiently gauge the blurring of a distinction between opposing Israel and opposing Jews, which expands European antisemitism, or the degree to which European antisemitism has been spiking—without much priority being given to fighting that trend—and fueling realistic worries about the future of Jewish life on that continent.[50] Much of the antisemitism documented in the ADL's findings is inflamed by hostility toward Israel and has direct links to Islamist radicals and their followers. But without Christian accountability regarding antisemitism's Christian roots, heritage, and lethal ties to the Holocaust, the content, tone, and implications of contemporary antisemitism cannot be adequately assessed and resisted. Whenever and wherever antisemitism exists, including in a largely post-Christian Europe, Christians should be vigilant and outspoken against it.

Meanwhile, views such as Braverman's have gained traction. While it is too soon to tell how they will affect Christian-Jewish relations in the long run, such thinking adds problematic wrinkles to the place of the Holocaust within those relations. Overcoming Christianity's complicity in the Holocaust, a challenge that can never be fully met, is now complicated even further if it turns out that attention to the Holocaust, understood as Braverman thinks it should be, leads to the conclusion that "the meaning of the Holocaust" requires that an anti-Israel priority is given to "working for justice for Palestine."[51]

Despite these difficulties, and ironically because the Palestinian–Israeli conflict is likely to loom large in the foreseeable future, further complicated as it is becoming as uprisings, rebellions, war, and particularly the atrocities committed by ISIS destabilize the Muslim Middle East, the likelihood is that the Holocaust's impact on Christian-Jewish relations in the United States is waning. That prospect might reduce tensions between Christians and Jews, but the value and outcomes of dispersing attention about the Holocaust remain to be seen. To the extent that Christians and Jews underplay, distort, or grow complacent about the Holocaust's implications for their own religious and ethical traditions or allow attention to the Holocaust to be eclipsed by other events, the prospects for avoiding dangerous disruptions in the relationships between Christians and Jews are not improved but may be worsened.

CONTINUING REVERBERATIONS

This analysis, which is itself a modest part of the Holocaust's impact on Christian-Jewish relations in the United States, makes clear that descriptions of, and forecasts about, the Holocaust's impact on Christian-Jewish relations are as complex and fraught as they may be partially gratifying and cautiously hopeful. After—and, tragically, because of—the Holocaust, relations between Christians and Jews in the United States and elsewhere arguably are about as good as they have ever been. But stresses and strains on those relationships remain and may grow more intense.

Christians have not yet come to terms fully with the Holocaust's implication that Christianity can no longer take itself to be superior to Judaism. If that recognition can deepen, it would allow religious pluralism to grow, which would be a fitting development for American Christianity in particular to advance. Such an advancement would require profound changes in Christian thought and practice. And if religious pluralism advances in a post-Holocaust world, those developments will not leave Judaism untouched either.

Much still depends on whether and how the Holocaust is thoroughly encountered, and the obstacles to that possibility appear to be growing as the Holocaust recedes further into the past. In addition, the seemingly intractable Palestinian–Israeli conflict extends its increasingly divisive ways, and upheavals in the Muslim world and the global persistence of mass atrocity crimes create present-day urgencies that edge the Holocaust away from center stage and require re-evaluation of what the credibility of its "lessons" may be. Where are Christian-Jewish relations going? The Holocaust remains a civilization-sized trauma. Its reverberations will continue to affect Christian-Jewish relations in the United States and elsewhere, but how they will play out cannot be foreseen because that depends on teaching and research, policy and practice, discourse and dialogue that have yet to be enacted.

Numerous times in his writings and lectures, Elie Wiesel speaks of a "mysterious Talmudic scholar" who became his teacher for several years in postwar France. Equally brilliant and enigmatic, Shushani, as he was known, receives high tribute from Wiesel: "I would not be the man I am, the Jew I am, had not an astonishing, disconcerting vagabond [Shushani] accosted me one day to inform me that I understood nothing."[52] Wiesel learned much more than that from his teacher. One of the most important insights he took from Shushani—it became a key part of Wiesel's ethics—is that "man defines himself by what disturbs him and not by what reassures him. . . . God means movement and not explanation."[53] The Holocaust should forever disturb Christians and Jews together. That disturbance will scarcely be reassuring, but it can be defining in ways that keep protesting and resisting the failures of ethics that still haunt Christian-Jewish relations.

The Holocaust put the word genocide *into humanity's vocabulary. Encounters with the Shoah have led me back and forth in time to confront the effects denoted by that term. In the early 1970s, when my work began to focus on the Holocaust, I also tried to grasp the World War I-related genocide unleashed by the Turkish government, which took the lives of 1.5 million Armenians between 1915 and 1923. In addition, I made an effort to track the varied genocidal policies that reduced the American Indian population from some 600,000 in 1800 to about 250,000 in 1900.[1] No one, however, can fully comprehend even a single case of genocide, let alone more than that as I still try to do. With the arrival of the second half of the 1970s, the challenges grew as the policies of Pol Pot and the Khmer Rouge destroyed 1.7 million Cambodians—about one-fifth of Pol Pot's own people—between April 1975 and January 1979 during a "Year Zero" campaign intended to purge and reconstitute Cambodian life from the ground up, decimating multiple groups in the process.*

Subsequently, with awareness and analysis intensifying, comparative genocide studies increased. With them came the fraught question, "Is the Holocaust unique?"[2] For a time, especially in the 1990s, it drew heated attention because an affirmative answer seemed to banish other genocides to undeserved second-class status. A negative answer, on the other hand, appeared to open the door to misleading equivalencies and even Holocaust denial. Engagement with these issues drove home several insights, which ground the chapter that follows:

- *Although they do not dispel the realization that no one can fully comprehend even a single case of genocide, comparative genocide studies are invaluable because, among other things, they reveal the particularities, differences, and similarities in genocidal situations.*

- *Although no one can study all genocides, each compels attention and deserves to be remembered.*

- *The effects of genocide—always devastating and unrelenting— bear witness to the failures of ethics, which include any attempt to privilege one genocide at the expense of others.*

- *Historical understanding, even when focused on the failures of ethics, is not an end in itself. Its value hinges on the ways and degrees in which such understanding promotes resistance against those failures and encouragement for their correction.*

- *The Holocaust, genocide, and other mass atrocities demand attention primarily for ethical reasons, including the hope that humankind can do better in curbing the impulses and institutions that lend themselves to such destruction and the useless suffering inflicted by it.*

7

The Effects of Genocide

> "Genocide," short; easy to remember. The day it got into Webster's was the happiest day of my life.
>
> —Raphael Lemkin in Catherine Filloux's *The G Word*

Catherine Filloux is a gifted contemporary dramatist whose numerous scripts about the Holocaust, genocide, and other mass atrocities include a short play called *The G Word*. It creates an encounter between a thinly disguised General Roméo Dallaire and Raphael Lemkin. Dallaire's heroic efforts to stop genocide were thwarted by international inaction that included reluctance even to use "the G word" to identify the genocide that engulfed Rwanda in 1994. Meanwhile, Lemkin had coined that fateful "G word" fifty years earlier. In Filloux's exchange between the two, Lemkin reflects on his word creation as follows: "'Genocide,' short; easy to remember. The day it got into Webster's was the happiest day of my life."³

This purported moment of happiness came after another event that, arguably, gave Lemkin much more satisfaction. On December 9, 1948, the United Nations took a corrective action to identify a crime that had been nameless and without explicit international recognition. With its approval of the 1948 Convention on the Prevention and Punishment of the Crime of Genocide, the United Nations not only defined the concept to include a variety of acts "committed with intent to destroy, in whole or in part, a national, ethnical, racial, or religious group, as such" but also officially criminalized genocide in international law.

It took some time for dictionaries to catch up with Lemkin and the United Nations. According to Steven L. Jacobs, who has studied Lemkin's papers extensively, on or about February 13, 1950, Lemkin received a letter from the G. and C. Merriam Company of Springfield,

Massachusetts. The letter said that the word *genocide* would appear in the 1950 Addenda section of the second edition of *Webster's New International Dictionary.* The correspondence further stated that *Webster's* definition of the term, not written explicitly by Lemkin himself but basically according with his broad understanding of the term's meaning, would be as follows: "The use of deliberate, systematic measures such as killing, bodily or mental injury, unlivable conditions, prevention of births calculated to bring about the extermination of a racial, political, or cultural group or to destroy the language, religion, or culture of a group." Still further, the correspondence from the dictionary company noted that *genocide* "is also entered and defined in Webster's New Collegiate Dictionary, although the definition is, of necessity, a shorter one."[4]

My search to find the date that Filloux's play calls the happiest of Lemkin's life produced some additional results of interest. For example, Merriam-Webster maintains an Internet site that tracks the frequency with which words are "looked up" online. For some time, *genocide* has been in the top third of those searches.[5] Further investigation on the Merriam-Webster site led to a list of the all-time top ten most frequently searched words. A pair of words—*effect/affect*—ranked tenth on that list, no doubt placing highly because the proper usage of the two terms is often confusing and confused. *Affect* usually functions as a verb, meaning "to influence, have an effect on." *Effect* usually functions as a noun, referring to an outcome or a result, but it can also be a verb, meaning "to make happen, produce."[6] As I thought about these meanings and their differences, questions began to form. They not only help to focus the ethical dilemmas highlighted in this chapter but also have relevance for resisting the failures of ethics. Here are two of those questions: (1) What have been the *effects* of genocide, what happens when genocide goes into *effect*, what takes place when genocide is *effected*? (2) How has genocide *affected* humanity, and how should it *affect* people today?

SOME EFFECTS OF GENOCIDE

Books are among the effects of genocide. One example is a volume called *Centuries of Genocide.*[7] It is not the only book of its kind, but like the term *genocide* itself, the existence and proliferation of such studies are fairly recent. Something else, however, may be even more striking: studies of genocide, in books or other formats, have to be updated. The updating is necessary because research about the past uncovers instances of and details about genocide that may not have been previously recognized and also because perpetrators find new places, occasions, and ways to effect genocide, to bring it about. Thus, *Centuries of Genocide* is the fourth edition a book that used to be called *Century of Genocide* until mass atrocities committed in the twenty-first century, as well as attention to some nineteenth-century cases, made clear that the title could not refer to the twentieth century alone.

In all of its editions, *Centuries of Genocide* is long—about six hundred pages—because there are so many genocides to consider. No single book can deal with all the candidates for inclusion, a reality documented by the fact that the editors of the fourth edition had to cut some previous chapters in order to direct attention to regions and atrocities that had not received the attention they deserved. Sooner or later, a fifth edition of *Centuries of Genocide*—and more—will be required because there is little reason to think that any genocidal campaign currently under way will be the last.

The effects of genocide have not stopped. To the contrary, genocide has gone on and on. Despite "early warning systems," genocide's methods are virus-like in their evolution, adaptability, and mutation. The 2013 edition of *Centuries of Genocide* has chapters that discuss at least fifteen genocidal cases: (1) the obliteration of California's Yana people; (2) the annihilation of indigenous groups in Australia; (3) the genocide of the Herero and Nama in German South West Africa, 1904–7; (4) the Turkish onslaught against the Armenians; (5) the Soviet Union's human-made famine in Ukraine; (6) the Third Reich's genocidal actions against Jews, Sinti and Roma (Gypsies), and disabled people; (7) Pakistani atrocities in Bangladesh; (8) massive killing unleashed by Indonesian military forces in East Timor; (9) the devastation carried out in Cambodia by Pol Pot and the Khmer Rouge, 1975–9; (10) genocidal destruction in Guatemala; (11) the murderous operations against the Kurds carried out by Saddam Hussein; (12) onslaughts in the Nuba Mountains region of Sudan; (13) the Hutu campaign against Tutsi in Rwanda; (14) the savagery that engulfed Bosnia and Herzegovina in the 1990s; and (15) the genocide in Darfur, Sudan.

While *Centuries of Genocide* explains that its cases come from the mid-nineteenth century to the early years of the twenty-first, the book's title still contains an ambiguity as dismal as it is instructive. Centuries of genocide? "Which ones?" it could be asked. Clearly, the twentieth century qualifies as a century of genocide, signifying—at least in part—that it takes modern means and mentalities to effect genocide, to unleash it on the scale and scope that genocide's twentieth-century perpetrators made all too real. But as the book's fourth edition indicates, the nineteenth and twenty-first centuries have been genocidal too. Even that expansion, however, does not contain all that the scourge of genocide has wasted. Lemkin knew as much, for despite the fact that he coined the term *genocide* to refer to the "modern development" of intentional group elimination, he acknowledged that it also denoted "an old practice."[8]

The genocide scholar Kurt Jonassohn answered the question "how old?" by contending that "attempts to eliminate entire groups of people have probably been a part of human conflicts for the past 10,000 years."[9] Nicholas Wade adds that "warfare between pre-state societies was incessant, merciless, and conducted with the general purpose, often achieved, of annihilating the opponent." These societies understood, he continues, that "killing a few of the enemy leaves the remainder thirsting for revenge, so a more effective solution is extermination."[10] No one, of course, knows for sure when the first genocide took place, but allusions to early examples can be found in the Hebrew Bible, which highlights a factor that turns out to be persistent in genocide: namely, that whenever genocide takes place, religion is involved—before, during, or after—in one way or another.[11] In some of the biblical narratives, the elimination of a group even appears to be commanded by God. That prospect makes one wonder.

Such wondering includes asking about the motivations that put genocide into effect. Jonassohn and his colleague Frank Chalk argued persuasively that genocide—ancient or modern—typically involves one or more of at least four motivational drives. They contend that perpetrators commit genocide: (1) "to eliminate a real or potential threat"; (2) "to spread terror among real or potential enemies"; (3) "to acquire economic wealth"; or (4) "to implement a belief, a theory, or an ideology."[12] Meanwhile, no effect of genocide is more pronounced than death itself. So the following question looms large: How much death has genocide, ancient and modern, effected? The answer to that question is one that nobody knows precisely. One reason is that genocide's toll cannot be confined to numbers, even if the numbers of dead could be fully tabulated, which they will never be. Genocide targets groups; individuals die in genocide because they are identified in terms of and sentenced to death because of group membership. So when one tries to calculate genocide's death toll, calculations of the incalculable are unavoidably involved. How much Armenian life did the Turks destroy? How vast was the destruction of the European Jews? How extensive was the damage to Tutsi existence as Hutu machetes hacked away? What losses are accumulating for tribes in Darfur as the catastrophe inflicted by Khartoum and the Janjaweed continues to unfold?

Not only are individual lives taken by genocide but culture and tradition are also imperiled if not destroyed. In one sense, genocides are rarely completely successful. They destroy not so much "in whole," to use the language of the United Nations, but "in part." In the latter regard, however, genocides are quite effective. Among their effects is the memory they leave in their wake, which can make genocide survivors recall that their identity includes belonging to a group that was targeted for annihilation while too little was done to prevent or intervene against that lethal effect. Such memory, more-over, often involves the anguished presence of an absence that includes awareness of what might have been as one ponders the loss of family and friends and what their decimation means as far as a group's future and vitality are concerned. A people's resilience against those losses can be remarkable, but the losses and their aftereffects do not go away, at least not completely. At the end of every genocidal day, the losses do add up. Some real number would encompass them, even if no one knows what it is. Millions?—without question. Tens of millions?—little doubt. Even more than that?—probably so. At the very least, the number is immense and growing. Whatever it will turn out to be, the figure signifies stupendous failures of ethics.

The effects of genocide are immeasurable. No restitution, repar-ation, or legal proceeding can redeem them, although the modicum of justice that may be retrieved from the ruins of genocide demands commitment to pursue those efforts. Meanwhile, at least one more effect of genocide must be mentioned. Paradoxically, the crime of genocide and our naming that crime with the word *genocide* create puzzles, problems, and disagreements that can hinder efforts to prevent or to intervene against that mass atrocity.

Illustrating aspects of this effect, Adam Jones's *Genocide: A Comprehensive Introduction* contains more than twenty definitions of genocide, a number that could be enlarged.[13] Developed by reliable scholars between 1959 and 2009, the definitions compiled by Jones have much in common, for they all indicate that genocide entails group destruction. In detail, however, the definitions are not in agreement, and they often collide with the one propounded in the 1948 United Nations Convention, which remains the legal standard. In Jones's catalog, for example, Henry Huttenbach's entry is perhaps the broadest in scope: "Genocide is any act that puts the very existence of a group in jeopardy."

Huttenbach's statement minimizes intentionality, which is emphasized in other definitions that define genocidal destruction as deliberate, planned, aimed, organized, purposeful, and so on. The definitions that underscore variations on the theme of intentionality do not, however, pin down the meaning of their terms to everyone's satisfaction. Significant differences also exist in the ways that these definitions identify the targets of genocide. Some accounts refer to human collectivities or minority groups; others refer more specifically to national, racial, sexual, religious, tribal, economic, or political groups, but the definitions' categories are not identical. As Scott Straus points out, the concept of genocide does not have a one-size-fits-all function. "From its inception," he correctly observes, "genocide has been an empirical, moral, legal, and political concept."[14] The effects of that development are multiple, but two of them are: (1) that genocide is a contested concept and (2) that debate about its meaning and application may even hamper efforts to intervene against the harm that perpetrators inflict.

For related reasons, Benjamin Valentino argues that it may make sense to find ways to dispense with the term *genocide* and to replace it with another. His suggested substitute is *mass killing*, which he defines as "the intentional killing of a massive number of noncombatants."[15] Valentino tries to elude the problem of determining intentionality by broadening that concept to include reasonable expectation that enacted policies would result in widespread death. Unfortunately, that move scarcely puts ambiguity to rest. As for his "massive number" category, which is intended to circumvent the idea that genocide has to target an entire group or some percentage of it, Valentino thinks that "a massive number [can be] defined simply as at least fifty thousand intentional deaths over the course of five or fewer years." When Valentino adds that "these specific numerical criteria are to some extent arbitrary," his understatement does little to convince that his substitution of *mass killing* for *genocide* is likely to fulfill the promise he offers for it.

A perplexing effect of genocide, then, is that there may never be a fully adequate definition of the term, at least not if we expect universal agreement about its meaning and about how to apply its meaning to the particularities of political circumstances.[16] The struggle to prevent genocide, to intervene against it, to prosecute its perpetrators may have to go on without the luxury of settled definitions. Such work will be daunting, for those who commit genocide will take advantage of the ambiguities that give genocide room to hide. No doubt work will continue to refine genocide's definition, but it would be folly to be hesitant to act while genocide's toll rises. Facing the question, "What is genocide?" we apparently are left to say that we cannot define it to everyone's satisfaction. Nevertheless, enough has been effected, enough has been seen, to make clear that *genocide* refers to a reality that deserves no more victories.

Like so much else in human experience, more than half the battle depends on the force of will to say, in spite of imperfect definitions, that the most reliable evidence and straightforward clarity insist that genocide is taking place *there* and it must be stopped, or that genocide is likely to take place *here* and it must be prevented. Failing such determination, yet another effect of genocide may be in store, namely, that the answer to the question "What is genocide?" is likely to be, in a word, *unending*.

NEGOTIATING WITH KILLERS

Considering how genocide has affected human existence leads to the question: "How should it affect men and women today?" The right answer, I believe, is that people should stop genocide and, if possible, eliminate it completely. In this case, the right answer is as complicated as it is obvious because pursuing it may involve negotiating with killers, dealing and compromising with hateful and loathsome people, among them "spoilers," those who benefit from the mayhem and do not want it to end. After enduring Auschwitz, Primo Levi wrote that "there are no problems that cannot be solved around a table, provided there is good will and reciprocal trust—or even reciprocal fear."[17]

Seeming to concur with Levi, the Holocaust scholar Raul Hilberg remarked that "there are some things that can be done only so long as they are not discussed, for once they are discussed they can no longer be done."[18] Hilberg primarily had in mind how the perpetrators of the Holocaust resorted to euphemisms and silence to mask their genocidal acts. Nevertheless, Hilberg's perspective, far from contradicting Levi's, left open the possibility that persuasion and negotiation could curb the conduct of those who, in the words of genocide scholar Martin Shaw, "aim to destroy civilian social groups."[19] It is instructive to probe further what Levi and Hilberg did and did not mean as they thought about discussion and negotiation concerning killing.

In *The Drowned and the Saved*, Levi devoted a chapter to what he called "useless violence," which was characterized by the infliction of pain that was "always redundant, always disproportionate." Levi's chapter went deep down because he did not dwell on the obvious—beatings, hangings, or even gassings, for example. Instead his catalog of useless violence recalled the cattle cars that shipped Jews to Auschwitz. Their "total bareness" revealed a "gratuitous viciousness" that left people neither privacy nor dignity when they had to relieve themselves. He pointed out that the loot collected from arrivals at Auschwitz meant that there were tens of thousands of spoons in that place. But none were given to prisoners; they had to fend as best they could, which might mean spending precious food from the camp's starvation rations to buy a spoon on the camp's black market. Plenty of ways existed to identify prisoners, but at Auschwitz the Germans implemented "the violence of the tattoo," which Levi described as "an end in itself, pure offense." Levi acknowledged, however, that National Socialism's useless violence did have one unredeeming element of utility: "Before dying," he observed, "the victim must be degraded, so that the murderer will be less burdened by guilt. This is an explanation not devoid of logic but it shouts to heaven: it is the sole usefulness of useless violence."[20] Levi might have added that the Nazi goal was not simply to lessen guilt's burden but to create practitioners of useless violence who would feel no guilt at all.

In spite of all that Levi said about useless violence, *The Drowned and the Saved* draws to a close with his contention that "there are no problems that cannot be solved around a table, provided there is good will and reciprocal trust—or even reciprocal fear." Levi knew how scarce those provisions, even reciprocal fear, could be, for he knew that killers, especially those who employ useless violence, have little use for questions that call into question what they are doing.

One of Levi's most telling descriptions of Auschwitz involves his camp initiation. On one occasion, he reached out a window to quench his painful thirst with an icicle. An SS guard immediately snatched it away from him. "*Warum?*" Levi asked him, only to be told with a shove, "*Hier ist kein warum*" (Here there is no why).[21] Levi's question "Why?" sought explanation, to say nothing of negotiation, but he got none because questions of life and death were already settled there. No asking was permitted for the likes of Levi. In Auschwitz no "why" existed—not as a question and certainly not as a satisfying explanation, either.

Levi would have agreed with another Holocaust survivor, the philosopher Sarah Kofman, who held that "no community is possible with the SS."[22] The impossibility of community scarcely encourages the possibility that there can be meaningful negotiation with killers who bear even faint resemblance to the SS men whose actions still scar the world. Negotiation, in fact, might buy them more time to do their worst. And yet, if one takes into account the larger outlooks of Levi and Kofman, they reflect dispositions that refuse to give up on approaches that entail reasoning and discussion, negotiation and persuasion. Those two writers remain convinced that events are not determined or fated to be what they are. Contingency and change remain, and so long as that is the case, there should not be premature closure when options regarding atrocity-stopping negotiation with killers remain.

The immediate goal is to stop the killing and the useless violence, and to do so as quickly as possible. Before one gives up on negotiation as a means to that end, one must have good and sufficient reasons to be convinced that good will, reciprocal trust, or reciprocal fear can never be found. Short of that conclusion, Levi and Kofman, who experienced immense losses at the hands of Nazi killers, would probably leave the door open for negotiation. Doing so, however, would not preclude pursuit of other means, including the threat or concurrent use of violence to defend against and stop killing assaults that are already under way.

Among the reasons why Levi and Kofman would not prematurely close the door to negotiation is the point Raul Hilberg made when he said that "there are some things that can be done only so long as they are not discussed, for once they are discussed they can no longer be done." Here it is also important to consider what Hilberg did and did not mean.

In 1971, Hilberg published a book called *Documents of Destruction: Germany and Jewry 1933–1945*. This edited volume, which contains Hilberg's commentary, includes documents from German and Jewish sources that recorded and constituted actions in the destruction of the European Jews. The book's front matter contains two epigraphs that highlight the most important imperative in what can be called Hilberg's ethics.[23] The first comes from Heinrich Himmler's speech to senior SS officers on October 4, 1943. Himmler praises his men for remaining decent and for having been "hardened" under the stress and strain resulting from having "gone through this"—Himmler's non-specific way of referring to mass killing. What has been accomplished, Himmler states, "is a page of glory in our history," but also one "never written and never to be written." In juxtaposition to Himmler's injunction that silence must cover the "page of glory," Hilberg sets the following words from a Jewish survivor named Jacob Celemenski: "Today I am one of the survivors. For twenty years I have constantly heard within my mind the very cry of the murdered: Tell it to the world!"

The contrast between these two passages is of fundamental importance. Himmler refers to a "page of glory" but counsels silence about it. Celemenski breaks silence in multiple ways. He unmasks the "glory" by indicating that it refers to mass murder. Himmler may want the "page of glory" to be unwritten, but the absence of the dead Jews resounds in the cries that reverberate in Celemenski's mind. Those cries insist upon remembrance and testimony, protest and resistance: Tell it to the world!

Ethical imperatives direct attention and guide action, but their meaning is not always self-evident. If, for example, one important imperative is to love one's neighbor as oneself, then questions such as "Who is my neighbor?" and "What is and is not involved in loving oneself?" have their place. The same can be said of Celemenski's "Tell it to the world!" What is one to tell and how should the telling be done? One can even reflect on what "telling" does and does not involve, and how "telling" might be related to negotiation as well. Hilberg's work sheds light on his most crucial imperative by illustrating what it means and what is entailed by it.

The *it* that must be told has at least three dimensions. First, paramount importance must be given to telling what has happened, to doing so as thoroughly, honestly, accurately, and persistently as possible. To do that, one has to reckon with both Himmler and Celemenski, with who they were, what they did, and what they said. Himmler and Celemenski, of course, are not only particular persons; they are also emblematic of countless others caught up in the destruction of the European Jews or in any other genocide.

Second, recording and telling the history of the Holocaust is both an end in itself and the means to something more. "Telling it to the world" may be the best that one can do to remember the dead, to mourn the loss, and to hold accountable those who perpetrated the Holocaust but have eluded justice. Such telling has value that is not reducible to instrumentality. Among other things, it is distinctive for its power to differentiate between *right* and *wrong*. It may not be universally impossible but it would certainly be difficult to read the epigraphs in Hilberg's edition of documents, to study those items, and then to return to the difference between the statements of Himmler and Celemenski without feeling that the Holocaust was wrong.

Third, when "telling it to the world" arouses and deepens feelings about the difference between right and wrong, the juncture is reached when the telling becomes more than an end in itself. If wrong has been done, then it ought to be set right as far as possible, and, at the very least the wrong ought not to be repeated. "Telling it to the world" means persistent, ongoing, and ever-more detailed and firmly documented reporting so that forgetfulness does not make it easier for others to create more never-to-be-written pages of "glory." Commenting on Himmler's speech of October 1943, Hilberg puts the point as follows: "There are some things that can be done only so long as they are not discussed, for once they are discussed they can no longer be done." If Hilberg is right, then should negotiating with killers include and even require "telling" of the kind that he identified?

Hilberg's strategy might turn out to be more—or less—sanguine than Levi's hopes for discussion around a table and depending on good will, reciprocal trust, or reciprocal fear. Hilberg's strategy seems to favor negotiation of an especially moral kind, one that could take place at a distance or at close quarters. Involving "telling," it requires calling acts what they are—mass murder, if the circumstances warrant—naming and, if possible, shaming, insisting that useless violence and mass murder are wrong and unacceptable, and then having the courage of those convictions to back them up so that the useless violence and mass murder cease.

Something more is at issue in Hilberg's insistence on the importance of telling it like it is. One can put the dilemma as follows: To what extent, if any, do perpetrators of useless violence or killing know that what they are doing is wrong? Hilberg's position on that question helps to show why he stressed the importance of calling actions by their right names, instead of obscuring them as Himmler did in this 1943 speech. In addition, his perspective helps to clarify what judgments need to be made as one considers whether to negotiate with killers and, if negotiation does take place, how it might best be done.

As noted in Chapter 1, Hilberg affirmed that ethics is the same today as it was yesterday and even the day before yesterday; it is the same after Auschwitz as it was before and during the lethal operations at that place. Especially with regard to needless and wanton killing, he emphasized, ethics is the same for everyone, everywhere. Hilberg left no unclarity. Such killing is wrong. We know that, "in our bones," he said, for such knowledge is the heritage of many years. But if such knowledge is deeply rooted in human experience, and if Hilberg's "we" does not exclude genocidal perpetrators, then it seems to follow that at some level those people did know that what they were doing to their targeted victims was wrong.

That issue is crucial for considerations about the failures of ethics and for questions about negotiating with killers in particular. Hilberg's analysis in *The Destruction of the European Jews* dwells on this problem at some length. One cannot be sure, of course, that the Nazis and their collaborators knew deep down that their policies toward the Jews were ethically wrong. To have clinching evidence about that fact, trustworthy confessions would be needed, including honest and convincing explanation of why the perpetrators violated their own ethical sensibilities. Such confessions and explanations we do not have, at least not for the most part, from the perpetrators who were most responsible for the Holocaust.[24] Hilberg, however, pointed to less direct and more circumstantial evidence to make a case that the perpetrators acted in spite of "knowing better."

Hilberg knew that the destruction process "had meaning to its perpetrators," but despite the imperatives of a "Nazi ethic" that declared a world without Jews to be right and good, he argued that the meaning of the destruction process had to vie with "growing uneasiness that pervaded the bureaucracy from the lowest strata to the highest. That uneasiness was the product of moral scruples that were the lingering effect of two thousand years of Western morality and ethics. A Western bureaucracy had never before faced such a chasm between moral precepts and administrative action; an administrative machine had never been burdened with such a drastic task."[25] Rising to the occasion, the German bureaucrats, according to Hilberg, took into account "that at crucial junctures every individual makes decisions, and that every decision is individual," and thus they developed a two-pronged approach that could trump, if not entirely assuage, bad conscience: repression and rationalization.[26]

Illustrated well in Himmler's previously mentioned speech, repression included hiding the truth about mass murder and limiting the flow of information about it; making sure that those who knew were also directly involved in some aspect of the killing; prohibiting criticism; urging perpetrators not to talk about their work; and making no explicit mention of killing in reports. Repression was insufficient to do the job of neutralizing conscience, however, and thus rationalizations were provided as well. Two were especially important. First, the destruction of the European Jews was a defensive measure or a preventive countermeasure. Second, it was acknowledged that the individual's role was difficult but also that the hard and dirty work was both necessary and excusable, all the more so with respect to excusability because the anti-Jewish actions were not being taken out of any personal vindictiveness. According to the Nazi ideology, the Jews were conspiratorial, criminal, and inferior. Not only their actions but also their very existence threatened German interests. Thus, orders against the Jews had to be followed, but if there were those who were not up to any particular task, opportunities to step aside were available. Furthermore, the division of labor in the destruction process made it possible for one to say that somebody might be doing unethical deeds—outright killing, for instance: *But I was not unethical because I was simply doing my duty at this desk or in that office.* There was always a receding moral horizon that provided safety for one's conscience, but if one was in the thick of going "through this," as Himmler put it, then there was what Hilberg called "the jungle theory," a last-ditch defense emphasizing that life is a struggle and those who refused to do what was necessary to preserve their way of life would lose it.

If Hilberg was right when he said that, from the German perspective, "the most important problems of the destruction process were not administrative but psychological," then it is also crucial to see that those problems, too, were solved, at least long enough for the "Final

Solution" to sustain itself until Nazi Germany was crushed by the Allies' superior military might. If ethics is in our bones, they are precariously fragile. If ethics is the result of the heritage of many years, that heritage guarantees very little. If ethics is the same today as it was yesterday and even the day before yesterday, its status remains as vulnerable and problematic as it is fundamental and important. Such realizations remain important as one considers when or how to negotiate with killers. Negotiation with killers—whether to pursue it, how to do it, what expectations to place upon it—requires lucidity about the failures of ethics and also about the fact that Levi, Kofman, and Hilberg insistently recognized: namely, that silence and neutrality are not options, at least not ones that will help the victims.

WILL GENOCIDE EVER END?

The effects of genocide affect people in various ways. Its effects lead perpetrators to deny that they are producing them, to evade responsibility for them, and to try to escape punishment when the tide turns. Meanwhile, women, children, and men who are targeted by those who commit genocide are definitely affected as they lose life in all sorts of ways. Rescuers and relief workers engage in dangerous and sacrificial efforts to reduce suffering, save lives, and to keep at least glimmers of hope alive. At the very least, genocide fatigue affects them. Genocide affects political leaders, too, but they deplore genocide rhetorically, often without using the G-word, more than they prevent and resist it effectively. At least in post-Holocaust times, scholars hold conferences about genocide, write and publish about it, often at great length, and provide "early warnings" about where genocide may next erupt. Some professors feel compelled to teach about genocide. Genocide affects people still in other ways: from time to time, students rally, marches are held, television announcements appear—all of them focused on responding to mass atrocities of one kind or another. Thus far, those efforts have not overcome the inertia and indifference that help to make such disasters ongoing.

In many cases, genocide affects people by causing depression and despair along with death. How could it not? That question, however, ought to be taken as more than a rhetorical flourish that underscores how devastating genocide's effects turn out to be. No crime is more human or inhumane than genocide. Other creatures do not make and enact such catastrophic plans. In particular, genocide has nothing to do with the fleet-footed and vulnerable antelopes that are widespread in Africa, and yet, in a way it does, because *The Antelope's Strategy* is an apt title for one of Jean Hatzfeld's memorable reports about Rwanda's life after genocide.

In a chapter entitled "Forest Exploits," Hatzfeld focuses on Eugénie Kayierere, who "gave the most prodigious athletic performance" ever known to him.[27] It took place not in a sporting event but in a five-week run for her life in the Kayumba Forest during April and May 1994. This forest stands on the hills above Nyamata, a town about twenty miles south of Kigali, the Rwandan capital. The context for what happened there includes the fact that in 1994 the Nyamata district was a Tutsi-dominated region in a small, predominantly Christian country, the most densely populated in Africa, whose people numbered approximately eight million, 85 percent of them Hutus.

Systematic killing of Tutsis began in Nyamata on April 11, after Juvénal Habyarimana, the Hutu president of Rwanda, was assassinated when a missile likely launched by Hutu extremists brought down his plane as it approached Kigali's airport on the night of April 6. In circumstances inflamed by pre-existing ethnic violence and the extremist Hutu leadership's fear that a Tutsi takeover was imminent, Hutu troops, supported by militias known as *interahamwe* ("those who attack together") and soon augmented by large numbers of local Hutu men, unleashed a planned—and in their eyes justifiable—slaughter of the "cockroaches," as Hutu propaganda dehumanized the Tutsi people.

Genocide engulfed the Nyamata district in frenzied massacres that left 50,000 Tutsis dead—five of every six in the region—including 5,000 murdered in or around Nyamata's main church and an equal number who met the same fate in another church at nearby Ntarama. By May 12, the genocide in Nyamata was over, as Hutus fled from the troops of the Rwandan Patriotic Front (RPF), who returned from exile to take control of the country. The RPF arrived too late, however, to prevent the national death toll from reaching 800,000. Nearly all of the dead, including moderate Hutus and about one-third of Rwanda's 80,0000 Twa (commonly known as Pygmies), were butchered by the machete "cuts" that tens of thousands of Hutu killers delivered in a mere hundred days.

Two of Hatzfeld's earlier books documented this history. Concentrating on the Nyamata district, *Life Laid Bare* presented testimony by Tutsi survivors. *Machete Season* was Hatzfeld's stunning account of ten Hutu men from the Nyamata area—friends and neighbors, mostly in their 20s and 30s—who became machete-wielding killers, hunting their Tutsi prey day after day in the marshes and hills and profiting from the loot that mass murder brought them.

Eventually captured, tried, and imprisoned in the penitentiary in Rilima, not far from their homes, these killers spoke with Hatzfeld freely, if not always honestly, anticipating neither release from their sentences nor further recriminations from the testimony they gave him. In early January 2003, however, President Paul Kagame decreed that thousands of perpetrators whose confessions had been accepted and who had served at least half of their prison sentences would be released from captivity. By early May, most of Hatzfeld's interview cohort was home again. Throughout Rwanda, known perpetrators and survivors of their onslaughts had to live together. Hatzfeld felt compelled to return to Rwanda, to re-establish contact with friends and acquaintances in the Nyamata district, and document how the Hutu–Tutsi encounters were unfolding in the genocide's aftermath. Those decisions led him to tell Eugénie Kayierere's story, a vital part of his book's message, says Hatzfeld, and to reflect on the antelope's strategy.

Hatzfeld notes that his earlier work barely mentioned the killings in Nyamata's hilltop forests, which are by no means lush but sparse with "thorny shrubs and stunted eucalyptus trees."[28] Unlike the thick marshes in Nyamata's lowlands, Rwandan hilltop forests such as the one at Kayumba lacked hiding places. Hatzfeld estimates that equal numbers of Nyamata's Tutsis fled to the marshes and to the forests to escape the Hutu predators. Those who survived in the slime and muck of the swamps far outnumbered the few who escaped the Hutu killers in the forested hills. Hatzfeld thinks that only "twenty people out of six thousand survived the hunting expeditions in Kayumba Forest."[29] One was Innocent Rwililiza, who became Hatzfeld's trusted interpreter and close friend. Two others, the only women among them as far as Hatzfeld knows, were Eugénie Kayierere and Médiatrice, "then a desperate little eleven-year-old who sneaked back down the hill after twelve days to lose herself amid the Hutu population of Nyamata."[30]

When the killings began in the Nyamata district, Eugénie and her husband ran for their lives but lost each other in the panic.

Surrounded by *interahamwe*, she and some of her neighbors hid in the bush for four days, not moving even to relieve themselves. On the move at night, they reached the forest, where thousands of Tutsis sought refuge. Hutus had carried out pogroms against Tutsis before. Some Tutsis thought that the violence soon would subside, making it possible for them to return home. Their hope was too optimistic.

For five weeks, a lethal routine brought Hutu hunters—sometimes 2,000 of them—to the forest at nine in the morning. Tutsis who had not been "cut" by four in the afternoon might live another day, but staying alive required outrunning the killers. As Innocent put it, "We ran for about six hours during the day. Some days threatened more than others, but never, never, was there a day without an attack."[31] Chances for survival—they were minimal at best and nonexistent for the elderly, young children, and mothers with babies—depended not only on stamina and speed but also on sticking together with those who knew the terrain or tactics that might confuse the hunters. "You had to latch onto a gang that kept up its morale," says Eugénie, but "when the killers seemed to be upon us, we'd scatter in all directions to give everyone a chance: basically, we adopted the antelope's strategy."[32]

Eugénie recalls "the hiss of the machetes swiping at your back."[33] She thinks she escaped more by luck than by strategy or speed. One day, she recalls, "I was trapped by a neighbor I'd known for a long time. Our eyes locked so suddenly that his first blow missed me, and I ran off." Another time, when she ran from nine to three o'clock— "sprinting, dodging, leaping"—her group started with a hundred and ended with thirty, all the others cut down. "We knew we were racing toward death," she adds, "but we wanted to dodge through life for as long as possible."[34]

When Hatzfeld took the title of his book from Eugénie's comment about the antelope's strategy and called her story vital to the message of his book, he neither emphasized nor discounted that her narrative contains elements of a "happy ending." Eugénie survived the genocide, found her husband alive, established a popular *cabaret* filled nightly with folks drinking *urwagwa* (banana beer), and gave birth to the first of her six children only ten months after returning from the forest. With those children at the center of her attention, she says that "the genocide simplified happiness for me."[35] But Eugénie does not forget the genocide's brutality and how people were "chopped up so viciously" and how she felt "already among the dead" during the genocidal hunt. She thinks it dishonors and humiliates the dead to give "details about how they were stripped naked or cut short, how they dragged themselves along, how they pleaded for mercy, how they screamed or groaned or vomited or bled."[36] Without her saying so, however, such details afflict her "simplified happiness," a point crucial to Hatzfeld's "message" and to the antelope's strategy in post-genocide Rwanda.

Neither the strategy nor the message brims with hope about reconciliation, justice, and trust, three of the most challenging themes threaded through Hatzfeld's book. Government policy, international influence, and everyday necessities in post-genocide Rwanda seemingly have suppressed Tutsi desires for revenge and Hutu regrets that the genocide was less than completely successful. Hatzfeld found Tutsis and Hutus living and working together, even to some extent socializing and worshipping together. This civility is not superficial, for Tutsis and Hutus need each other to sustain a viable economy in Rwanda, but relationships and respect between Tutsis and Hutus do not run deep enough, at least not yet, to assuage the grief and grievances that linger and fester after all that happened in Rwanda's swamps, forests, and other slaughter sites.

The Gacaca Court proceedings, which in Nyamata began on Thursday mornings in 2002, seem to be an exception to the rule. *Gaçaça*, meaning "justice on the grass," refers to the locations where tribal people's courts sat for centuries until they were largely supplanted by colonial courtrooms. But when the genocide left Rwanda's justice system in ruins, the government reinstituted Gacaca deliberations, hoping that their organized encounters between perpetrators and survivors would advance accountability, rebuild trust, enhance reconciliation, and restore at least some sense of justice.

These aims are essential if Rwandan life is to move beyond its genocidal past. To some extent they are being achieved, but Hatzfeld's conversations with Tutsis and Hutus underscore that success is sporadic and fragile. While time's passage will bring some mending to Rwanda, Hatzfeld suggests that many of Rwanda's wounds are beyond healing. The ongoing predicament is how Tutsis and Hutus will live together in those circumstances.

The antelope's strategy contributes to the dilemma. Tutsis and Hutus continue to run in their ethnic groups. As the past pursues them into the future, those groups stick together but unavoidably individuals must go their own ways, as Eugénie said, to give everyone a chance. That dynamic means that the genocide remains—one could even say continues—inside individuals, ultimately leaving them alone to cope with its memories and effects as best they can. The results of that struggle do little to encourage trust, reconciliation, and hope for justice.

A survivor named Berthe Mwanankabandi speaks for many in Nyamata and elsewhere when she says that "justice finds no place after a genocide."[37] Innocent Rwililiza told Hatzfeld that when Tutsis "talk among ourselves, the word *forgiveness* has no place," even though the international humanitarian organizations active in Rwanda have insisted on its reconciling importance.[38] Ignace Rukiramacumu, one of the Hutu killers interviewed by Hatzfeld, claims that "convincing a Tutsi you are telling the truth is impossible," and his fellow perpetrator, Alphonse Hitiyaremye, added that "the real truth, the atmosphere, if I may say so, cannot be told."[39] A survivor named Claudine Kayitesi would agree with Alphonse. "The future has already been eaten up by what I lived through," she laments with profound awareness of how much is lost "when you cannot trust those who live close by."[40] Appropriately, Hatzfeld offers no one-size-fits-all summation for the personal testimonies in his book; their perspectives and contents are diverse and at times conflicting. *The Antelope's Strategy*, however, moves unrelentingly to a telling conclusion: trust between Tutsis and Hutus, tenuous as it has long been, arguably remains damaged beyond repair by the genocide and its aftermath.

Hatzfeld's message is as sober as it is vital: the effects of genocide are incalculable. Innocent says that living through the genocide brought him "no enriching knowledge," but he has learned "to be ready for anything, to think on the alert. . . . I always want to know what's going on behind what's going on."[41] Such knowing, *The Antelope's Strategy* makes clear, is one of the necessary factors for correcting the failures of ethics and for responding well to the effects of genocide.

POSTSCRIPT

In 1935, several years prior to Raphael Lemkin's invention of the term *genocide* and long before Catherine Filloux's script for *The G Word* had him say, " 'Genocide,' short; easy to remember," Nazi Germany's Nuremberg Laws stripped German Jews of citizenship, established race as the fundamental legal principle in German life, and did much to pave the way toward the Holocaust, the genocide that annihilated most of Lemkin's family. While those steps were taken in 1935, American movie-goers could see a now-forgotten film called *Mississippi*. If that film remains noteworthy at all, it is because the Jewish song-writing team, Richard Rodgers and Lorenz Hart, composed music for its soundtrack, including a ballad called "It's Easy to Remember," a theme coupled with the line that follows, "But so hard to forget."

"It's easy to remember"—Lemkin wanted his word *genocide* to be like that.[42] The theme "but so hard to forget" also applies to the term and the reality it denotes. The relationships between those phrases with regard to genocide are far more fraught than the ones that Rodgers and Hart grasped in their song about love lost and hope crushed. Lemkin's word may be easy to remember, but it is a question whether remembering genocide, really remembering it, is easy at all. Put another way, it is not so hard to forget that genocide has happened and that its threats continue. And yet, the song's part of about being so hard to forget still has its haunting impact: forgetting genocide is very hard indeed because that atrocity exacts a cost that no one should demand or have to pay.

How should genocide affect humankind? Genocide should be both so easy and so hard to remember that the impossibility of forgetting it compels the resistance and action needed to bring genocide at least closer to ending.

Late on a summer afternoon at Auschwitz-Birkenau in 1996, a thunderstorm drenched the remains of that Nazi killing center where more than a million Jews were murdered. As the storm passed and the sun came out, a rainbow appeared over Auschwitz. The juxtaposition of Birkenau, the reality and aftereffects of that death camp, and a rainbow, with its awesome beauty and symbolic, even biblical, meanings of life, hope, and promise, remains jarring and poignant to me. Memory of that intersection, even collision, between history and nature makes me wonder whether humankind can begin to repair the damage we have inflicted on each other and the natural world.

My work on this chapter brought to mind a book called How Green Were the Nazis? It concentrates on environmental concerns and objectives in the Third Reich—those regarding the German landscape among them—especially before World War II ravaged the European continent. The book's cover features a haunting aerial photograph that depicts a German pine forest. Formed by larch trees, the deciduous conifers that turn bright yellow in the autumn before shedding their needle-like leaves, a large swastika stands out amidst the evergreens. The editors' note about the cover explains: "Presumably a zealous forester planted the sylvan swastika, with a diameter of nearly two hundred feet, in the 1930s as a sign of his allegiance to the Nazi regime. The swastika survived not only World War II but also four decades of East German communist rule. Visible only from the air during the fall and winter months, the larch trees were detected in 1992 and felled in 2000."[1]

A few years ago, I planted a small larch tree at my home in the Cascade Mountains of north central Washington State. It has grown from three feet to nearly thirty. Planting that tree was a small protest against Nazi pride that found it good to use those tall, thin, magnificent specimens to deface nature itself with the swastika. No tree—no world—deserved that fate. As I consider the failures of ethics and resistance against them, the cover photo from How Green Were the Nazis? helps me to focus what I want to say in response to the question, What has been learned from the Holocaust?

8

What Has Been Learned?

> The unremitting effort continues for the small incremental gains . . . lest all be relinquished and forgotten.
>
> —Raul Hilberg, *Sources of Holocaust Research*

What importance will studies about the Holocaust have in ten, twenty, a hundred years, even a millennium from now? Presently, the Holocaust and study about it are deeply embedded in human memory, memorialization, scholarship, and teaching. A generation of younger scholars will carry forward the work that those before them have done. But the world will not be the same as time passes. Holocaust scholars and Holocaust-related institutions and education programs will continue their work. Assessment of their accomplishments will be needed, too, but to what end all of this effort will be expended is less than clear. What will happen to the "warnings" and "lessons" of the Holocaust in a world where mass atrocities and genocides show few signs of abating? Who can say with certainty that catastrophes worse than the Holocaust are not in store? What of the Holocaust's status—so often claimed—as a watershed event unprecedented, if not unique, in human history? Events may be in play that will lead eventually to the extinction of much, or all, of human life. What would Holocaust studies amount to, then?

Considering the failures of ethics and resistance against them, the question raised in this chapter's title comes to mind. A sobering response to the question, "What has been learned from the Holocaust?" is *not enough*. Fortunately, if we not only recognize but also take to heart the fact that *not enough* has been learned, then it could be that the outcome will be better than bleak. Knowing that we lack something, that we fall short, even that we might do better, is *maybe something*, which is the second response that governs the explorations that follow. They focus, first, on knowledge about the Holocaust and, second, on some of the implications of that knowledge that most need to be taken to heart if we are to protect and care for the world that is our home.

GETTING IT RIGHT

In the spring of 1993, the year before genocide erupted in Rwanda, the United States Holocaust Memorial Museum opened in Washington, DC. Interest in the Holocaust was high in the United States, and urgency about preserving and transmitting memory of it was intensified by awareness that the survivors of the Shoah were aging and dying. That same perception governed Steven Spielberg's 1994 establishment of the Survivors of the Shoah Visual History Foundation (now the USC Shoah Foundation—The Institute for Visual History and Education), an initiative that followed his pivotal film *Schindler's List*, which debuted in 1993. Archives established even earlier, such as the Fortunoff Video Archive for Holocaust Testimonies, which came into existence at Yale University in the early 1980s, had influenced some currents in Holocaust studies research, but the scope and size of the Spielberg project, which currently holds more than 53,000 genocide survivor testimonies, ensured that survivor testimony and Jewish experience would be at least as central to scholarly study of the Holocaust as the attention that scholars have given to the German perpetrators and their collaborators.

The recognition that living Holocaust survivors would not be alive to testify and teach forever drove still other initiatives in the mid-1990s, including the founding of Holocaust Museum Houston, which opened in that Texas city in March 1996. At that time, the field of Holocaust studies looked different than it does two decades later. If one recalls books and debates that occupied center stage in Holocaust studies in 1996, the most important publications from that year included Daniel Goldhagen's still controversial *Hitler's Willing Executioners: Ordinary Germans and the Holocaust* and a volume edited by Alan Rosenbaum, *Is the Holocaust Unique? Perspectives on Comparative Genocide*.

Goldhagen argued that an "eliminationist antisemitism" had been widespread in Germany during and even before the time that the Nazis held power, and that such distinctively German antisemitism went far to explain why and how the Holocaust took place. Many scholars found Goldhagen's claims overblown, insufficiently contextualized, and inadequately nuanced. But that ferment went beyond arguments among scholars; it helped to generate renewed research about European antisemitism and the role such ideology played in the multiple dimensions of Jewish plight under Hitler. Meanwhile, Goldhagen went on to publish *Worse Than War: Genocide, Eliminationism, and the Ongoing Assault on Humanity*. By no means did he abandon study of the Holocaust, but, as the title of that 2009 book suggests, Goldhagen broadened the context in which he considers the Shoah.

Arguably, when Rosenbaum's collection *Is the Holocaust Unique?* appeared in 1996, a fairly widespread presumption held that, indeed, the Holocaust was a unique event. Nothing quite as cataclysmic, many people believed, had happened before or since. Rosenbaum's book did not reject that view, at least not entirely—some of its contents defended the uniqueness of the Holocaust—but the book did question the presumption of uniqueness. The furor surrounding questions about the uniqueness of the Holocaust was considerable in the mid- and late 1990s. That debate's intensity subsided, but versions of the issue remain in play. Rosenbaum's book, expanded and revised, is now in its third edition, which appeared in 2009, eight years after the second was published in 2001. Scholars increasingly grapple with questions about relationships between the Holocaust and other mass atrocities and, in particular, with issues regarding the comparative place of the Holocaust in relation to other genocides.

The year before the books by Goldhagen and Rosenbaum appeared—on June 23, 1995, to be exact—I finished some of the most challenging work I have ever done in the field of Holocaust studies. I had the privilege of working with Ralph Appelbaum Associates and Holocaust Museum Houston to write the text for the museum's permanent exhibition. The challenges included ensuring that the text's facts were accurate, its narrative valid and vivid, the writing clear and compact so that it would be accessible to the Museum's visitors and suitable for the size of the exhibition panels. At every turn, decisions had to be made about what to include and emphasize, what interpretive framework to employ, and what to leave out. The scholarly, pedagogical, and ethical imperative was to do as best one could to *get it right*. Ultimately, *getting it right* is what the field of Holocaust studies tries to do. In that process, much is at stake, because *getting it right* is easier said than done, as difficult as it is important. To illustrate that point, consider two brief passages from the 1995 Houston Museum text.

The plans for Holocaust Museum Houston wisely emphasized that testimony from, and narration about, the numerous Holocaust survivors who then lived in the Houston area ought to be highlighted in the permanent exhibition. As a result, I received written transcripts of the oral testimony that had been given by many of those women and men. My text for the permanent exhibition included excerpts from them. That text began with a question that is not as simple as it looks: What was the Holocaust? Obviously, if there is to be a museum about the Holocaust, if there are to be studies about the Holocaust, some definitional clarity has to be provided about the content, scope, and meaning of the subject. Here are two ways in which my text began to deal with those problems.

One of the Houston survivor testimonies came from Irving Berk. Words I excerpted from his testimony provided a first response to the question, What was the Holocaust? The excerpt, Berk's words, went as follows: "I probably skipped something. I covered my whole life in a couple of hours. . . . I didn't have as bad a time, I guess, as some people did in the camps, but I lost most of my family there. My mother, my younger brothers and sisters came in and never went out."

Such testimony says a lot about what the Holocaust was—and is—but note something especially important in that excerpt. Berk observed that his testimony "probably skipped something," and how could it not, given that he had limited time to tell what had happened to him? At the same time, what he did say underscored that "my mother, my younger brothers and sisters came in and never went out." We remember and honor those who were murdered in the Holocaust, but mostly we do not have their testimony. The silence that surrounds them, I believe, is important in thinking about what the Holocaust was and is, and in considering what studies of the Holocaust can and cannot do.

One thing more about Irving Berk deserves attention with regard to the scope, development, and significance of Holocaust studies. Retrieving his testimony more than a decade after I had written about it in 1995, I realized that I did not know what had happened to him in recent years. So I wrote to my friend, Susan Llanes-Myers, the museum's executive director at the time, to see if she might be able to give me an update. Almost immediately, I had an informative reply from Pam Hamilton, Llanes-Myers's assistant and the person who was keeping track of Houston-related survivors. Hamilton's records showed that Berk was still living but had relocated to Arizona. Then her message reminded me of some earlier facts about him. Irving Berk had been born Irving Berkovicz on October 10, 1924, in an eastern European town called Khust Zakarpatska, which at that time was part of Czechoslovakia; later it came under Hungarian control and today is situated in western Ukraine.[2] Before coming to the United States and Texas in 1950, Berk spent time in the following camps: Auschwitz, Mauthausen, Buchenwald, and Ebensee.

"I didn't have as bad a time, I guess, as some people did in the camps," Berk said. How should one fathom that statement, given that he endured Auschwitz, Mauthausen, Buchenwald, and Ebensee? Very few prisoners entered all of those places and came out alive to testify about them. How did he get from one place to another? How did those camps come to be? What about his home town in Czechoslovakia and the Jews who lived there? The briefest, simplest statement about the Holocaust opens up a thousand questions, each one of them inviting study and research, each one of them revealing the importance of *getting it right*.

As an ethical imperative, *getting it right* matters. Fidelity to it is crucial not only for sound scholarship and education but also for resisting the failures of ethics. In fact, the two—sound scholarship and education and resistance against the failures of ethics—are profoundly related. Without careful study and research, it is impossible to know what the Holocaust was and is. Without careful study and research, no museum, exhibit, or teaching about the Holocaust can be reliable. Without careful study and research, erroneous judgments, invidious comparisons, misleading equivalencies, and even outright denial of events may gain undeserved belief and undesirable traction. Without careful study and research, we cannot keep fresh, credible, and relevant the most important lessons that the Holocaust may be able to teach us.

Returning to my text for Holocaust Museum Houston, I intended the excerpt from Irving Berk to be a reminder that what we think we know about the Holocaust, and however deeply held our convictions may be about those matters, research and study about that catastrophe, about any genocide or mass atrocity, need to be tempered with senses of humility and fallibility, with awareness, as Raul Hilberg puts it, that "there is no finality. Findings are always subject to correction and reformulation."[3] Like Berk, scholars and studies of the Holocaust need constantly to be aware that "I probably skipped something," and how could we not because the *vastness* of the Holocaust is one of its defining characteristics. No person or perspective can grasp it completely, although as Hilberg further observed, we keep trying to make gains "lest all be relinquished and forgotten."

Opening with the excerpt from Irving Berk's testimony, my text for Holocaust Museum Houston quickly changed its voice and perspective, as the following words from that text indicate: "The Holocaust," I wrote, "was the systematic, state-organized persecution and murder of nearly 6 million Jews by Nazi Germany and its collaborators. Two-thirds of Europe's Jews and one-third of the world's Jewish population were slaughtered in the Holocaust. More than half of the dead came from Poland, where the Nazi annihilation effort was 90 percent successful."

Consider two questions about such a statement. First, when I wrote those words, how could I be confident—as I was in 1995 and still am today—about their truth? Holocaust scholars and researchers, like scholars and researchers everywhere, depend on each other, since no one can begin to know everything. The coin of the realm in Holocaust studies is immersion in primary sources, which can be of various kinds, depending on what the focus of the scholarship may be. For instance, if one's focus is on art, film, or novels related to the Holocaust, then the primary sources may be paintings, movies, and stories and all that one can find out about them. If one is dealing with quantitative generalizations—for example, that nearly six million Jews were murdered by Nazi Germany and its collaborators—then one must rely on those who have studied, documented, and retested the data, much of it retrieved from archives of one kind or another, that substantiate the claims. In the process of doing that work, one will discover that scholars are not entirely in agreement, let alone of one interpretive mind, which means that what can be called "false precision" about Holocaust-related statistics has to be avoided, along with claims for finality.

So the second question to raise about that opening paragraph in my Houston Museum text is as follows: Can statements about the Holocaust be true and still not be adequate? I think nothing in that opening paragraph of my Houston Museum text is less than true, but I also have no doubt that what is stated in that paragraph is incomplete, not the whole story, and therefore in need of expansion and contextualization that only further study and ongoing research can provide. Furthermore, the state of Holocaust studies in 1995 or 1996 would not have allowed the kinds of amplification and interpretation that are possible now, or that will be ten or twenty years on. For instance, when I wrote that the Holocaust was "systematic, state-sponsored persecution and murder of nearly 6 million Jews by Nazi Germany and its collaborators," a good deal was known about how that destruction process worked, but by no means everything, especially about what the historian Timothy Snyder later came to call the "bloodlands" of Eastern Europe—Poland, the Baltic States, Belarus, Ukraine, and western Russia—where most of the Holocaust's killing took place.[4] My opening paragraph in the Houston text remains valid, but its meaning and complexity are bound to change and require updating as more is discovered and documented.

DISCOVERY AND DOCUMENTATION

Fast-forward from the opening of Holocaust Museum Houston in March 1996 to September 5, 2005. On that date, I received a message from Lucy Qureshi, who at the time was the commissioning editor for religion and theology at Oxford University Press. Qureshi wanted to know about the feasibility of an Oxford Handbook of Holocaust Studies. She indicated that such a work would be a tall order, for it would need to be an authoritative, up-to-date guide to the most important findings, issues, and debates that were driving research about the Holocaust and would likely do so in the future. Discussion between Qureshi and me soon included the Northwestern University historian Peter Hayes.

Cutting to the chase, in late 2010 Oxford University Press published *The Oxford Handbook of Holocaust Studies*, which Hayes and I compiled and edited. That five years elapsed between the commissioning and publication of the book indicates something else about Holocaust-related scholarship, namely, that it takes time. Hayes and I had to establish the book's topics and recruit reliable scholars to write about them. Then the forty-seven commissioned authors had to do considerable study and research to identify and assess the state of their subjects within the broader field of Holocaust studies. Spotlighting three of the book's five parts to illustrate some of the contributors' findings, here are glimpses of ways in which scholars have been working to keep understanding of the Holocaust focused, accurate, and timely.[5]

Conventional treatments of the Holocaust have often emphasized a three-dimensional analysis that concentrates on perpetrators, victims (including survivors), and bystanders. Gestures are made to the pre-1933 context and to some of the post-Holocaust implications and reverberations of the Nazi genocide, but typically the latter topics are not discussed in much detail. Without abandoning insights from the perpetrator-victim-bystander rubric, *The Oxford Handbook of Holocaust Studies* re-evaluated and disaggregated that three-part approach. The *Handbook*'s second part, for example, concentrates on the principal *protagonists* in the Holocaust. It explores not only the agency of Nazi leaders and the killers who showed initiative even as they executed orders from above, but also the efforts of Jews, including children and women, to resist and survive the onslaught against them, even as this assault struck them in distinct ways. The chapters under this heading also examine the motives and actions of institutions, such as the Christian churches and Allied and neutral governments, whose behavior affected the course of the Holocaust and its aftereffects. Taking the time-worn term *bystander* to be too general and vague, the *Handbook* suggests that the term *onlooker* may do better justice to the internal diversity of the category and includes a chapter on a subgroup that hardly fits under the usual tripartite division, namely those who risked their lives to rescue Jews.

Looking beyond Adolf Hitler and Heinrich Himmler, the most prominent Nazi leaders, Christopher Browning showed how recent research has concentrated on the lesser-known "problem-solvers" who were essential Holocaust protagonists during four phases of Nazi Jewish policy: 1933–9, when the regime disemancipated, isolated, and impoverished the Jews of Greater Germany and drove over half of them abroad; 1939–40, when the regime sought to clear its expanding empire of Jews through schemes of massive ethnic cleansing; 1941, when the definition of a "Final Solution" to the self-imposed Jewish Question became systematic and total mass murder; and 1942–5, when the Third Reich tried to achieve that goal. At every turn, the regime encountered myriad problems. In a political culture encouraging activism and initiative, cadres of middle-echelon experts, functionaries, and technocrats "working toward the Führer" made many of the decisions and devised many of the measures that drove this lethal radicalization.

Meanwhile, identifying Jews solely as *victims* of the Holocaust begs more questions than it answers because this approach tends to underplay the active and even proactive stance of Jews who at every turn did what they could to defend and preserve their lives, a description, Nicholas Stargardt showed, that applies to Jewish children as well as to adults. That the Holocaust took an immense toll on children is a fact both well known and under-researched in Holocaust studies. Typically overlooking how children took action rather than were acted upon, the popular depiction of them in the Holocaust tends towards the sentimental, with murdered innocence at its center. Stargardt explored how historians, at least since the late 1980s, have subjected the experience of children to more searching analysis, without making their fate any less shocking. Nazism had a special interest in children, both in shaping the next generation of German children and in eliminating the offspring of Jews, Sinti and Roma ("gypsies"), and so-called degenerates. At every stage of persecution, children were targeted in specific ways, from "Jew benches" in schools, through the medical killing of children in psychiatric asylums, to selection in the death camps. Children, however, were not passive victims. New research has revealed, for example, much about their experience of ghettoization, including their adeptness at smuggling, as well as their ingenuity in hiding, which often required adopting new identities, languages, and religious beliefs.

Recognizing that the Holocaust happened in specific places, sites, and physical circumstances, the *Holocaust Handbook*'s third part concentrates on key Holocaust *settings*. It has long been known that Nazi ideology and Hitler's ambition envisioned an expansion of German-dominated "living space" (*Lebensraum*), which oriented Hitler's regime eastward. Drawing on recent studies that expand understanding well beyond its scope in 1996, Wendy Lower assessed Nazi intentions for eastern Europe, which were colonial by design, and showed how Nazi leaders sought to restructure Germanized "living space" economically and racially. In addition, every analysis of the Holocaust must deal with places such as ghettos and labor sites, but what are the most current findings and issues about them? Narratives about the ghettos in Warsaw and Łódź have dominated the depiction of Jewish ghettoization during the Holocaust, but Martin Dean indicated that these two cases diverged considerably and were hardly representative. The Germans created more than 140 ghettos in the Polish territories incorporated into the Reich, approximately 380 in the General Government (Polish territory colonized but not annexed), and more than 600 in other occupied areas. Dean explored the similarities and differences that characterized this grisly and still incompletely researched aspect of the Holocaust. Meanwhile, recent studies reveal that Nazi Germany established some 30,000 slave labor camps, a number much larger than previously thought. Holding that the term "slave labor" understates the condition of Jewish workers during the Nazi era, Mark Spoerer provided a taxonomy of the Nazi regime's use of forced, especially Jewish, labor from 1938 to 1945 and outlined the circumstances that made such labor lethal to greater or lesser degrees in particular times and places.

The Holocaust's magnitude and devastation are known from documents and diaries, testimonies and trials, artifacts and places, and because literature, film, art, music, memorials, museums and other acts of remembering keep directing attention toward those realities. At every turn, however, questions remain about how the Holocaust can and should be grasped—detailed, described, depicted—for the event's vastness and particularity, its horrors and implications seem to confound articulation and comprehension. In response to those challenges, Holocaust studies rely on historical analysis, interpretation of texts, artistic creation and criticism, and philosophical and religious reflection to find the most adequate, if always fallible and limited, ways to state what happened and what the meaning of the events—or their lack of meaning—may be. The *Holocaust Handbook*'s fourth part turns to such issues by considering *representations* of the Holocaust.

Without documentation provided by German sources, understanding of the Holocaust would be severely hampered. Peter Fritzsche amplified this point by showing that German government offices and private diarists and correspondents kept widely scattered but extensive records of the unfolding of the "Final Solution." Adding to understanding about what was known by Germans regarding the assault against the Jews, Fritzsche showed how anti-Jewish legislation ensured that the paper trails of persecution ran to the far corners of the German bureaucracy. Moreover, the perpetrators of anti-Jewish actions at local and national levels commemorated their deeds, in effect preparing initial drafts for a victorious history of the destruction of Jewish life. Private diaries and letters confirm not only the widespread knowledge that Germans came to share about the "Final Solution" but also the process by which many of them came to endorse cruelty toward Jews.

Few artistic expressions stir human feeling more than music. Not surprisingly, therefore, music played key parts in the Holocaust. Richard Wagner's operas deeply affected Hitler. The Nazis suppressed music by Jewish composers and dismissed Jewish professional musicians. But in the Theresienstadt ghetto, concerts were given, operas staged, and musical works were written by Jewish musicians. Prisoner musicians in Auschwitz accompanied the comings and goings of wretched labor brigades. As the "Partisans' Song" illustrates, music encouraged Jewish resistance as well. Music continues to be important in relation to the Holocaust, posing and responding to challenges and prospects for representing that event. The musicologist Bret Werb surveyed the repertoire of Holocaust-related music—a category encompassing commemorative music, musical settings of relevant texts, and works dramatizing events in Holocaust history—in classical and popular genres, and he placed these works in the context of stylistic trends and cultural-political developments. He also identified the repertoire's most frequently employed subjects and texts—the Warsaw ghetto, Auschwitz, Anne Frank, children's poetry from Theresienstadt—and discussed Holocaust representation in folk song, rock and roll, jazz, and rap.

Holocaust memorials and museums depend on diverse forms of representation, but as James Young indicated, they become places and provide occasions that represent the Holocaust in their own distinctive ways. Public memorialization of the Holocaust era began early, with every affected group remembering its own fate. The more events of World War II and the Holocaust recede in time, the more prominent museums and memorials about them become. As survivors have struggled to bequeath memory of their experiences to the next generations and governments have sought to unify disparate people with "common" national narratives, a veritable "boom" of Holocaust memorials and museums has occurred. Since 1990, hundreds of museums and institutions have been established worldwide to remember and tell the history of Nazi Germany's destruction of the European Jews. Young emphasized that depending on who builds these memorials and museums and where, they recollect this past according to particular national myths, ideals, and political needs. At a more specific level, these museums also reflect the temper of the memory-artists' time, their architects' schools of design, and their physical locations in national memorial landscapes.

The contributors to *The Oxford Handbook of Holocaust Studies* tried their best to *get it right*, to provide an authoritative, up-to-date guide to the most important issues and salient debates that inform research—currently and yet to come—about the Holocaust. Unfinished and future events, however, affect the book's durability and shelf life. These prospects reflect a governing principle in the field: desires for finality and closure should never trump critical inquiry that corrects and reformulates what is "known" and searches for discoveries about what is still unknown. That principle means not only that no book can claim finality and closure regarding Holocaust studies but also that the endings of the Holocaust itself have not achieved closure and never will.

What persists, however, is the recognition that, like the Holocaust itself, the field of Holocaust studies does little to encourage optimism about humanity's future and progress. Both entail darkness and invite despair, because the more one learns about the Holocaust, genocide, and other mass atrocities, the worse those disasters turn out to be. Nevertheless, while *The Oxford Handbook of Holocaust Studies* is but a fleeting episode in history's unfolding, the fate of both depends on time's passage. How the Holocaust is studied, the care given to that work, may or may not affect the outcomes that await, but while *not enough* remains a key answer to the question "What has been learned from the Holocaust?" it is also true that more than *maybe something*—indeed, a great deal—has been added to knowledge about the Holocaust, not least that the Shoah, resisting finality and closure, must keep summoning inquiry, discovery, and resistance lest we relinquish and abandon what is precious and good. That process leads to the second dimension of the *maybe something* that is the counterpoint response to *not enough* when the question is "What has been learned from the Holocaust?"

NATURE AND THE HOLOCAUST

One thing to learn from the Holocaust is that many Jews—the murdered ones as well as those who survived—resisted relinquishing what is precious and abandoning what is good by writing about what happened to them and their families. As those diaries and memoirs describe an unrelenting catastrophe, they frequently include observations about the seasons of the year, the weather, the sky, and other features of the natural world. Elie Wiesel's *Night* is one significant example. That memoir notes small but significant details as the seasonal cycle moved from the spring of 1944 toward the spring of 1945. A listing of Wiesel's comments, almost poetic in their combination, reads as follows:

> Spring 1944.... The trees were in bloom.
> The eight days of Passover.... The weather was sublime.
> Some two weeks before Shavuot. A sunny spring day...
> All this under a magnificent blue sky.
> A summer sun.
> The lucky ones found themselves near a window; they could watch the blooming countryside flit by.
> The night had passed completely. The morning star shone in the sky.
> It was a beautiful day in May. The fragrances of spring were in the air. The sun was setting.
> "All of creation bears witness to the Greatness of God!"
> Winter had arrived.
> An icy wind was blowing violently.
> Snow was falling heavily.[6]

Taken by themselves in this listing, removed as the individual descriptions are from the context in which they are embedded, these references to the natural environment are more ordinary than ominous. In fact, however, they create an extraordinary contrast and backdrop to the events that make *Night* as disquieting as it is unforgettable. One more brief passage from Wiesel's testimony depicts this reality in a particularly powerful way: "Never shall I forget," writes Wiesel, "the small faces of the children whose bodies I saw transformed into smoke under a silent sky."[7] That sentence is part of a tipping point in *Night*, for upon Wiesel's entry to Birkenau, the part of Auschwitz that was both the destination for his deportation transport and the main killing center in the vast Auschwitz complex, he was forever changed as he saw children, alive and dead, thrown into flaming pits. "Never shall I forget," he repeats seven times. "Never shall I forget those things, even were I condemned to live as long as God Himself. Never."[8]

Each of *Night*'s descriptions of nature anticipates, foreshadows, or recalls what Wiesel cannot forget and what human beings should remember as a warning. At least three dimensions define these relationships in Wiesel's memoir and in those of other Holocaust victims and survivors. First, the beauty of nature contrasts with the brutality that human beings have inflicted, which included cattle-car deportations to human-made places of human-created degradation, filth, starvation, disease, death-dealing labor, violence, murder, and graves unmarked or nonexistent. Second, in *Night* and other Holocaust memoirs, nature sometimes appears to be conspiratorial in compounding the suffering that the Jews experienced at the hands of their German captors. Particularly the extreme heat of summer or the icy cold of winter diminished life chances for those who had no protection against the elements. Even more pronounced, a third implication in *Night* is that nature was indifferent to Jewish plight during the Holocaust. The sun rose and set, night came and went, the stars shone and the moon beamed, the seasons passed, and the earth stayed in its orbit while devastation raged and seemed to make no difference in nature's indifferent order.

These three dimensions imply a fourth: much of what needs to be learned from the Holocaust will be missed if we overlook how that event did and should affect the natural environment that is our home.[9] Disrespect for human life and disregard for the natural world are intertwined. Usually perpetrated under the cover of war, genocide, including the Holocaust, wreaks havoc on the natural world as well as on human life itself. Conversely, where human life is fully respected, the likelihood that the natural world will be better cared for is enhanced. Where the natural world is cared for well, it is also likely—although, unfortunately, not automatically guaranteed—that human life will be well respected too.[10]

Ignored or underestimated at our peril, the scientific evidence is unmistakable: Climate change is happening at alarming and probably irreversible rates.[11] As far as the long-term future of humanity as a whole is concerned, no reality facing humanity may be more important. Driven by human-made factors—such as deforestation and carbon pollution produced by burning fossil fuel—droughts, wildfires, superstorms, and other climate disruptions portend the kinds of economic and political instability that lead to human rights abuses, war, mass atrocities, and genocide as unsustainable consumption, resource scarcity, impoverished populations, and unwanted refugees ramp up danger in the world. Allowed to proceed unchecked, climate change will incite genocidal violence, breed immense human suffering, and threaten the very existence of civilization.[12] An internet site linked to the solar panels on my house estimates that the average tree removes about seventeen pounds of carbon dioxide from the atmosphere each year. Even the modest renewable solar energy output from my small system can replace or add the equivalent of some five hundred trees annually. If humanity's carbon footprints are to be reduced, if global warming and climate change are to be checked and the environment on which human life depends is to be preserved, trees—forests of them—are of immense importance. Trees—forests of them—were of immense importance in Nazi Germany and eventually in the Holocaust as well.

According to the geographer and environmentalist Michael Imort, the Nazi leader Hermann Göring, one of Hitler's most trusted lieutenants, became "the self-anointed *Reichsforstmeister* or 'Reich master of forestry,'" enforcing the *Dauerwald* policy, a term best translated, says Imort, as "perpetual forest" or "eternal forest." Under this plan, ecologically advanced at the time, German foresters abandoned practices that "planted, thinned, and cut" simply to maximize economic yield. *Dauerwald* strategies focused not on the individual tree as a product but on the forest as an organism or ecosystem. Economic interests remained paramount and, in fact, were enhanced, but the stakes of the *Dauerwald* concept were higher than that because it emphasized not only sustainability but also cultivation of "*bodenständige* (native) species" and "exclusion of introduced, 'foreign' species."

This forestry philosophy enabled Göring to proclaim: "Forest and people are much alike in the doctrines of National Socialism. . . . *Eternal forest and eternal nation are ideas that are indissolubly linked*" (Göring's emphasis). On December 13, 1934, the Third Reich anticipated those remarks, which Göring made about a year later, by establishing its Law Concerning the Protection of Racial Purity of Forest Plants. "Ask the trees," an influential forester would write in 1939, "they will teach you how to become National Socialists!"[13] In unintended ways, those words proved prophetic. The world war that Nazi Germany started that same year meant that vast forests in Nazi-occupied Poland, France and Norway, along with those in the expanded Third Reich itself, were exploited for military and genocidal purposes. Those purposes included production of railroad ties that facilitated transports to Auschwitz and lumber from which that camp's primitive barracks were constructed to house Jews and others who were spared from the gas chambers but starved, beaten, or worked to death.

Meanwhile, especially in eastern Europe, the forest became a place where some Jews escaped, hid, and resisted as partisans. For them, trees meant resistance, hope, and even life itself, which indicates that it is too narrow to underscore only nature's seeming conspiracy with human-made atrocity, a point driven home all the more by what is likely the best known tree related to the Holocaust.

Until a few years ago, a distinctive 170-year-old horse-chestnut tree stood not in a forest but in the courtyard garden of the house at Keizersgracht 188 in the Dutch city of Amsterdam. Anne Frank could see that tree from the hiding place at Prinsengracht 263, where she and her family took refuge from July 6, 1942, until their betrayal on August 4, 1944, which resulted in Anne's deportation to Auschwitz and her death from typhus at Bergen-Belsen in early March 1945.

Several entries in Anne Frank's celebrated diary, including three touching examples from 1944, focus on the Amsterdam chestnut tree and have made it famous too. February 23: "The two of us looked out at the blue sky, the bare chestnut tree glistening with dew, the seagulls and other birds glinting with silver as they swooped through the air, and we were so moved and entranced that we couldn't speak." April 18: "April is glorious, not too hot and not too cold, with occasional light showers. Our chestnut tree is in leaf, and here and there you can already see a few small blossoms." May 13: "Our chestnut tree is in full bloom. It's covered with leaves and is even more beautiful than last year."[14]

In the early twenty-first century, more than 260 schools in at least sixteen countries bear Anne Frank's name. Typically, they commit themselves to be centers of learning that highlight freedom, justice, human dignity, and Holocaust remembrance. Anne was born on June 12, 1929. In recent years, children from those schools have celebrated her birthday by planting seedlings germinated from the Amsterdam tree's chestnuts. That project took off when it became clear that the old tree, weakened by disease, had become a safety hazard, one that could even endanger the secret annex where the Frank family hid. By the autumn of 2007, plans to axe the tree were far along. That November, however, Dutch officials and conservationists got a court injunction that spared it. Despite special care and support, the tree fell in a windstorm on August 23, 2010, but around the world today, saplings from Anne Frank's tree live on. On April 30, 2014, for example, one of them was planted in the west lawn of the United States Capitol.

Linked with details about Nazi forestry and the parts that the woods played in Jewish resistance and survival, the story of the Anne Frank tree becomes a kind of parable-commentary on an important realization: Just as it is true that the natural world can kindle and support hope where atrocity rages, even while nature in other guises may seem indifferent to, or complicit in, injustice and suffering, there is no easy continuity between respect for human life and respect for the natural world. The credibility of claims about that continuity depends on whether the right kinds of respect are in play. Everything hinges on their qualities.

The Nazis could be good foresters, but only up to a point. Their philosophy of forestry itself was inseparable from an ideology that was fundamentally disrespectful of human equality and human rights. They could not fully and truly be good foresters because their worldview—steeped in racism, militarism, and genocidal outcomes that had much to do with God-denying and scripture-burning arrogance—entailed that ultimately they would ravage forests, and much more, instead of saving and nurturing them in ways that respected the trees themselves as well as benefiting humankind.

The genocidal catastrophe that the Nazis unleashed did immense harm to the natural world as it also took an incalculable toll on human existence, Jewish life in particular, including damage to the ways in which the natural world can appear to us. A rainbow ought not to produce senses of irony and skepticism, unavoidable though such senses can be when one arches an Auschwitz sky. Instead, it ought to be a sign of hope and even covenant. It can be that way if, among other things, we become truly good foresters—figuratively and literally. What that means can be glimpsed by paying further attention to Anne Frank's chestnut tree.

A tree is just a tree, of course, but that tree is not just any tree, and it may help us to realize that no tree, indeed nothing in creation, is insignificant. A tree in Amsterdam did not and could not save Anne Frank's life, but it helped to sustain and encourage her. The Holocaust's perpetrators and the natural world's typhus killed her—the natural world is not necessarily a friendly place—but those facts do not render meaningless the ethical sensibilities and spiritual convictions that her diary underscores.

One can be cynical about the passion aroused to save the Anne Frank tree and to raise saplings from it. Those efforts do not ensure what is needed even more, namely, concerted efforts to reduce needless suffering, to curtail human rights abuses, and to intervene against genocide, if not to prevent it. Nevertheless, in the determination to save a particular chestnut tree, just as in the determination to try to *get it right* as far as scholarship about the Holocaust is concerned, one can identify elements of what is needed if humankind is to advance much larger and more desirable goals. Those elements include devotion to truth and honesty as well as dedication to protecting and saving life, resisting the human and natural forces that destroy what is good, and refusing to give up when success seems to be a forlorn hope.

The continuity between respect for the natural and the human world is fragile, complex, and difficult. One rightly cares for and about the Anne Frank tree and its seedlings both as a means to human good and as ends in themselves. Tension-filled though that relationship may sometimes be—especially when we think, mistakenly, that the natural order exists for human use and consumption alone—the integrity of the natural world and the dignity of humankind, individually and communally, go hand in hand. They do so because human life cannot flourish without a healthy natural environment, and because a natural world in which human life is absent, abused, or abusive with regard to itself or its environment compromises and even lacks elements of awareness, responsibility, and awe on which the presence of sense and meaning within and about the natural world depends.

We cannot fully and truly respect human life without caring for the natural world, and we cannot fully and truly respect the natural world without caring for humanity both in individual and communal terms. We are part of the natural world, and the natural world is not fully and truly itself without us, partly because the natural world is itself in process. What we do within and for it and ourselves makes a great deal of difference with regard to the order and meaning of existence itself. And, if we listen well to the best that these two inseparable realms—the human and the natural—can say to us, neither of them exhausts reality, let alone completes it. They point toward, they even embody in ways that transcend themselves, at least traces of the divine. If we will let them, such traces can compel and focus properly our stewardship on earth.

EXPAND THE BLUE

These reflections about *not enough* and *maybe something* in response to the question "What have we learned from the Holocaust?" are deeply informed by a story that the American Jewish philosopher Philip Hallie loved to tell. As an artillery officer during World War II, Hallie helped to destroy Nazi Germany, but he was best known as an ethicist whose belief in the preciousness of human life led him to write about cruelty and also about a French village called Le Chambon-sur-Lignon, where several thousand Jews found a war-time haven in the 1940s. Hallie often recalled a hurricane that battered New England. The storm's devastating power became his metaphor for the human predicament. "It's the hurricane we're in," Hallie liked to say, amplifying his conviction with the admonition, "Don't forget it."

Hallie's concern about "the hurricane" was not limited to lethal weather. Human existence, he thought, is always contending with hurricanes of one kind or another. Significantly, however, when Hallie tracked the hurricane that reached his Connecticut home, havoc was not all he saw. As the storm raged, he noticed that there seemed to be space for calm and quiet within the hurricane's eye. Hallie's eye, moreover, was drawn to the pale blue sky overhead. That blue was his favorite color, for, as he put it, his passion, his hope, was to "expand the blue." Some persons, Hallie added, "make a larger space for blue, for peace, for love." Such work, he insisted, "takes power as well as love. It takes force of will. It takes assertion and commitment."[15] As one considers the failures of ethics and ways to resist them, as we think about and act on what has—and has not—been learned from the Holocaust, moving beyond *not enough* and adding what is needed to *maybe something* depend on expanding the blue and on cultivating the qualities required for that mending of the world.

In the late summer of 1994, I received a telephone call from Joseph Freeman, a resident of Pasadena, California, and a Holocaust survivor from Radom, Poland. He asked me to read and comment on the autobiographical manuscript he had written. Thus began a long friendship, which soon included his wife, Helen, an Auschwitz survivor. Joe is no longer alive, but I can still hear his voice.

Joe Freeman's testimony included three books. Especially significant is the one that resulted from the manuscript he asked me to read. It is a distinctive and significant account of a death march that took place from March 16 to April 26, 1945, with Nazi Germany's surrender only days away and well after its killing centers on Polish soil—Auschwitz-Birkenau among them—had been shut down and evacuated.[1] Joe and Helen often met with students in courses about the Holocaust that I taught at Claremont McKenna College. Nothing in those courses made a deeper impression upon those students than the Freemans' testimony. When Joe spoke, two characteristics stood out. First, in spite of the inhumanity he experienced, he had a firm commitment to mend the world. Second, he often repeated the phrase, "It's not so easy." The phrase and the commitment belong together when resistance against the failures of ethics is at stake.

"It's not so easy"—when Joe voiced those words, he was doing what the Holocaust scholar James Young calls "memory-work."[2] Such work not only recalled catastrophe and suffering but also relived it. "It's not so easy" because those requirements permitted little optimism. Freeman's memory-work was done to communicate what he had experienced. But that task was not easy because my students and I could scarcely imagine what he described. He wanted us to understand and be warned by what he had endured. Even though we could not comprehend him fully, perhaps our learning was deepest, our grasp as great as it could be, just when we saw how much he struggled to make clear and vivid what we could only glimpse from afar.

Joseph Freeman and his "It's not so easy" are my companions in this chapter's reflections about the politics of testimony. Joe wanted his testimony to make a good difference in the world. When my students and I heard him say, "It's not so easy," we heard that anguished hope in his voice. Joe's presence conferred responsibilities upon us. How could that not be the case whenever testimony about genocide and other mass atrocities is given and received?

9

The Politics of Testimony

You cannot go down into hell with impunity. You must pay an entrance fee, and an exit fee too.

—Philip Hallie, *Tales of Good and Evil, Help and Harm*

Without testimony spoken and written by, and about, persons whose lives have been destroyed by genocide and other mass atrocities, awareness would be dimmed, understanding diminished, memory dulled, forgetting made easier, and accountability betrayed. Jarring, disruptive, and destabilizing, the presence of such testimony often makes clear that those who give it have paid and in some cases continue to pay the enormous price exacted by entry into the hell of genocide and mass atrocities and then by survival in the times and circumstances where life's continuation follows. For those of us fortunately spared the direct experience that produces testimony about genocide and other mass atrocities, even engagement at a distance through hearing or reading such testimony can exact costs related to those that the philosopher Philip Hallie had in mind when he said, "You cannot go down into hell with impunity. You must pay an entrance fee, and an exit fee too."[3]

Almost without relief, testimony about genocide and other mass atrocities plunges one into abysmal darkness. Disorientation, melancholy, despair, even shame—those are among the somber moods that result. Once touched by such testimony, a person does not easily walk away. One reason is that these encounters raise questions as disturbing as they are challenging: What effects should this testimony have? What responsibilities, if any, does it confer upon me? How must I live differently? What must communities do better? Such questions are ethical and therefore political too.

The latter point invites clarification of the meanings of the word *politics* in this chapter on "The Politics of Testimony." Inescapable and essential, politics typically refers to at least three dimensions of human activity: believing, governing, and maneuvering. The first instance—believing—centers on a person's or a group's attitudes, perspectives, values, visions, and convictions, especially insofar as those outlooks involve interpretations and commitments about action and policy. In the second case—governing—politics points toward the organization, management, and implementation of beliefs and the actions and policies toward which beliefs point. In the third category—maneuvering—politics emphasizes strategies devised to advance special interests and tactics employed to serve particular constituencies. Depending on the substance and style of these three dimensions, politics is more or less contentious or congenial, more or less cut-throat or constructive.

The politics of testimony moves back and forth. On the one hand, it involves the ways, often conflicting, in which the giving and receiving of testimony about genocide and other mass atrocities inform and affect human belief, organization, and strategy. On the other hand, the politics of testimony refers to the ways, often conflicting, in which human belief, organization, and strategy inform and influence how testimony is shared, especially with regard to the testimony's impact on policies that accept or shirk responsibilities when genocide and mass atrocities threaten. Our attitudes and priorities are among the factors that determine the characteristics and the quality of the politics of testimony. To illustrate and justify these points, consider four areas where the politics of testimony looms large: (1) in scholarship and education about genocide and other mass atrocities; (2) in the pursuit of justice; (3) in post-conflict relationships; (4) in the prospects for ethics.

THE POLITICS OF SCHOLARSHIP AND EDUCATION

A highly important but unfortunately not widely studied book about Holocaust scholarship is *Sources of Holocaust Research*, published in 2001 by Raul Hilberg. Although focused on the Holocaust, that book has implications for the study of every genocide and mass atrocity and for the parts that testimony may play in such study. Having focused on the Holocaust for five decades, Hilberg said that he had thought of his sources as "raw material that would enable me to fashion a description of the destruction process.... But then I stopped to ask myself: what is the nature of my sources? They are not identical to the subject matter. They have their own history and qualities, which are different from the actions they depict and which require a separate approach."[4]

Hilberg's taxonomy identified a vast array of sources, which included what he labeled "testimony," accounts given "after the end of the Nazi regime by perpetrators, onlookers, and survivors."[5] He put this testimony into four categories: legal testimony; interviews of specific persons; oral history; memoir literature. As Hilberg's book indicates, he utilized a wide range of sources for his research and writing, but it is also true that his "gold standard" for reliability was the written document, preferably from official German sources—a position that suited his intention to grasp how the Germans had been drawn toward and then implemented the "Final Solution." As for "testimony," legal proceedings could be useful because they were "hemmed in" by "laws of evidence," but when it came to oral history and memoir literature, Hilberg retained considerable skepticism about their usefulness—even though he sometimes drew upon them to advance his quest to understand the processes that led to the destruction of the European Jews.

Hilberg's skepticism about oral history and memoir literature reflected three concerns. Noting especially the surge of oral history gathering that resulted in the collection of thousands of survivor testimonies at places such as Yale University, Yad Vashem in Jerusalem, the United States Holocaust Memorial Museum, and what today is the USC Shoah Foundation—rather disdainfully he dubbed them "oral history depots"—Hilberg made the following evaluation: "Notwithstanding the quantity of words in oral history, it is inherently limited in three respects: (1) The survivors as a whole are not a random sample of the Jewish community that was destroyed. (2) Those who testified are not a random sample of the survivors. (3) Their testimony does not contain a random sample of their experiences."[6] Hilberg argued further that "the limits and limitations of oral delivery apply also to books [memoir literature], and on occasion even more so. The authors had to make themselves available. They had to invest their time and step forward with an idea, outline, draft, or manuscript. What they finally offered remained a personal account with selected revelations."[7]

The historian Timothy Snyder echoes aspects of this critique of survivor testimony in commentary about what he calls "the literature of Auschwitz written by its survivors," including Primo Levi and Elie Wiesel. Their testimony has contributed to an overemphasis on the importance of Auschwitz and thus to misunderstandings about the Holocaust. "Today," says Snyder, "Auschwitz stands for the Holocaust," but that impression overlooks or at least downplays the fact that "by the time the gas chambers and crematoria complexes at Birkenau came on line in spring 1943, more than three quarters of the Jews who would be killed in the Holocaust were already dead." Starvation, shooting, and gassing at other places had already done more damage. "Auschwitz," concludes Snyder, "is the coda to the death fugue." Throughout his work on the "bloodlands" of eastern Europe, "the zone of the Holocaust" where most of the killing took place, Snyder recalls "the voices of the victims themselves, and those of their friends and families," but it remains essential to ensure that those voices contribute to accurate historical understanding.[8]

Despite criticisms such as Hilberg's or Snyder's, skepticism about oral history and memoir literature has scarcely prevailed in Holocaust and genocide studies and certainly not in Holocaust- and genocide-related education, where, if anything, the "gold standard"—especially where emphasis is placed on the "lessons" communicated by genocide and mass atrocities—often centers on survivors and their testimonies. Conviction of that kind is at least partly behind the frequently expressed concern about what will happen to Holocaust-related education when the last survivor passes away. Even as that time rapidly approaches, issues remain about how to interpret and use testimony about the Holocaust as well as testimony about other genocides and mass atrocities. In that regard, two significant concerns deserve attention. One pertains to the scope and analysis of survivor testimony, the other focuses on the "lessons" that such testimony may contain.

Especially with regard to the Holocaust—but other genocides and mass atrocities reveal something similar—the gathering of survivor testimony has concentrated on obtaining as many testimonies as possible, a methodology that frequently makes the gathering of an individual's testimony a one-time occurrence that also entails formulaic interviewing techniques. Cataloging and organizing these testimonies so they are accessible has posed numerous logistical problems—for example, how to cope with multiple languages, how to index and catalog the testimonies, how to store them, and how to make them accessible to scholars, teachers, and students. While those problems continue to be solved, a "what if" question remains: namely, what if follow-up took place? If testimony were less closed and more ongoing, what would be found?

Although opportunities for follow-up interviews are rapidly dwindling among Holocaust survivors, owing to aging and death, this matter is not hypothetical, at least not entirely, because in-depth gathering of Holocaust testimony has taken place in some cases, and it might happen more thoroughly with the survivors of more recent mass atrocities. One of the leaders in such work is the Holocaust scholar Henry Greenspan, who has devoted attention to repeated and in-depth conversations with Holocaust survivors. Rather than speaking about *testimony*, Greenspan emphasizes the survivors' *recounting* of their experiences, construing that word as a verb and concentrating on what he calls "the process of retelling."[9] This process reveals that testimony lacks closure and involves layers that include the untellable and the silences that enclose it.

Greenspan rightly points out that "we do a lot more living than speaking. . . . Silence, in the sense of experience never discussed, is the rule. Talk is the exception."[10] Particularly with regard to the survivors of genocide and other mass atrocities, silence involves a range and complexity that disaggregate the untellable into the unsaid and the incommunicable, the unbearable and the irretrievable. Greenspan shows that listening to, or reading, the recounting of survivors of genocide and other mass atrocities is far more complicated and unsettling than we are accustomed to thinking. It is that way because testimony both reveals and hides the worst. As my survivor-friend, Joe Freeman, once said to me, "There are things we will never talk about."

Turning now to questions about the lessons that may—or may not—be communicated through testimony about genocide and mass atrocities, few people have listened more persistently or carefully to the oral testimony of Holocaust survivors than Lawrence Langer.[11] With some of that testimony in mind, Langer once said that "there is nothing to be learned from a baby torn in two or a woman buried alive."[12] That trenchant comment epitomizes his rejection regarding the idea that moral lessons about "the triumph of the human spirit" or "the transcendence of good over evil" can be learned from the testimony of "former victims," Langer's preferred way of referring to Holocaust survivors and one that also could identify those who escaped death in other genocides and mass atrocities.

Langer's listening convinced him that the testimony of former victims is laden with what the Auschwitz survivor Charlotte Delbo called "useless knowledge." Such knowledge does not unify, edify, or dignify the lives of former victims. It divides, besieges, and diminishes them instead. If we really let testimony in and do not preempt it for inappropriately optimistic goals, the effects on those of us who receive testimony may be similar. Langer's unflinching analysis of survivor testimonies insists that the truth they tell resists interpretations that console. Instead, the disruption, absence, and irreversible loss recalled by them are a reminder and a warning pointing to the failures of ethics and to other dimensions of the politics of testimony. The reminder is that the testimonies of former victims need not have existed if the power of those who perpetrate genocide and other mass atrocities had been checked in time and if those targeted for destruction had not been so defenseless. The warning is related: Although safety and security are never guaranteed, they do depend on the strength and commitment of the communities in which one dwells.

THE POLITICS OF JUSTICE

Raul Hilberg included legal proceedings as an important resource of testimony about the Holocaust. The work carried out by the International Military Tribunal at Nuremberg after World War II, as well as numerous similar proceedings in the postwar years, aimed at bringing to justice at least some of the most heinous perpetrators of mass atrocity crimes. More recently, the International Criminal Tribunal for the former Yugoslavia (ICTY), the International Criminal Tribunal for Rwanda (ICTR), and the International Criminal Court (ICC) have carried on related work. In these settings the testimony of survivors often plays crucial roles in which the politics of testimony and the politics of justice are intertwined. As an example, the following excerpt from the transcript of a trial conducted by the ICTY warrants attention. It features a woman identified in the transcript as Witness 50. As the scholar Tazreena Sajjad points out, Witness 50, a Bosnian Muslim woman, was 16 in 1992 when she was taken prisoner by Bosnian Serbs, held for two months, and repeatedly raped.[13] She was one of thousands of Bosnian Muslim women and girls who experienced such abuse. Standing trial for Witness 50's abuse was a man named Zoran Vukovic, a member of the Bosnian Serb Army. Here is part of Witness 50's testimony against him, delivered on March 29, 2000:

PROSECUTOR: Where did he take you?

WITNESS: He took me to an apartment. I assume that it had been abandoned because I didn't see anybody there. When he brought me to that apartment, he took me into one of the rooms, which was to the left-hand side of the hallway. There was a big bed for sleeping in. I don't remember exactly whether there was a cupboard or what there was there, but it was a bedroom. And then it happened once again; I was raped again.

PROSECUTOR: Did Zoran Vukovic say anything to you?

WITNESS: Well, yes. They would always say things. But once he had done what he was about—I mean, once he had raped me, when he finished raping me, he sat down and lit a cigarette, and he said that he could perhaps do more, much more, but that I was about the same age as his daughter, and so he wouldn't do anything more for the moment.

PROSECUTOR: Can you—would you be able to recognize Zoran Vukovic today?

WITNESS: Yes, I could.

PROSECUTOR: I'm going to ask you to look around the courtroom, and please take your time. Let us know if you recognize somebody here who was the Zoran Vukovic you have described.

WITNESS: If I look from the door going down, the first person next to the guard with dark hair is Zoran Vukovic.

PROSECUTOR: To help clarify the record, could you just describe something he's wearing?

WITNESS: He is wearing a light blue shirt, a dark blue suit.

PROSECUTOR: Your Honor, may the record reflect that the witness has pointed out the accused, Zoran Vukovic.

Vukovic was found guilty and sentenced to twelve years in prison for raping Witness 50. Was justice done in this case? Did this trial and others aid or hinder reconciliation between perpetrators and those they assaulted?[14] How should Witness 50 and her testimony, including their silences, be heard? Surely testifying was courageous, but it left her vulnerable and even at risk. Probably she would agree with Joe Freeman's "It's not so easy." The testimony of Witness 50 was politically necessary lest a culture of impunity be given strength greater than it already has, but what resources are still needed, and probably are greatly lacking, to help Witness 50 and her many sisters to regain and sustain health and to repair the damage that has been done? At least in part, the politics of testimony, the politics of justice, and issues about resistance against the failures of ethics are ensnared and unresolved in questions such as those.

THE POLITICS OF POST-CONFLICT RELATIONSHIPS

On January 8, 2008, *Gazeta Wyborcza*, the largest daily news publication in Poland, published a previously obscure photograph whose original date was uncertain. Subsequent research carried out by the Holocaust historian Jan Gross revealed that the photograph depicts "a group of local peasants caught by the police shortly after the war, while digging at Treblinka."[15] Apparently those scavengers were digging through the ashes in the remains of that extermination camp, hoping to find jewelry and dental gold that German plunderers at Treblinka had overlooked during the "Final Solution" and the eventual evacuation from, and dismantling of, that dreadful place.

While the presence of policemen in the photograph suggested that the diggers were not in full compliance with the law, the photo also indicated that the men and women engaged in the sifting process were probably not under anything approaching arrest. For the photo, replete with skulls and bones arranged in the foreground, was posed and snapped so as to include more than thirty persons, some with shovels in hand, who had gathered in comradely fashion to mark an occasion that would turn out not to be unusual but routine and repeated as Polish "gleaners . . . sifted through the ashes and remains of murdered Jews at sites of all the Nazi extermination camps in Poland (Treblinka, Belzec, Sobibor, Chelmno, and Auschwitz) for many years after the war."[16]

Gross's 2012 book *Golden Harvest: Events at the Periphery of the Holocaust* is a study based on that Treblinka photograph. If a picture is worth a thousand words, Gross also draws extensively on testimony to unpack the photograph's meaning and significance. In the process, he illustrates how politics is not only intertwined with testimony but also driven by it. In this case, that relationship is especially pronounced regarding post-conflict relationships.

Although the untold harm done by genocide and other mass atrocities can be limitless, the mayhem and slaughter do not continue unabated. In the aftermath, perpetrators and survivors, sometimes living side by side as "neighbors," are left to negotiate their relationships in post-conflict situations. Those relationships cannot be set right by international tribunals, important though they are. Other ways of coping have to be found. Examples include attempts at restorative justice such as the South African Truth and Reconciliation Commission or the community justice efforts located in the Rwandan Gacaca courts. The weight placed on these institutions, which combine traditional local justice with modern jurisprudence, may be more than they can bear, but the proceedings show that testimony can often have mitigating and mending effects, if not completely healing ones. Such outcomes, however, are hard-won, because the suffering and loss go so deep down. In some cases, testimony, far from facilitating "getting along," may work in the opposite direction. Particularly in that regard, Gross's study of the "golden harvest" offers an instructive perspective on the politics of testimony.

Using the Treblinka photograph as a point of departure, Gross found that its scenario was, as he suspected, the tip of an iceberg, one that would exacerbate friction in post-Holocaust Polish-Jewish relations. Typically, genocides and mass atrocities are perpetrated for multiple reasons. Material advantage and economic gain are regularly among them. The Nazi genocide against the European Jews was a massive theft and plunder operation. Jewish life was to be destroyed root and branch, but Jewish property was not. It was to be harvested—everything from entire businesses and art collections to the dental gold extracted from Jewish bodies before they were buried in massive unmarked graves or turned into smoke and ashes by the consuming fires of crematorium furnaces.

In Nazi-occupied Poland, the Polish people were under duress and in peril for their lives, but for the most part they were not under the sentences of terror and death that befell the Jews who found themselves in Poland under the swastika, either because they had lived in Poland for years or because they had been deported to the ghettos and camps established by Germans in Polish places. In recent years, emphasis has frequently been placed on Polish solidarity with Jews, something exemplified by the fact that more than six thousand Poles have been designated Righteous of the Nations by Yad Vashem and the State of Israel because those women and men selflessly rescued Jews during the Holocaust. Those uplifting events, however, continue to exist uneasily in a context where Polish antisemitism has cast a long and, to some extent, continuing shadow. Findings of the kind in Gross's research show that the Polish rescuers are the exceptions that prove the rule of a much darker history of Polish-Jewish relationships during the Holocaust, one that is not likely to improve those relationships in post-Holocaust times, at least not until the realities of the past are faced openly and honestly.[17]

Gross worked detective-like to locate testimony that would contextualize the Treblinka photograph. His exploration took him far and wide as he located evidence, much of it in case files of one kind or another, to show that Polish complicity in the plunder and destruction of Jewish life was widespread and not at all restricted to odd, exceptional instances here and there. In a word, Gross found that during the German occupation of Poland, "the inhabitants of Polish towns and villages ceased to perceive their Jewish neighbors as human beings and began to treat them as if they were 'the deceased on leave.'"[18] (Gross took the latter phrase from Emanuel Ringelblum, leader of the Jewish historians who documented life and death in the Warsaw ghetto.) As far as post-conflict relations in Poland are concerned, the effects of Gross's *Golden Harvest* remain in suspense, but debate about Polish-Jewish relations has swirled as a result of his contributions to the politics of testimony.

THE POLITICS OF TESTIMONY AND THE PROSPECTS FOR ETHICS

Testimony and the politics that churns through and beyond it may sometimes buoy our spirits and encourage us. But when testimony is an unfiltered aftereffect of genocide and other mass atrocities, more often than not it produces discouragement and even despair, for, to paraphrase Lawrence Langer, it contains too many children torn in two, too many persons buried alive, and too much from which little, if any, hope can be salvaged. Arguably, no aspect of the politics of testimony is more significant than awareness that testimony about genocide and other mass atrocities tends to weaken confidence about ethics, about the status of right and wrong, about the conviction that what is good and just can and will prevail over corruption and injustice. Testimony about genocide and other mass atrocities does little to support the view that the universe can accurately be called moral.

The politics of testimony and ethical dilemmas go hand in hand. Resistance against the failures of ethics may prove insufficient to save the day; nevertheless, it remains crucial, and it is ignored at our peril. The Auschwitz survivor Primo Levi was skeptical about the existence of human conscience, an innate and shared moral compass that would guide us all, if only we would pay attention and follow it. Nevertheless, his testimony about responses to mass atrocities included other notes as well. They, too, are part of the politics of testimony because they contain crucial reminders about obligations and possibilities that can resist the failures of ethics, even when it may seem hopeless to do so.

In his book *Moments of Reprieve*, Levi recalled his friend Lorenzo Perrone, the person Levi had identified earlier in *Survival in Auschwitz* as the one to whom he owed his life. Not a Jew but an Italian civilian, Lorenzo, a skilled mason, was "officially" a "voluntary" worker helping to build the industrial plants that the Germans were constructing at Auschwitz III. (Established in 1942, this subcamp in the vast Auschwitz complex, also called Buna or Monowitz, housed prisoners—Elie Wiesel and Levi among them—who toiled at the Buna synthetic rubber works, located on the outskirts of the Polish village of Monowice.) In fact, however, Lorenzo was more like a labor conscript, and he despised the German cruelty that he saw at Auschwitz.

After meeting Levi in late June 1944, he decided to help his fellow Italian, although it was a crime with grave consequences for Lorenzo even to speak to an Auschwitz prisoner. For months, Lorenzo got Levi extra food, which was the physical difference between life and death. "I believe that it was really due to Lorenzo that I am alive today," Levi would write, underscoring that Lorenzo's help meant much more than food alone. What also sustained him was that Lorenzo "constantly reminded me by his presence, by his natural and plain manner of being good, that there still existed a just world outside our own, something and someone still pure and whole, not corrupt, not savage, extraneous to hatred and terror; something difficult to define, a remote possibility of good, but for which it was worth surviving."[19]

When liberation came, Levi lost track of Lorenzo, but later he became determined to find out what had happened to his life-saving friend. They reconnected for a short time in Italy after the war, but soon Lorenzo died. At one of their postwar meetings, Levi learned that he was not the only Auschwitz prisoner whom Lorenzo had helped, but Levi's friend had rarely told that story. In Lorenzo's view, wrote Levi, "We are in this world to do good, not to boast about it."[20]

Lorenzo's actions and Levi's testimony about them bear witness to the reminders that can make the difference between accepting and resisting the failures of ethics. Levi may have been right in thinking that no universal human conscience exists, that there is no innate and shared moral compass to guide us all, if only we would pay attention and follow it. But that sensibility does not negate, at least not completely, the reminding presence of Lorenzo, which testifies that "we are in this world to do good." Remote though it often seems, difficult to define though it may be, that possibility remains. More than that, the possibility becomes an imperative if the world is to be less corrupt and savage and more opposed to hatred and terror.

Levi was right to suggest that it is difficult to define precisely how it is that we are in this world to do good, but it was not difficult for Levi to feel Lorenzo's "presence" and to discern his "natural and plain manner of being good." Those characteristics were oppression-resisting, hope-sustaining, death-defying, and life-giving. More often than not, ethics at its best involves reminders of the kind embedded in Lorenzo's actions. Reminders are not always welcome or heeded. But good reminders of the kind that Lorenzo gave Levi are testimonies about sometimes difficult-to-define realities—justice, compassion, respect, love—that have been experienced, at least at times, in word and deed. Reminders about those realities may be especially acute when such qualities are threatened and in short supply, but Levi testified with insistence that the reminder of Lorenzo—we are in this world to do good—should always be vivid and never abandoned. As Joe Freeman would say, "It's not so easy," but these realizations are key ingredients in the exit fee that must be paid, in the response we need to make, as testimony about genocide and other mass atrocities confers responsibilities upon us.

I was with my father, Josiah, when he died in the early morning of Tuesday, October 2, 2001, at the age of 96. During the fall semester of that academic year, Tuesdays were teaching days for me at Claremont McKenna College. That morning, my class on the Holocaust was scheduled to meet at 9:40. I made the decision that I knew my father would want: go and teach. With respect and care, the students received the news about my loss, and then they agreed that the most meaningful thing to do was to keep studying together. That hour with them remains as vivid as my memory of my father's face.

The lesson for that October morning concentrated on reading from Christopher Browning's book, Nazi Policy, Jewish Workers, German Killers. *Specifically, we focused on Browning's findings about the dispositions and motivations that characterized the units of the German Order Police who killed tens of thousands of Jews in eastern Europe during the Holocaust. Those units were not monolithic. They typically contained three cohorts. The largest group, says Browning, "followed orders and complied with standard procedures but did not evince any eagerness to kill Jews."[1] Smaller in number was "a significant core of eager and enthusiastic killers." Smaller still was "a minority of men who sought not to participate in the regime's racial killing." Browning concluded that they "had no measurable effect whatsoever," but the eager killers "formed a crucial nucleus for the killing process in the same way as eager and ambitious initiators at middle echelons and Hitler, Himmler, and Heydrich at the top." The influence of such ambitious and determined people, added Browning, "was far out of proportion to their numbers in German society." Nevertheless, combined with a compliant majority, that zealous minority produced untold suffering and death. That day my students and I wondered about the meaning of such results, what they imply about justice, and whether death is the last word.*

In the contexts of the Holocaust, genocide, and other mass atrocities, facing death involves at least two unsettling apprehensions. First, the murdered dead have faces—defaced, devoured, and now completely obliterated though they may be. What meanings or lack of meanings do those faces possess and perhaps communicate? Second, as one faces the murdered dead, trying to see their lifeless and mutilated faces, how does doing so affect deep-down understanding of the Holocaust and other atrocities and even our grasp of their place in reality itself?

The latter question is fundamental, because if death is the last word, if at the end, the void, the abyss, nothingness (call it what you will) consume and prevail, there arguably are senses in which the Holocaust, genocide, and other mass atrocities vanish too. No trace of them remains; our sound and fury about them, including our historical research and our ethical passions about memory, justice, and "repairing the world" (tikkun olam) evaporate in insignificance. Could that prospect help to explain why even scholars of the Holocaust and other genocides, who immerse themselves in the dark sides of history, are reluctant to fully face death and its implications? Could that same prospect provoke inquiry and even action that might go in a different direction, one that would not consign the Holocaust, genocide, and the murdered dead to oblivion? My career as a scholar of the Holocaust and genocide, indeed my life itself, will end before long. So these questions and dilemmas loom large, at least for me, because meaning itself is at stake.

10

Death and Meaning

A corpse. The left eye devoured by a rat. The other open with its fringe of lashes. Try to look. Just try and see.

—Charlotte Delbo, *Auschwitz and After*

One cannot encounter the Holocaust, genocide, and other crimes against humanity without confronting death as atrocity—brutal, unjust, and relentless. In the ghettos, killing fields, and gas chambers of the Holocaust, a "good death," one that comes with a person "at peace," perhaps surrounded by loving family and friends, was scarcely possible, except as a release from useless suffering. Before and after the Holocaust—in Armenia, the former Yugoslavia, Rwanda, Darfur, and so many other places that they elude the comprehension of even the most dedicated scholars—genocidal actions escalate death as atrocity to overwhelming enormity, which includes the desecration that robs the dead of respect, consigning their bodies to unmarked mass graves, to decay and rot, to incineration, to disrespect and disappearance.[2] Scholarship about these atrocities typically converts the murdered dead into statistics, but even when it goes further, taking account of who the dead were before they were murdered, depicting how their lives were destroyed, or even exploring how their killers tried to dispose of the remains of their work, too little attention is paid to facing death. That shortcoming is one of the failures of ethics that must be resisted. This chapter explores how important issues about *meaning*—focused by questions about the meaning of the Holocaust—swirl around that proposition.

CHANGING, CONTESTED, CATASTROPHIC

Meaning can be defined in various ways, but here that word refers to the sense or significance, the purpose or outcome of something. Understood in that way, the *meaning* of the Holocaust is *changing*, *contested*, and *catastrophic*. My understanding of that claim involves the fact that I collect Holocaust-related items that come to my attention in news stories and other communications. I will cite some of these items, beginning with one that highlights how and why the meaning of the Holocaust is changing. In recent fund-raising communications from the United States Holocaust Museum, director Sara Bloomfield said, "For a child born today, the Holocaust will be a distant event that he or she will know through the pages of history alone."[3] The passage of time changes the meaning of events. With that passage, events, including the Holocaust, lose their immediacy. The time is soon coming when no one living will have first-hand experience or eyewitness memory of the time of Nazi Germany's genocide against the Jewish people, let alone direct awareness of specific details about that onslaught.

More and more, the Holocaust will be mediated and represented, so much so that a good question will be: Is it possible to encounter, to know, the Holocaust directly, or will our encounters, our knowing, be of the mediations, the representations, of that history? Soon after World War II ended, Charlotte Delbo, one of the most eloquent and insightful survivors of Auschwitz, was already well aware of the changes and challenges that could not be avoided: "Today," she wrote, "people know / have known for several years / that this dot on the map / is Auschwitz / This much they know / as for the rest / they think they know."[4]

Delbo, of course, would admit that today our "knowledge" about the Holocaust, or at least what we think we know about that disaster, is much greater than it was when she began in 1946 to write her memoir-trilogy, *Auschwitz and After*. The advances in research not only about the Holocaust itself but also about the conditions and circumstances that led to it—including the long history of antisemitism—and the aftereffects and reverberations of the Shoah affect our understanding of what the name *Holocaust* denotes and connotes. Current subfields in Holocaust studies (for example, a focus on what happened to Jewish women and children during those times) did not exist twenty years ago, but now they do. We seem capable of knowing more and more about the Holocaust; no end to research about the topic is coming. At the same time, this work has an unintended consequence and a paradoxical implication because no one, no institution or person, can undertake, comprehend or absorb it all, thus leaving us to ask, "What does all of the research, the study, the knowledge about the Holocaust mean? What have we really *learned* from it? How will further changes in the study of the Holocaust affect our grasp of its meaning?

Many of the changes that affect the meaning of the Holocaust in the world today do so by making that meaning *contested*. Consider, for example, a statement attributed to Avner Shalev, chairman of Yad Vashem, Israel's memorial to the Holocaust. In a *New York Times* article that discussed Yad Vashem's outreach, he was quoted as saying that "this [the Holocaust] is the most complicated phenomenon in human history."[5] What responses should be made to such a statement? Is the claim that the Holocaust is "the most complicated phenomenon in human history" true, false, some mixture of the two, or perhaps less a factual claim than a way of underwriting a privileged position for the Holocaust, one undergirding the view that no effort should be spared to educate the world about that catastrophe and to advance the "lessons" that are embedded in it?

If Shalev was quoted correctly in the *New York Times* article, it seems likely that his proposition would have to be contested, if only to ask how one would *know* and *show* that the Holocaust is the most complicated phenomenon in human history. The same would be true of any claim that took the form "the Holocaust is the most _____ phenomenon in human history." Think of the adjectives that could fill the blank. Terms such as *devastating, destructive, extreme, important, unique* would be among them, but any and all of those formulations are contestable, and not least because of their ideological undercurrents and political implications.

The fact that the meaning of the Holocaust is *contested* will not be eliminated by forgoing language that describes the Holocaust as *the most* of "anything" in human history. It remains imperative, moreover, to emphasize that the fact of the Holocaust itself is beyond contesting, and that this catastrophe continues to be, in Christopher Browning's words, "a watershed event in history."[6] Yet what more there is to say about the place and status of that event in human history also remains a question and is very much contested. How, for instance, should the Holocaust be understood in relation to other genocides? It can be argued that the Holocaust was an instance of genocide or nothing could be, but what kind of genocide was the Holocaust: the most extreme, the worst of any genocide to date? What snares and delusions lurk if one is tempted to go there or if one does not make such comparative judgments?

Another Auschwitz survivor, Jean Améry, saw other ways in which the Holocaust's meaning was bound to be contested. "What happened, happened" he said with reference to the Holocaust, "but *that* it happened cannot be so easily accepted."[7] Améry deeply *resented* what Germans had done to him and his Jewish people. Yes, he argued, "the atrocity as atrocity has no objective character. Mass murder, torture, injury of every kind are objectively nothing but chains of physical events, describable in the formalized language of the natural sciences. . . . But," he continued, "my resentments are there in order that the crime become a moral reality for the criminal, in order that he be swept into the truth of his atrocity."[8] For Améry, the Holocaust was *outrageous*, as deeply wrong ethically as anything could be, and his refusal of reconciliation with the Holocaust's perpetrators, let alone forgiveness of them, remains a vital element in any meaning that the Holocaust may have. Nevertheless, Améry sensed, feared, and anticipated that this meaning of the Holocaust would be eroded. "All recognizable signs suggest," he wrote, "that natural time will reject the moral demands of our resentment and finally extinguish them."[9]

Améry took his own life in 1978, before his sense of the Holocaust's meaning was contested by later distortions and denials of the Holocaust that include the volatile claims that Jews and their allies use the "Holocaust" to extort reparations, to exploit Palestinians, and to excuse Israeli policies that abuse human rights. Thus, in a reversal that even Jean Améry could hardly anticipate, the meaning of the Holocaust now includes awareness that the Nazi genocide against the Jewish people reignites antisemitism and reinvigorates a sensibility, prominent in certain Muslim quarters, that the Holocaust points toward unfinished business that could only be completed by the destruction of the State of Israel, by nothing less than a "second Holocaust."

It is no exaggeration to say that the contested meaning of the Holocaust is a matter of life and death, a realization illustrated in an editorial that appeared on the Vatican's internet news site on January 27, 2012, the anniversary of the Holocaust Memorial Day established by the United Nations in 2005, its January date coinciding with the liberation of Auschwitz in 1945. Warning against "the risk that people will forget, or even worse, deny the Holocaust," the Vatican editorial underscored that "the memory of the Holocaust is a crucial point of reference in the history of mankind, when we try to understand what is at stake when we speak of the essential dignity of every human person, the universality of human rights, and commitment to their defense." Then the editorial added that the Holocaust is also "a place for the most radical questions about God and about evil."[10]

Many of the important developments in international law emerged, in one way or another, in the wake of the Holocaust. One thinks of the United Nations Convention on the Prevention and Punishment of the Crime of Genocide, the Universal Declaration of Human Rights, and the establishment of various international tribunals to prosecute those who commit crimes against humanity. Nothing about the Holocaust, however, guarantees that its meaning will include success in deterring mass atrocity crimes, preventing genocide, or honoring human rights. To the contrary, the meaning of the Holocaust is catastrophic because that event has done so much to undermine confidence about human rights, ethics, reason, humanitarian progress, and the hope that "never again" would be so much more than the bereft slogan it has become. Furthermore, while the Vatican editorial was correct to point out that the Holocaust raises "radical questions about God and about evil," what about attempts to respond to those questions in convincing ways? The Holocaust is not the only event that does so, but it continues to scar religious and philosophical life. At least it does so if we let the Holocaust in and do not ignore, forget, preempt, sanitize, or overly instrumentalize it.

In his 1968 book *Legends of Our Time*, Elie Wiesel included an essay called "The Guilt We Share." Its point of departure was the 1961 trial of Adolf Eichmann, a key architect and perpetrator of the "Final Solution." Early in that essay, Wiesel recalls asking the literary critic Alfred Kazin "if he thought the death of six million Jews could have any meaning." The reply, says Wiesel, was that Kazin "hoped not."[11]

Wiesel's question and Kazin's reply are worth pondering. The reply "I hope not" might seem utterly disrespectful, but Wiesel did not take it that way. Instead, I believe, Wiesel took Kazin's rejection of meaning to be a cautionary injunction, for if we say quickly and easily, "Oh, yes, the Holocaust has meaning," then not only would one have to say what the meaning is, but also in doing that, one might run the risk of *justifying* or *legitimizing* the Holocaust by turning the Holocaust into the means that supports or tends toward some great end, or by proclaiming an answer to what Wiesel called "the metaphysical *why*," which would give the Holocaust its "proper" place in the "meaning" of life or the "meaning" of history or in "God's plan."

More than *having* meaning, the Holocaust *destroyed* meaning. That perspective may give the Holocaust meaning, but, if it does, the meaning is primarily and catastrophically negative. Put another way, as Wiesel does in his essay on "The Guilt We Share," the Holocaust and its aftereffects reveal massive human failure, which is catastrophic presently and may portend even greater catastrophe to come. Whether events trend in those directions depends, at least in part, on responses to the question: "What if death is the last word?"

TRY TO LOOK

Attending to the dying and the dead, Charlotte Delbo's *Auschwitz and After* challenges her readers to try to look and see. Her challenge, indeed her task in focusing her readers' attention so the challenge can be felt, is immense because Delbo knew that her readers had not viewed what her eyes had seen and could really never behold what she remembered. Delbo wanted her words to do their best to inform her readers' vision and to deepen their insight. Her accomplishment is not only that her readers may *begin* to envision what she saw and recollected but also that her word depictions make one aware that the beginning cannot be sustained. In and through that disruption, however, sensitivity about the meanings of death as atrocity may intensify where even the mind's eye unavoidably dims.

One spring evening in Auschwitz, Delbo and her worn-out prisoner companions returned to the camp after another long and punishing day of slave labor. This time, her work detail carried the bodies of Berthe and Anne-Marie, two comrades beaten to death—helplessly, hopelessly—when they collapsed from exhaustion that afternoon. Every evening, the Germans required that the prisoners, dead or alive, must be counted, and so it was with Berthe and Anne-Marie, who were lined up for "roll call" with those who had carried their lifeless bodies back for the tally. When the count ended, darkness had fallen, but Delbo writes that while the roll call lasted, "we never looked at them." And then her depiction continues, but less with continuity than with disruption: "A corpse. The left eye devoured by a rat. The other open with its fringe of lashes. Try to look. Just try and see."[12]

Whose corpse did Delbo's description identify? During the roll call, Delbo says, "we never looked at them," and yet she urges her readers—and perhaps even herself?—to look. But whose body does she want her readers—and perhaps even herself?—to see? Berthe's? Anne-Marie's? Delbo leaves the corpse unnamed. It is just the one with the rat-devoured left eye, the one whose right eye is fringed with lashes and still as open as it is sightless. Delbo leaves her readers—and perhaps even herself?—to bridge the disruption, if that can be done.

This much can be said: The corpse Delbo had in mind was once a living person, a woman or a man with a name, one who had parents and friends, one who probably loved and was loved, and definitely one who deserved neither to be robbed of life by genocidal perpetrators nor to be left in degradation after being senselessly beaten to death and reduced to a mark in the death column of an Auschwitz roll call.

This much more must be said: What happened to that person was wrong. But what happened to that person has been repeated and continues to be repeated again and again. The corpse/person Delbo remembers should be remembered forever, but in spite of monumental human efforts—including museums and their walls of names, collections of survivor testimonies, libraries of research, and mandates for education—the odds against that outcome are grave.

The main reason for that grim judgment is not that people are forgetful or indifferent, although those characteristics are prevalent even where the worst atrocities are concerned. Nor is the main reason to be found in the fact that, with relatively few exceptions, concern about events diminishes as they recede into the past. The main reason remembrance is likely to fail and meaning is likely to go missing is that if we human beings look, if we "just try and see," the empirical evidence overwhelmingly leads to the conclusion that human consciousness and history, indeed human life itself, are neither everlasting nor eternal but instead are finite and temporary, long-lived though they may be. Birth and death: human life came into existence; it will pass away as well. The cosmic process has been and will be in play for ages exceeding recorded history. It is not restricted to particular persons, communities, nations, and traditions but engulfs them all without exception or remainder.

Fond assumptions say otherwise, and so do hopeful faiths, but such assumptions are more problematic than self-evident, and such faiths are more doubtful than assured. In fact, their persistence and tenacity depend on apprehension that even though one generation follows and precedes another, that passage is not an undying process. The absence of human life from existence foreshadows and outlasts the presence, which includes the consciousness and awareness on which history and its meanings depend.

THE WORLD WITHOUT US

The preceding considerations make it worthwhile to recall Alan Weisman's book called *The World Without Us*.[13] Packed with insights about climate change and global warming, which could signal the end of human life, at least as we know it, Weisman's study did not concentrate on the Holocaust, genocide, and other mass atrocities, but its perspective is nonetheless significant in that context and for the outlook about facing death that is developing here.

In his book, which is based on extensive scientific, anthropological, and historical research, Weisman invited his readers to consider what would happen to planet earth if human life disappeared completely. Over time, he asked, how would the natural world change? As centuries and millennia passed, what traces of human existence, if any, would remain? Humanity, Weisman emphasized, arrived in the cosmos recently, at least if one considers how long the galaxies and earlier life forms existed before anything resembling human life evolved.[14] The emergence of that life made history. Consciousness of past, present, and future grew and expanded. Eventually, human memory led to the recording of experience in storytelling, art, and writing. Then through contemporary forms of communication such as radio, film, television, and the internet, people became linked together ever more closely. In time's eons, however, these developments, their spectacular appearance notwithstanding, are but brief and fleeting episodes.

The World Without Us is a reminder that, in the cosmic scheme of things, one's life and the existence of one's people, nation, culture, or religion may turn out to be insignificant. Weisman's purpose, however, was not to argue that humanity's existence lacks importance and meaning. To the contrary, while urging perspective about humanity's finite and frail place in reality, Weisman wanted people to appreciate intensely that human life is distinctive and precious, that what we think and do makes a huge difference. Human activity has tremendous implications, not only in history but also for our world's environment and even for the vast universe that is earth's home and ours as well.

Weisman also wanted his readers to understand that humanity has done great harm in, and to, the world. He emphasized the importance of realizing that there are ways in which the world would be better off without human beings who consume, plunder, and destroy its splendor. His predominant points remained, however, that nature has immense recuperative power and that too much of irretrievable value would be lost if the world were really to exist without us. The need, he urged, is to nurture a renewed sense of respect, reverence, and responsibility for the gift of life and the wondrous universe in which it develops.

Unfortunately, Weisman's account harbors implications that require further examination of his most fundamental assumption, namely, that the existence of the world, at least as we think we know it, can persist without us. To examine that assumption, note that Weisman's thought experiment leads to reflection on the significance of history and on the importance of particular events within it. A part of his analysis suggests that human consciousness may eventually disappear from reality. If that happened, history arguably would be null and void; it would be as if no particular event had happened, because our historical awareness, and in that sense, history itself, depends on human consciousness and, in particular, on memory. Absent memory and the conscious life that sustains it, historical documents would decay, artifacts would erode, and places would eventually disappear virtually without a trace. If anything human did remain—Weisman thinks plastics of various kinds are among the human artifacts that have the best prospect of lasting longest—the chances of detecting their meaning would be slim or none. By this cosmic standard, no human events, not even the Holocaust, genocide, or other mass atrocities loom very large.

The implications of the disappearance of human consciousness from reality do not stop with the disappearance of identifiable human events and the evaporation of history. The very ideas of *world* and *nature* and their senses of reality are shaken up as well.

Weisman's thought experiment contains the seeds of its impossibility. Strictly speaking, we cannot even imagine the world without us. Every intention to do so requires us; all attempts to do so unavoidably involve us. The point is not that human experience and consciousness create the world and that nothing would exist if they did not. Such a view would be as arrogant as it is ungrounded, as incredible as it is contrary to understanding and to what we like to call "common sense." But insofar as concepts and terms such as *world* and *nature* have meaning, which they do, those meanings are not only inseparable from human awareness but are also informed by, and even constituted or constructed within, experience.

When Charlotte Delbo urged her readers—and perhaps even herself?—to look and to see that corpse with its "left eye devoured by a rat," the world changed and nature was not the same as it was before. In spite of that death, the world also went on and so did history. The meanings of both, however, have been affected in ways that can make us see more clearly what fully facing death entails: Absent human experience, absent looking and feeling, understanding and incomprehension, absent outrage and resentment about what happened to that person in Auschwitz and to every victim of genocide and atrocity, there may be nothing to see, let alone any justice that will be done.

NO WOUND THAT WILL NOT HEAL?

In *Auschwitz and After*, poetry mixes and mingles with the death that Delbo wants the living to face. A portion of her verse recalls the post-Holocaust act of kindness she experienced one day in Sicily when a boy gave her a flower. That day, Delbo says, she told herself "there is no wound that will not heal." She repeats that thought from time to time, but, she adds, "not enough to believe it."[15] Delbo's yearning and disbelief have much to do with her saying, "I know the difference between before and after," an outlook that encompassed the fact that death, especially death in and through atrocity, leaves the world too bereft of justice.[16]

Delbo lost her life to cancer in 1985. More than forty years earlier, on January 24, 1943, she had been deported to Auschwitz from her native France. Of the 230 women in her convoy—most of them, like Delbo herself, non-Jews who had served in the French Resistance—

only 49 survived.[17] For Delbo, *after* irrevocably referred to Auschwitz. Its reality, she emphasized, was "so deeply etched in my memory that I cannot forget one moment of it."[18] Among other things, her Auschwitz experience left her acutely aware that the Holocaust and its aftermath had fragmented the meaning of words. "There are people," she observed, "who say, 'I'm thirsty.' They step into a café and order a beer."[19] Those words are her ironic conclusion to a chapter called "Thirst." It attempts to describe what the "free word" *thirst* can never capture, an experience incompletely grasped by her reader even when Delbo writes that it took her to "the point of losing my mind." The parching that she found no words to describe was so all-consuming that it was only relieved by drinking and drinking some more from a pail, as she was finally able to do in Auschwitz, "like a horse, no, like a dog."[20]

After the Holocaust, genocide, and other mass atrocities, even apparently simple words such as *after* cannot mean what they did before. What happens, then, to *justice*, a word whose meanings were already fragile, problematic, and contested before genocidal atrocity struck and the Holocaust raged? The word remains and persists. The fact that it has not been silenced but is still spoken and heard indicates that *justice* is a needed word. But *justice* is also a wounded word because it is primarily and unavoidably an *after*-word.[21]

Cries for, and appeals to, justice are usually pronounced when something has gone badly wrong. If life were fair, unscarred by failure, greed, terror, war, rape, or genocide, there would be little need to dwell on justice. The Holocaust and other atrocities intensify the need for justice but also make justice impossible, at least as far as the traditional idea of justice as a balancing of scales is concerned. Attempts to restore order, to provide restitution and recompense, even to mete out punishment to perpetrators, can be made. Tribunals try to handle matters of this kind. Noble and partially successful though these efforts are, their shortcomings are more striking, because within history no compensation for atrocity is adequate. For the dead, nothing can be done except to remember them. Far from bringing comfort, that remembering—to the extent that it is not swallowed by forgetting and by the death of those left behind—underscores the absence of justice. Memory can encourage efforts to rectify the absence of justice, but when driven by injustice, memory can produce more of the same. It can intensify hostility; it can fuel hate and inflame revenge.

No human quality is more virtuous than the protest and resistance that take the realities of injustice—defined in key ways by the corpses of the Holocaust, genocide, and other mass atrocities—as spurs to try yet again to curb their destructiveness. Absent such determination and defiance, history most likely would be much bloodier. Nevertheless, evidence is scarce to support the hope that this struggle can transcend the fate of Sisyphus. Defying the gods by thwarting death, Sisyphus was punished by a ceaseless repetition requiring him to push a weighty rock up a mountain only to have it roll back to the bottom as he neared the top. In *The Myth of Sisyphus*, the philosopher Albert Camus, a contemporary of Delbo's in the French Resistance, depicted Sisyphus defiantly taking up his unending task again, contending that "there is no fate that cannot be surmounted by scorn."[22] Camus experienced the Nazi occupation of France but not Auschwitz. He imagined Sisyphus happy, but would Delbo agree?

A MEANS OF JOY

The philosopher Philip Hallie studied and wrote movingly about Le Chambon-sur-Lignon, the French community that saved several thousand Jews during the Holocaust.[23] His deep admiration for Camus included knowledge that the French writer had lived near the village while the rescue operation was under way. That action probably influenced the development of Camus's enduring novel, *The Plague*, which he was writing at the time. In Paris during the late spring of 1959, less than a year before Camus lost his life in a car crash, Hallie had his only personal meeting with him. One of Hallie's most touching essays, published posthumously, describes the visit and the meaning that Hallie took from it.[24] Camus, wrote Hallie,

> wanted to put himself at the service, not of the makers of history, but rather of the victims of that history. And he would have to do this again and again and again, knowing that his revolt against death would never defeat death. He would just try to limit the harm done. The world is not benign; there will always be victims, but we can feel solidarity with the victims we can embrace; we can feel the joy of helping a few people a few times. The rock will roll down the hill again; but when we are pushing it up the hill with our cheeks against it and our arms spread out on it, we can be close to that hardness and make a little difference, though only

temporarily. We can have the joy of friendship, of love, even while we
forget nothing, not even murder.[25]

In that passage, Hallie emphasizes *joy*—the joy of helping, the joy of
friendship and love, while never forgetting murder and always trying
to see the murdered dead. Such joy, I believe, is related to the scorn
that Camus attributed to Sisyphus, for that joy is in spite of even the
worst crimes against humanity. Refusing to be driven to despair, such
joy defies atrocity, even if not victoriously. With that sense of joy in
mind, Camus rightly called Sisyphus happy, and I believe that Delbo
could agree.

Hallie went one step further. He rightly thought that ethics—
including, I believe, responses to the failures of ethics—should be "a
means of joy."[26] The joy he had in mind is not sentimental, occasional, or fleeting but transforming and converting; it is an in-spite-of
joy, reflecting the hope of nevertheless, insisting on the mending
opportunities of "and yet... and yet," and encouraging solidarity
with those who resist and limit harm, relieve suffering, and save
lives. Absent that joy of living, said Hallie, ethics is "a blinding,
puritanical, dried up, self-destructive and life-destructive force."[27]
But what Hallie called "moral beauty" can happen "when someone
carves out a place for compassion in a largely ruthless universe."[28]

When ethics is a means of joy, that in-spite-of joy is as hard-won as
it is important because human experience is real, or, for us, nothing
can be. Embedded in and constituted by that experience, history and,
in particular, the Holocaust, genocide, and other mass atrocities—
denials to the contrary notwithstanding—are also as real as anything
can possibly be. Within history, justice remains an *after*-word. Not
only will it primarily be voiced in the wake of useless destruction,
harm, and suffering, but also justice will remain elusive. It will be
what humanity does not have, what it lacks, and what it is *after* in the
sense of seeking. At best, justice can obtain only in part and incompletely. The extent to which that judgment is the last word, however,
might depend on whether human experience itself has aspects and
dimensions that extend beyond history. Put another way, as one tries
to follow Charlotte Delbo's insistence to look, to try and see, could
facing death, could envisioning a Holocaust corpse, its left eye
devoured by a rat, make one yearn, if not believe, that history does
not exhaust human experience?

For justice to prevail, for it to be complete, more than history and more than human lives that utterly end with death are minimal requirements. Arguably, God would be required as well. The philosopher Immanuel Kant saw those relationships when he held that if ethics and the ideal of justice are fully reasonable—he thought they must be—at least three postulates, as he called them, were fundamental: freedom, human life beyond history and death, and God. The validity of these prerequisites could not be proved, but Kant's insight was a version of the principles that justice makes no sense apart from the freedom to choose and that justice delayed is justice denied. To the extent that justice is incomplete, injustice prevails, and what is reasonable is thwarted.

So, for the sake of inquiry and perhaps for the sake of justice itself, ponder what the good news might be if human life does not end with death, if history is not all there is for us, and if a God exists to ensure that justice does prevail completely, a restoration whose full goodness would vanquish past evils. Next, imagine once more Berthe and Anne-Marie, the two Auschwitz women Delbo saw beaten to death because they could no longer do the slave labor that the Germans demanded. Furthermore, consider again the corpse that Delbo wanted her readers to see. Envision them—Berthe, Anne-Marie, the unnamed corpse—alive beyond death. Try to conceive a reality in which justice prevails completely over the injustice of genocide's death camps and killing fields. Perhaps God can do so. Perhaps human beings can be transformed beyond death so that they can too. Anything, people sometimes say, is possible. But this scenario of healing and restoration is scarcely imaginable. In fact, if that outcome emerged, ethics and justice would require suspicion about its validity and integrity.

When ethics is a means of joy, the joy is as hard-won as it is important because what happened happened, and unless memory is erased, the injustice will not be forgotten, nor should it be. Even beyond death and with a God who would try to make justice whole, reality is too flawed for that result's credibility to hold. No doubt healing and restoration are badly needed—within history and beyond. They can be obtained in part, a cause for joy, but not to an extent that will set everything right. Existence is permanently scarred. Facing death, especially its atrocity in the Holocaust and other genocides, forever diminishes good news about justice but does not make impossible the joy evoked and encouraged by someone's carving out "a place for compassion in a largely ruthless universe."

Charlotte Delbo and Elie Wiesel were imprisoned in different parts of Auschwitz, but both unavoidably found corpses filling their fields of vision. "Try to look," wrote Delbo. "Just try and see." The more genocidal death is faced, the more likely that heartbreak, melancholy, futility, and despair will invade our minds and occupy our hearts. Anticipation that such moods stalk us, awareness that they can be paralyzing, may make even scholars of the Holocaust and genocide reluctant to do the looking and seeing that Delbo emphasized. But in spite of those moods, the very looking and seeing that evoke them can have other and better outcomes without preempting those gloomy dispositions and their validity, persistence, and insight.

In Wiesel's memoir *Night*, two moments of facing death refuse to go away. One involves his report about the hanging of a young boy in Auschwitz. The Germans suspected him of complicity in sabotage. Along with two adults, the tortured boy was executed while the assembled prisoners had to watch and then march past the victims. The two adults died quickly, but the boy lingered, "struggling between life and death, dying in slow agony under our eyes. And we had to look him full in the face."[29] The other episode forms *Night*'s conclusion. Force marched from Auschwitz to Buchenwald, the camp from which he was "liberated" in April 1945, Wiesel was transferred to a hospital where he "spent two weeks between life and death." One day he looked at himself in a mirror, something he had not been able to do for many months. "From the depths of the mirror," says Wiesel, "a corpse was contemplating me. The look in his eyes as he gazed at me has never left me."[30]

Wiesel importantly insists that facing death involves not only looking and seeing the dead but also setting eyes on the dying of the dead. More than that, he suggests that our looking and seeing should include the murdered dead looking at and seeing us, mute and visionless though atrocity has made their eyes. Still more, Wiesel's self-description makes one see that even those who have "survived" atrocity may have experienced—and still do experience—dying and death in their own living. Mado, one of Delbo's Auschwitz sisters, puts it this way: "People believe memories grow vague, are erased by time, since nothing endures against the passage of time. That's the difference; time does not pass over me, over us. It doesn't erase anything, doesn't undo it. I'm not alive. I died in Auschwitz but no one knows it."[31]

Once a person has these perspectives, once the senses of heart-break, melancholy, failure, futility, and despair have been felt and have even gone deep down, the question remains: What will happen when we look in a mirror and a gaze back contemplates and questions us? What shall we do with our living? Writing after heart surgery at the age of 82, Wiesel answered: "indifference and resignation are not the answer."[32] Delbo replied: "I beg you / do something . . . / something to justify your existence . . . / because it would be too senseless / after all / for so many to have died / while you live / doing nothing with your life."[33] In spite of the failures of ethics, Camus and Hallie affirmed that we can, and must, feel "the joy of helping . . . the joy of friendship, of love."

My conclusion follows theirs: We neither should nor can eliminate the darkness into which facing death and, in particular, the death unleashed by the Holocaust, genocide, and other mass atrocities plunges us, but working together with others, and standing in solidarity with those who resisted and rescued during the Holocaust, I can try my best to be sure that memory of the Holocaust and other atrocities continues, that education about those catastrophes advances, and that the purposes of those activities include equipping us to resist injustice, to protest when life is disrespected, to live in ways that, in spite of mass atrocity crimes, still seek to mend the world, and to find and encourage joy when those steps are taken.

We cannot avoid despair over the fact that memory of the Holocaust, genocide, and other mass atrocities, including education about them, have not dislodged the likelihood that death by atrocity will be faced again and again. But working together with others, and standing in solidarity with those who resist and rescue, we can try our best to make human existence better than it otherwise would be. Facing death inflicted by the Holocaust and other atrocities reveals the failures of ethics as nothing else can. Facing death with that understanding still leaves us to ask what we will do next—today, tomorrow, and the day after tomorrow. Within resistance against the failures of ethics, satisfied contentment cannot be found. But in that resistance, meaning and joy must be ours.

Epilogue

The Right Side of History?

The salvage trucks / back in and / the salvage men / begin to sort / and stack, / whistling as / they work.

—Kay Ryan, "Salvage"

Three poets have influenced what this book has to say. William Stafford emphasized that "there's a thread you follow." In the epigraph with which the book began, Paul Hunter anticipated that the thread is about failure and, in particular, the failures of ethics. In the poem from which the epigraph is taken, Hunter gives his reader ownership of a farm field that will not yield a crop this year. Too much rain, or not enough, has fallen. The sun has been too hot or the temperature has dipped too low. Bugs and blights have wreaked their havoc. Cultivation has not worked, and what is to be made of the loss? If it is not to be the end, "if there is to be another crop," writes Hunter, someone must "clear away or turn under / mow rake and burn off this failure."[1]

This book tries to nurture responsible owning of world fields that appear fruitless and barren because of ethical failings. It aims to encourage the determination needed for new and better crops to flourish. In a poem called "Salvage," Kay Ryan's urban imagery contrasts with Hunter's pastoral theme, but her mood is much the same. "The worst has happened," she writes, but the salvage begins, the self-taught crew looking for what is needed to keep unthinkable wreckage at bay. As if invoking a spirit of in-spite-of joy, Ryan's poem seems to ask its reader to hear the salvage crew "whistling as they work."[2] This book seeks to amplify that whistling so that the salvage crew responding to the failures of ethics is larger, better equipped, and stronger.

The thread followed by Paul Hunter's resilient, field-owning care-takers and by Kay Ryan's defiantly whistling salvage workers permits no slack for illusion or loose ends that obscure lucidity. So this book draws to a close by raising one more question: Does it make sense to speak of *the right side of history*? An internet search provides many references to indicate that this intriguing concept is widely used in contemporary discourse, much of it involving partisan political debate about which sides are "right" or "wrong." The American president Barack Obama provided an instructive international example on September 24, 2014, when he addressed the United Nations General Assembly.[3]

Obama contended that, at least for young people in the United States, "this is the best time in human history to be born, for you are more likely than ever before to be literate, to be healthy, to be free to pursue your dreams." Given that reality and especially history are so riddled by failure and especially by the failures of ethics, how should such rhetoric be understood? Is Obama's claim verifiable or is it cheerleading? Is the encouragement profound or hollow? To which "young people" does the claim apply? Its sweeping generality collides with the inconvenient fact that in the United States, let alone in less affluent countries, young people who are poor or from a declining middle class are likely to experience shrinking rather than expanding opportunity. Obama himself may have sensed that his lofty optimism was more puzzling than persuasive because he quickly went on to note "a pervasive unease in our world," its current causes including the outbreak of Ebola, Russian aggression in Europe, and brutal violence, especially escalated by ISIS, in Syria and Iraq. Underscoring American determination and promising leadership to deal effectively with those challenges, he called for an international response to join the United States "on the right side of history." That concept implies that history itself has an ethical structure, which would support and vindicate—at least in the long run—decisions and actions that are on the right side. Likewise, decisions and actions that are on the wrong side of history, a reality implied by the existence of history's right side, would not enjoy such support and vindication. Such thinking is not new. The idea of the right side of history is as old as it is problematic, as persistent as it is loaded with assumptions, hopes, and aspirations.

Four points about the meaning of the idea are important to ensure that efforts to curb the failures of ethics do not harbor illusion or abet mystification. First, the concept presumes that history itself is a reality, a social process—perhaps in some ways metaphysical—that is larger than the actions of specific human individuals or groups, something not restricted to particular times, places, or epochs but encompassing, at least, the entire scope of human existence in the universe. Second, the right side of history seems to entail *destiny*—a direction that history is taking and a trajectory toward one or more destinations that history will reach. If that view is true, then history is neither absurd nor meaningless; it is infused with meaning that is not transitory but possibly of ultimate significance. Third, the concept is tied to the idea of truth. Judgments that are contrary to fact, not to mention lies, may hold sway for a time, but they will not be on the right side of history, at least not at the end of the day, because being on the right side of history entails paying attention to what is genuinely known—and not just a matter of opinion—and heeding what reliable and well-documented inquiry reveals. Fourth, the concept of the right side of history seems to be a profoundly ethical and even religious idea that, in one way or another, signifies *progress*. The ethical dimensions of the concept are illustrated in claims that the right side of history is the side that favors what are taken to be basic human rights.

In addition, it is important to underscore that the right side of history is an idea that itself has a history. At least in Western civilization, biblical religion is one of its key underpinnings, especially insofar as people think that history's source and ultimate governance are not only divine but also providential. The latter outlook envisions judgment and justice, redemption and renewal, expectation and hope. The Christian hymn, "This Is My Father's World," voices such yearnings, affirming that "though the wrong seems oft so strong, God is the Ruler yet." Martin Luther King, Jr., had that theme in mind during his "Where Do We Go from Here?" address to the Southern Christian Leadership Conference on August 16, 1967. "When our days become dreary with low-hovering clouds of despair," said King, "and when our nights become darker than a thousand midnights, let us remember that there is a creative force in this universe working to pull down the gigantic mountains of evil, a power that is able to make a way out of no way and transform dark yesterdays into bright tomorrows. Let us realize," King emphasized, "that the arc of the moral universe is long, but it bends toward justice."[4] In such a context, the right side of history has to do with God's will, humanity's conformity to or alienation from it, and the proposition that, no matter what hell breaks out on earth, God's ways shall prevail.

The German philosopher G. W. F. Hegel built his grand, some would say grandiose, philosophy of history on foundations akin to biblical ones, but his outlook emphasized that the arc of the universe, moral, progressive, and freedom-directed though it might be, far transcended the interests and inclinations of any particular people, time, and place. History, said Hegel, is a "slaughter-bench, upon which the happiness of nations, the wisdom of states, and the virtues of individuals were sacrificed."[5] Still, although it is full of destruction and negation, history is moving progressively. Karl Marx agreed but only in part. Attempting to stand Hegel's philosophy of history on its head, as he put it, Marx claimed that an economic dialectic drove history far more than any spiritual powers. He envisioned that the right side of history would eventuate in the demise of repressive capitalism and the triumph of human liberation. Additional sources exist for the idea of the right side of history, but the ones mentioned are sufficient to suggest how varied and potent the idea can be.

But is there such a thing as the right side of history? To sharpen the focus of that question, consider what typically happened in classrooms of mine. In courses on genocide, I early on asked students: *Will genocide ever end?* The students never answered *yes*. My follow-up to that initial result produced, with some prodding, a few tentative "maybes" but not much more conviction than that. By the end of the semester, the students' responses were more affirmative than they were in the early going, if only because they became convinced that there is nothing necessary or inevitable about genocide. But what continued to interest me through the work we did together was whether the students, or any of us, have found that "the right side of history" exists—not just in the sense of an apparently faint hope but in the much more robust sense of a direction or destiny, fundamentally moral in its character, that history is taking.

Some people have called the twentieth century a century of genocide. It was a century rife with massive human rights abuses and mass atrocity crimes. Not much progress has been made in ending crimes against humanity in the twenty-first century, allusions to the right side of history notwithstanding. But who among us would want to say that the Holocaust, genocide, and other mass atrocities are on the right side of history? Surely, they are on the wrong side of history or nothing could be. Yet the dilemma remains that the wrong is often so strong that we have to wonder about the purported moral arc of the universe.

It matters whether the right side of history exists, but arguably something else matters more, at least for us, who live and die in the fleeting moments and short-lived places of the time that is ours. What we choose to do matters more. How we confront the failures of ethics, protesting and resisting them so that human life can flourish, matters more. The best salvage crews do not rely on the right side of history; they are not motivated, at least not primarily, by belief in it. Nor are they disheartened or deterred by doubt that the right side of history exists. Awareness that disaster is a fact, that catastrophe has happened, is enough to keep them on the move. Never letting go of that thread can bring joy that makes all the difference in the world.

Acknowledgments

Following the thread that led to this book, I became keenly aware that I cannot name everyone who prompted me to write it. Sadly, that company includes all of the perpetrators of mass atrocities and their countless victims. I know that this book fails to do enough to hold the former responsible and to remember the latter with the respect they deserve. My shortcomings also encircle the many people who during my long life have helped and encouraged, befriended and taught me in ways small and large but whose names are likely to escape me. These acknowledgments will not do enough to credit them sufficiently or to thank them adequately, but I am mindful of the fact that while books are written in solitude, they are the result of social relationships in ways that are only dimly apparent to an author. Fortunately, vivid recollection can to some extent supplant dull awareness. So I name, remember, and thank especially the following persons who significantly influenced my thinking and focused my writing.

Friends at Claremont McKenna College—especially William Ascher, Hiram Chodosh, Leigh Crawford, Stephen Davis, Robert Fossum, Pamela Gann, Edward Haley, David Hetz, Wendy Lower, David and Margaret Mgrublian, Jonathan Petropoulos, Gaines Post, Jr., Steven Smith, John and Bonnie Snortum, Jack and Jil Stark, Peter Thum, and Christopher Walker—provided insight, support, and inspiration. Heartening guidance also came from Victoria Barnett, Yehuda Bauer, Michael Berenbaum, Donald Bloxham, Christopher Browning, Eva Fleischner, Peter Fredlake, Irving Greenberg, Peter Hayes, Raul Hilberg, Paul Hunter, Berel Lang, Lawrence Langer, Esther Mackintosh, Carolyn Manosevitz, Elisabeth Maxwell, Brett O'Bannon, Samuel Oliner, John Pawlikowski, Carol Rittner, Richard Rubenstein, Pierre Sauvage, Frederick Sontag, William Stafford, Zev and Alice Weiss, and Elie Wiesel. For many years and in ways unknown to them, they have generously taught, informed, and mentored me. Founded in 1996 by Leonard Grob and Henry Knight, the Stephen S. Weinstein Holocaust Symposium, which meets biennially at Wroxton College in the United Kingdom, has given me welcome friendship and immense support. I deeply appreciate the backing I have received from this symposium and, in addition to the founders,

I am particularly grateful to Rachel Baum, Margaret Brearley, Arie Galles, Dorota Glowacka, Myrna Goldenberg, Henry Greenspan, Peter Haas, Hubert Locke, Rochelle Millen, David Patterson, Sarah Pinnock, Didier Pollefeyt, Martin Rumscheidt, Bob Skloot, and James Waller. Finally, no author could ask for more from an editorial team than the one at Oxford University Press with whom I have been privileged to work. That team includes Tom Perridge, first and foremost, and his fine assistants Alexander Johnson, Karen Raith, and Aimee Wright, and also Alyssa Bender, Rosie Chambers, Gayathri Manoharan, and Rachel May. Special thanks go to Doreen Kruger for copyediting the book, Rebecca Francescatti for indexing it, and Tracy Hall, who did the proofreading.

As the book's completion approached, I celebrated the fiftieth anniversary of my marriage to Evelyn Austin, whom I love more than words can say. A dedicated teacher who taught many children how to read, she has been my teacher as well as my best friend each and every day. Her influence on me, and especially on my ethical sensibilities, is immense. Nothing I could say or do would ever thank her enough for loving me, but this book is gratefully dedicated to her and to those in my immediate family circle who would not be there without her. Apart from the parents who gave us life—Doris King and Josiah Roth, Marjorie Rice and Robert Austin—no marriage, let alone one lasting fifty years and more, would have been possible for Lyn and me. This book, I hope, honors them too, and helps to keep memory of them alive. The care, friendship, and love I have received from family and friends surpass my understanding and, at the end, words give way to silence—awed and humble but forever indebted and thankful.

* * *

Earlier versions of some of this book's chapters appeared in the following publications: chapter 3, in John K. Roth, ed., *Genocide and Human Rights: A Philosophical Guide* (New York: Palgrave Macmillan, 2005); chapter 4, in Carol Rittner, ed., *Holocaust Education: Challenges for the Future* (Greensburg, PA: Seton Hill University, National Catholic Center for Holocaust Education, 2014); chapter 5, in David Cesarani and Eric J. Sundquist, eds., *After the Holocaust: Challenging the Myth of Silence* (New York: Routledge, 2012); chapter 6, in Steven T. Katz and Alan Rosen, eds., *Elie Wiesel: Jewish, Literary, and Moral Perspectives* (Bloomington, IN: Indiana University Press, 2013), and chapter 7, in *International Journal for Philosophy of Religion* 68, nos.1–3 (2010). I am grateful for the opportunity to incorporate that work in this volume.

I also express thanks to authors and publishers for permission to use quotations that form the epigraphs for the book and its chapters. Those epigraphs include lines from: "This Failure" by Paul Hunter, reprinted from *Ripening* by permission of Silverfish Review Press, copyright © 2007; "The Way It Is" by William Stafford, from *Ask Me: 100 Essential Poems*, reprinted by permission of The Permissions Company Inc. on behalf of Graywolf Press, Minneapolis, Minnesota, copyright © 1998, 2014 by the Estate of William Stafford; *Hitler's Furies* by Wendy Lower, reprinted by permission of Houghton Mifflin Harcourt Publishing Company, copyright © 2013; *The Destruction of the European Jews* by Raul Hilberg, reprinted by permission of Yale University Press, copyright © 2003; *At the Mind's Limits* by Jean Améry, reprinted by permission of Indiana University Press, copyright © 1980; *Garden, Ashes* by Danilo Kiš, reprinted by permission of the Dalkey Archive Press, copyright © 2003; *One Generation After* by Elie Wiesel, reprinted by permission of Georges Borchardt, Inc., copyright © 1970; *A Jew Today* by Elie Wiesel, reprinted by permission of Random House and Georges Borchardt, Inc., copyright © 1978; *The G Word* by Catherine Filloux, reprinted by permission of the author, copyright © 2004; *Sources of Holocaust Research* by Raul Hilberg, reprinted by permission of Ivan R. Dee and Rowman & Littlefield, copyright © 2001; *Tales of Good and Evil, Help and Harm* by Philip Hallie, reprinted by permission of Harper Collins, copyright © 1997 by Doris Hallie; *Auschwitz and After* by Charlotte Delbo, reprinted by permission of Yale University Press, copyright © 1995; "Salvage," by Kay Ryan, from *The Niagara River*, reprinted by permission of Grove Press, copyright © 2005 (Any third party use of this material, outside of this publication, is prohibited.)

My gratitude also goes to Tommy Sands for permission to reprint lines from his song lyrics. Scripture quotations are from New Revised Standard Version Bible, copyright © 1989 National Council of the Churches of Christ in the United States of America. Used by permission. All rights reserved.

Notes

PROLOGUE

1. William Stafford, *The Way It Is: New & Selected Poems* (St. Paul, MN: Graywolf Press, 1998), 42.
2. Helpful reflection on failure, including cracks in reality as well as moral shortcomings and shortfalls in human character and conduct, can be found in Colin Feltham, *Failure* (New York: Routledge, 2014). See also Carolyn J. Dean, *The Fragility of Empathy after the Holocaust* (Ithaca, NY: Cornell University Press, 2004).
3. Paul Hunter, "This Failure," in his collection called *Ripenings* (Eugene, OR: Silverfish Review Press, 2007), 37.
4. This poem, as well as "This Failure," can be found at the PBS Internet site containing Hunter's interview with Gwen Ifill: <www.pbs.org/new shour/bb/entertainment/july-dec07/ripening_07-09.html>.
5. See Hunter's "Author's Note" in *Ripenings*, 83.
6. See David Grossman, "On Hope and Despair in the Middle East," *Haaretz*, July 8, 2014. The essay is available at: <www.haaretz.com/news/diplomacy-defense/israel-peace-conference/1.601993>. For instructive reflections on hope, see Adrienne M. Martin, *How We Hope: A Moral Psychology* (Princeton, NJ: Princeton University Press, 2014).
7. G. J. Warnock, *Contemporary Moral Philosophy* (London: Macmillan, 1967), 60. See also Philip Hallie, *Tales of Good and Evil, Help and Harm* (New York: HarperCollins, 1997), 54.
8. William Stafford, "Traveling through the Dark," in *The Way It Is*, 77.
9. William Stafford, "A Ritual to Read to Each Other," in *The Way It Is*, 75–6.
10. As defined by the International Criminal Court (ICC), crimes against humanity "include any of the following acts committed as part of a widespread or systematic attack directed against any civilian population, with knowledge of the attack: murder; extermination; enslavement; deportation or forcible transfer of population; imprisonment; torture; rape, sexual slavery, enforced prostitution, forced pregnancy, enforced sterilization, or any other form of sexual violence of comparable gravity; persecution against an identifiable group on political, racial, national, ethnic, cultural, religious or gender grounds; enforced disappearance of persons; the crime of apartheid; other inhumane acts of a similar character intentionally causing great suffering or serious bodily or mental injury." See the ICC website: <www.icc-cpi.int/en_menus/icc/about% 20the%20court/frequently%20asked%20questions/Pages/12.aspx>.

11. John Keegan, *The First World War* (New York: Vintage Books, 2000), 421.
12. Sigmund Freud, "The Disillusionment of the War," trans. E. C. Mayne, in *The Standard Edition of the Complete Works of Sigmund Freud*, vol. XIV, ed. James Strachey (London: Hogarth Press, 1957), 285.

PART I

1. For background on this story, see David Shatz, "'Yeah, Yeah': Eulogy for Sidney Morgenbesser, Philosopher with a Yiddish Accent," *Tablet Magazine*, June 27, 2014. The article is available at: <www.tabletmag. com/jewish-arts-and-culture/books/177249/sidney-morgenbesser?utm_ source=tabletmagazinelist&utm_campaign=236ab3f7c7-Friday_June_ 27_20146_26_2014&utm_medium=email&utm_term=0_c308bf8edb-236ab3f7c7-207179709>.

CHAPTER 1

1. William James, "The Teaching of Philosophy in Our Colleges," *The Nation* 23, no. 586 (1876): 178. I am indebted to Henry Greenspan for the quotation.
2. Wendy Lower, *Hitler's Furies: German Women in the Nazi Killing Fields* (Boston, MA: Houghton Mifflin Harcourt, 2013), 2.
3. See Carol Rittner and John K. Roth, eds., *Different Voices: Women and the Holocaust* (St. Paul, MN: Paragon House, 1993).
4. Lower, *Hitler's Furies*, 200.
5. Lower, *Hitler's Furies*, 166.
6. Lower, *Hitler's Furies*, 166.
7. For a helpful discussion on this point, see Paul A. Levine, "On-lookers," in *The Oxford Handbook of Holocaust Studies*, ed. Peter Hayes and John K. Roth (New York: Oxford University Press, 2010), 156–69.
8. See Victoria J. Barnett, *Bystanders: Conscience and Complicity During the Holocaust* (Westport, CT: Praeger Publishers, 2000). Barnett's book first appeared in a series called "Christianity and the Holocaust—Core Issues," which Carol Rittner and I edited for the Greenwood Publishing Group. For related matters, especially pertaining to rescue—and its lack—during the Holocaust, see David Gushee, *Righteous Gentiles of the Holocaust: Genocide and Moral Obligation*. 2nd edn. (St. Paul, MN: Paragon House, 2003) and Ervin Staub, *The Roots of Goodness and Resistance to Evil: Inclusive Caring, Moral Courage, Altruism Born of Suffering, Active Bystanding, and Heroism* (Oxford: Oxford University Press, 2015).

9. Raul Hilberg, *The Destruction of the European Jews*, 3rd edn. (New Haven, CN: Yale University Press, 2003), 3:1085.

10. The photo can be seen online at the website of the United States Holocaust Memorial Museum (USHMM): <www.ushmm.org/information/exhib itions/permanent/kristallnacht/explore-the-objects>. The USHMM special exhibition "Some Were Neighbors: Collaboration and Complicity in the Holocaust" is also significant in relation to bystanders and bystanding. For more information, see the website for this exhibition: <http://somewereneighbors.ushmm.org/>.

11. See Karl A. Schleunes, *The Twisted Road to Auschwitz: Nazi Policy toward German Jews, 1933–1939* (Urbana, IL: University of Illinois Press, 1990).

12. See Alexis Herr, "Fossoli di Carpi: The History and Memory of the Holocaust in Italy" (Ph.D. diss., Clark University, 2014). During the Holocaust, argues Herr, economic incentives motivated much complicity—hence her emphasis on compensated complicity.

13. Omer Bartov, ed., *The Holocaust: Origins, Implementation, Aftermath* (New York: Routledge, 2000), 204.

14. Bartov, ed., *The Holocaust*, 204.

15. For an important discussion of the ethical dilemmas and insights that thread through the tensions and collisions between the realization that "I must" and the recognition that "I can't," see Lisa Tessman, *Moral Failure: On the Impossible Demands of Morality* (Oxford: Oxford University Press, 2014).

16. For insights on these points, I am indebted to Ernesto Verdeja, "Moral Bystanders and Mass Violence," in *New Perspectives on Genocide Research*, ed. Adam Jones (New York: Routledge, 2012), 153–68.

17. See Samantha Power, *"A Problem from Hell": America and the Age of Genocide* (New York: Basic Books, 2002).

18. See Albert Camus, *The Rebel: An Essay on Man in Revolt*, trans. Anthony Bower (New York: Vintage Books, 1956), 297.

19. Gitta Sereny, *Into That Darkness: An Examination of Conscience* (New York: Vintage Books, 1983), 23.

20. Sereny, *Into That Darkness*, 15.

21. Sereny, *Into That Darkness*, 367.

22. The full texts of the Genocide Convention and the Universal Declaration of Human Rights are available online, respectively, at: <www.oas.org/dil/1948_Convention_on_the_Prevention_and_Punishment_of_the_Crime_of_Genocide.pdf and www.un.org/en/documents/udhr/>.

23. On the concept of choiceless choice(s), which he coined, see Lawrence L. Langer, "The Dilemma of Choice in the Deathcamps," in *Holocaust: Religious and Philosophical Implications*, ed. John K. Roth and Michael

Berenbaum (St. Paul, MN: Paragon House 1989), 222–32. See also Langer's *Versions of Survival: The Holocaust and the Human Spirit* (Albany, NY: State University of New York Press, 1982), esp. 72. Choiceless choices, writes Langer, do not "reflect options between life and death, but between one form of abnormal response and another, both imposed by a situation that was in no way of the victim's own choosing."

24. Jean Améry, *At the Mind's Limits: Contemplations by a Survivor on Auschwitz and Its Realities*, trans. Sidney Rosenfeld and Stella P. Rosenfeld (Bloomington, IN: Indiana University Press, 1980), 28.

25. Améry, *At the Mind's Limits*, 89.

26. Améry, *At the Mind's Limits*, 40, 95.

27. See, for example, Götz Aly, *Why the Germans? Why the Jews? Envy, Race Hatred, and the Prehistory of the Holocaust*, trans. Jefferson Chase (New York: Metropolitan Books, 2014), 205–18; Peter J. Haas, *Morality after Auschwitz: The Radical Challenge of the Nazi Ethic* (Philadelphia, PA: Fortress Press, 1988); Claudia Koonz, *The Nazi Conscience* (Cambridge, MA: Harvard University Press, 2003); John K. Roth, *Ethics During and After the Holocaust: In the Shadow of Birkenau* (New York: Palgrave Macmillan, 2005), 83–9; and Richard Weikart, *Hitler's Ethic: The Nazi Pursuit of Evolutionary Progress* (New York: Palgrave Macmillan, 2009).

28. Lower, *Hitler's Furies*, 197.

29. See Eric Lichtblau, *The Nazis Next Door: How America Became a Safe Haven for Hitler's Men* (Boston, MA: Houghton Mifflin Harcourt, 2014).

30. Michael Berenbaum, "Who Owns the Holocaust?" *Moment* 25, no. 6 (2000): 60.

31. See Roth, *Ethics During and After the Holocaust*, 70, 193–4.

32. See Jeffrey C. Alexander et al., *Remembering the Holocaust: A Debate* (New York: Oxford University Press, 2009).

33. One of those associates was the SS officer Adolf Eichmann, a key Holocaust perpetrator, whose actions facilitated the deportation and destruction of more than 1.5 million Jews. Bettina Stangneth's penetrating study, *Eichmann before Jerusalem: The Unexamined Life of a Mass Murderer*, trans. Ruth Martin (New York: Alfred A. Knopf, 2014) insightfully explores how Eichmann consciously and thoroughly "rejected traditional ideas of morality, in favor of the no-holds-barred struggle for survival that nature demanded. . . . The only thing that mattered was one's own people" (218). Stangneth shows that Eichmann's outlook took philosophical and religious ethics into account. He grasped the inclusive and universal implications of their appeals to conscience, justice, and rights, but he was unpersuaded. Eichmann was convinced instead that the ethnic values of blood and soil were worth much more. His morality, grounded in belief in "the final battle of the races," underscored that "the battle could never be over as along as a

single enemy was still alive" (222). Thus, his Nazi ethic required loyalty to, and fulfillment of, its non-negotiable imperative: Jewish existence must be obliterated. Importantly, Stangneth indicates, serious thinking and even a kind of philosophizing, one that rejected much of philosophy to be sure, were essential in the path that Eichmann took. That outcome shakes any easy assumptions about the ability of thought and philosophy in particular to prevent the failures of ethics.

34. Hilberg, *The Destruction of the European Jews*, 3:1085.
35. On this point, see Dan McMillan, *How Could This Happen: Explaining the Holocaust* (New York: Basic Books, 2014), 169–81.
36. See, for example, Christian Ingrao, *Believe and Destroy: Intellectuals in the SS War Machine*, trans. Andrew Brown (Cambridge, UK: Polity Press, 2013).
37. See Primo Levi, *The Drowned and the Saved*, trans. Raymond Rosenthal (New York: Summit Books, 1988), 36–69, and Primo Levi, *The Voice of Memory: Interviews, 1961–1987*, ed. Marco Belpoliti and Robert Gordon and trans. Robert Gordon (New York: The New Press, 2001), 175.
38. Levi, *The Voice of Memory*, 180, 232.
39. Primo Levi, *Other People's Trades*, trans. Raymond Rosenthal (New York: Summit Books, 1989), 20.
40. Levi, *Other People's Trades*, 22–3.
41. Levi, *The Drowned and the Saved*, 200.
42. Peter Hayes, "Ethics and Corporate History in Nazi Germany," in *Lessons and Legacies IX: Memory History, and Responsibility; Reassessments of the Holocaust, Implications for the Future*, ed. Jonathan Petropoulos, Lynn Rapaport, and John K. Roth (Evanston, IL: Northwestern University Press, 2010), 302.
43. William Stafford, *The Way It Is: New & Selected Poems* (St. Paul, MN: Graywolf Press, 1998), 85.

CHAPTER 2

1. See, for example, the United Nations Human Rights Council's "Report of the Independent International Commission of Inquiry on the Syrian Arab Republic" (February 22, 2012), especially paragraphs 58–70, which include discussion of torture and other human rights abuses. The document is available at: <www.nytimes.com/interactive/2012/02/23/world/middleeast/24syria-document.html?ref=warcrimesgenocideandcrimesagainsthumanity>. See also the CBS News report (July 12, 2012), "Syria Forces Reportedly Using Rape, Sexual Torture in Fight against Opposition," which is available at: <www.cbsnews.com/8301-503543_162-57470955-503543/syria-forces-reportedly-using-rape-sexual-torture-in-fight-against-opposition>. In addition, see Lauren Wolfe's report, "Syria Has a Massive Rape Crisis" (April 3, 2013), which is available at: <www.womenundersiegeproject.org/blog/

entry/syria-has-a-massive-rape-crisis>. Wolfe directs Women under Siege, an initiative of the Women's Media Center. Documenting how rape and other forms of sexualized violence are used as weapons of war and genocide, Women under Siege has recently devoted much of its attention to atrocities in Syria. See the project's web site at: <www. womenundersiegeproject.org/>.

2. See the UN News Centre's article, "First UN Report on Children in Syria's Civil War Paints Picture of 'Unspeakable' Horrors" (February 4, 2014), which is available at: <www.un.org/apps/news/story.asp?NewsID= 47077#.U0W5umdOWUl>. See also Somini Sengupta's *New York Times* article, "U.N. Report Details Abuse of Children in Syrian War" (February 4, 2014), available at: <www.nytimes.com/2014/02/05/world/middleeast/ at-least-10000-children-killed-in-syria-un-estimates.html>. The document itself, "Report of the Secretary-General on Children and Armed Conflict in the Syrian Arabic Republic," January 27, 2014, is available at: <http:// reliefweb.int/report/syrian-arab-republic/report-secretary-general-children- and-armed-conflict-syrian-arab>. Also relevant is the September 2014 report of the International Rescue Committee, *Are We Listening? Acting on Our Commitments to Women and Girls Affected by the Syrian Conflict*, which is accessible at: <www.rescue.org/sites/default/files/resource-file/ IRC_WomenInSyria_Report_WEB.pdf>.

3. Jean Améry, *At the Mind's Limits: Contemplations by a Survivor on Auschwitz and Its Realities*, trans. Sidney Rosenfeld and Stella P. Rosenfeld (Bloomington, IN: Indiana University Press, 1980), 24.

4. The phrase "done to death" is George Steiner's. See his *Language and Silence: Essays on Language, Literature, and the Inhuman* (New York: Atheneum, 1967), 157. I am indebted to Paul C. Santilli for this reference. Santilli's reflection about the importance of encountering the dead, especially the murdered dead, has influenced mine. See especially Paul C. Santilli, "Philosophy's Obligation to the Human Being in the Aftermath of Genocide," in *Genocide and Human Rights: A Philosophical Guide*, ed. John K. Roth (New York: Palgrave Macmillan, 2005), 220–32.

5. See Part I of the Convention, Article 1.1. The text is available at: <www. hrweb.org/legal/cat.html>.

6. See *Prosecutor v. Akayesu*, Judgment (paragraphs 597 and 598), International Criminal Tribunal for Rwanda, Case No. ICTR-96-4-T (1998). The relevant document is available at: <http://www.unictr.org/sites/uni ctr.org/files/case-documents/ictr-96-4/trial-judgements/en/980902.pdf>.

7. Améry, *At the Mind's Limits*, 28.

8. Améry, *At the Mind's Limits*, 28–9.

9. In this chapter, the terms *rape* and *rape/torture* will typically be used in synonymous ways. The same holds for the terms *rape-as-policy* and *rape/ torture-as-policy*.

10. Améry, *At the Mind's Limits*, 33.
11. See *Prosecutor v. Akayesu*, Judgment (paragraphs 597 and 731), International Criminal Tribunal for Rwanda, Case No. ICTR-96-4-T (1998). For access information regarding this document, see note 6 above.
12. In addition to Kristof's many *New York Times* editorials on these topics, see Nicholas D. Kristof and Sheryl WuDunn. *Half the Sky: Turning Oppression into Opportunity for Women Worldwide* (New York: Alfred A. Knopf, 2009).
13. Nicholas D. Kristof, "The Grotesque Vocabulary in Congo," *New York Times*, February 11, 2010, A33. The article is available at: <www.nytimes. com/2010/02/11/opinion/11kristof.html>.
14. Nicholas D. Kristof, "The World Capital of Killing," *New York Times*, February 7, 2010, WK12. The article is available at: <www.nytimes.com/ 2010/02/07/opinion/07kristof.html?_r=0>. The peer-reviewed study cited by Kristof is "Mortality in the Democratic Republic of Congo: An Ongoing Crisis," which is a special report by the highly respected International Rescue Committee. The report is available at: <www.rescue.org/sites/ default/files/migrated/resources/2007/2006-7_congomortalitysurvey.pdf>.
15. These paragraphs are from "2005 World Summit Outcome," a report from the General Assembly of the United Nations (October 24, 2005). For further information see: <http://responsibilitytoprotect.org/index. php/component/content/article/35-r2pcs-topics/398-general-assembly-r2p-excerpt-from-outcome-document>.
16. The Charter of the United Nations is available at: <www.un.org/en/ documents/charter/intro.shtml>. In addition to the preamble, see Chapter I, Article 2, Paragraph 7. The qualifications pertain to the conditions enumerated in Chapter VII.
17. For further information about these developments and for current events regarding R2P, consult the website for the International Coalition for the Responsibility to Protect, which is accessible at: <www. responsibilitytoprotect.org/>.
18. See Thomas G. Weiss, "R2P after 9/11 and the World Summit," *Wisconsin International Law Journal* 24, no. 3 (2006): 741. In addition, see his book *Humanitarian Intervention: Ideas in Action*, 2nd edn. (Cambridge, UK: Polity Press, 2012).
19. The report is available at: <www.un.org/en/ga/search/view_doc.asp?sym bol=A/63/677>.
20. This text and further information about the context of the three pillars is available at: <www.un.org/en/preventgenocide/adviser/responsibility.shtml>.
21. Further information about the Security Council's action on April 16, 2014, regarding the responsibility to protect, including a link to Resolution 2015, is available at: <www.responsibilitytoprotect.org/index.php/ component/content/article/136-latest-news/5365-security-council-adopts-

resolution-on-prevention-of-genocide-reaffirms-rtop-.un-member-states-told-they-must-act-now-to-uphold-their-responsibility-to-protect-popula tions-in-north-korea->.

22. Insightful assessments of R2P include three books by Alex J. Bellamy, *Responsibility to Protect: The Global Effort to End Mass Atrocities* (Cambridge, UK: Polity Press, 2009), *Global Politics and the Responsibility to Protect: From Words to Deeds* (New York: Routledge, 2011), and *The Responsibility to Protect: A Defense* (Oxford: Oxford University Press, 2015). See, too, Luke Glanville, *Sovereignty and the Responsibility to Protect: A New History* (Chicago, IL: University of Chicago Press, 2014); Aidan Hehir, *The Responsibility to Protect: Rhetoric, Reality, and the Future of Humanitarian Intervention* (New York: Palgrave Macmillan, 2012); and Anne Orford, *International Authority and the Responsibility to Protect* (Cambridge, UK: Cambridge University Press, 2011). Also relevant are Alex J. Bellamy, "Military Intervention," in *The Oxford Handbook of Genocide Studies*, ed. Donald Bloxham and A. Dirk Moses (Oxford: Oxford University Press, 2010), 597–616; Andrew Clapham and Paola Gaeta, eds., *The Oxford Handbook of International Law in Armed Conflict* (Oxford: Oxford University Press, 2014) and "The Failure of Prevention," a special issue of *Genocide Studies International* 8, no. 1 (2014).

23. See the International Commission on Intervention and State Sovereignty, *The Responsibility to Protect: Report of the International Commission on Intervention and State Sovereignty* (Ottawa, ON: International Development Research Centre, 2001). Citations refer to the report's internal enumeration of sections and paragraphs. The report can be found at: <http://responsibilitytoprotect.org/ICISS%20Report.pdf>. See also Gareth Evans, *The Responsibility to Protect: Ending Mass Atrocity Crimes Once and For All* (Washington, DC: Brookings Institution Press, 2008).

24. An American psychologist, Boder was among the first to interview survivors of the Holocaust and other Nazi crimes after World War II. Eight of these interviews were published by the University of Illinois Press in 1949. Boder ended the introduction to his book with these words: "The verbatim records presented in this book make uneasy reading. And yet," he added, "they are not the grimmest stories that could be told—I did not interview the dead." That last thought-provoking phrase—I did not interview the dead—became his book's title. See David P. Boder, *I Did Not Interview the Dead* (Urbana, IL: University of Illinois Press, 1949), xix. For a significant study of Boder and his work, see Alan Rosen, *The Wonder of Their Voices: The 1946 Holocaust Interviews of David Boder* (Oxford: Oxford University Press, 2010). The phrase "see through the gloom" comes from Robert Pogue Harrison, *The Dominion of the Dead* (Chicago, IL: University of Chicago Press, 2003), 159.

25. Harrison, *The Dominion of the Dead*, 158.
26. The phrase "giving a voice to the dead" is Victor Brombert's. See his *Musings on Mortality: From Tolstoy to Primo Levi* (Chicago, IL: University of Chicago Press, 2013), 6. This insightful and elegant book, which has significantly influenced my thinking about the failures of ethics, is the result of Brombert's long and distinguished career as a literary scholar. While Brombert notes that "musings on mortality are not to be mistaken for meditations on death," the particular musings he discusses—those of Franz Kafka, Albert Camus, and J. M Coetzee, among others—often concentrate on mortality linked to the fragile human body and the suffering to which it is susceptible, particularly when human intentions and actions aim to desecrate and destroy it. "Confronting mortality," concludes Brombert, "paradoxically implies being alive, questioning how to live, raising moral issues" (165). His understated conclusion is fundamental, especially when confronting mortality takes place in the context of mass atrocities such as those unleashed in rape/torture as policy.
27. Identified as United Nations document A/67/792-S/2013/149, the report is available at <www.securitycouncilreport.org/atf/cf/%7B65BFCF9B-6D27-4E9C-8CD3-CF6E4FF96FF9%7D/s_2013_149.pdf>.
28. Fortunately, scholarship is beginning to make up for lost time in this area. For recent examples, see Myrna Goldenberg and Amy H. Shapiro, eds., *Different Horrors, Same Hell: Gender and the Holocaust* (Seattle, WA: University of Washington Press, 2013), Sonja M. Hedgepeth and Rochelle G. Saidel, eds., *Sexual Violence against Jewish Women during the Holocaust* (Waltham, MA: Brandeis University Press, 2010), and Carol Rittner and John K. Roth, eds., *Rape: Weapon of War and Genocide* (St. Paul, MN: Paragon House, 2012). Also relevant is Lenore J. Weitzman, "Women," in *The Oxford Handbook of Holocaust Studies*, ed. Peter Hayes and John K. Roth (Oxford: Oxford University Press, 2010), 203–17.
29. Améry, *At the Mind's Limits*, 30.
30. See Patrick Desbois, *The Holocaust by Bullets* (New York: Palgrave Macmillan, 2008). A Catholic priest, Desbois has done pioneering research that has immense ethical significance. Further information about his work is available at the website for Yahad—In Unum, the organization he heads, which is dedicated to researching the Holocaust, fighting antisemitism, and advancing Catholic-Jewish relations: <www.yahadinunum.org/index.php?option=com_content&view=article&id=9&Itemid=16&lang=en>.
31. The text of this resolution, plus discussion that led to its passage, is available at: <www.un.org/News/Press/docs/2013/sc11043.doc.htm>.

32. See, for example, suggestions made by Roselyn Costantino and Lee Ann De Reus in *Rape: Weapon of War and Genocide*, ed. Rittner and Roth, 130–1 and 152–3. Further insight is available in Nicholas D. Kristof and Sheryl WuDunn, *A Path Appears: Transforming Lives, Creating Opportunity* (New York: Alfred A. Knopf, 2014).

33. Nicholas D. Kristof, "A Policy of Rape Continues," *New York Times*, July 25, 2013, A27. The article is available at: <www.nytimes.com/2013/07/25/opinion/kristof-a-policy-of-rape-continues.html?ref=nicholasdkristof&_r=0>.

34. In 2013, the Salamat were in the middle of inter-tribal and inter-ethnic fighting, especially with their rivals, the Miseriya. Government-linked militia and paramilitary groups have compounded the plight of the Salamat.

CHAPTER 3

1. Waller's sketch, which appears on the cover of the paperback edition of John K. Roth, ed., *Genocide and Human Rights: A Philosophical Guide* (New York: Palgrave Macmillan 2005), is accessible at: <http://jacketupload.macmillanusa.com/jackets/high_res/jpgs/9781403935489.jpg>.

2. Raphael Lemkin, *Axis Rule in Occupied Europe: Laws of Occupation, Analysis of Government, Proposals for Redress* (Washington, DC: Carnegie Endowment for International Peace, 1944), 79. For further information about Lemkin, his thought, and his crucial contributions to the 1948 United Nations Convention on the Prevention and Punishment of the Crime of Genocide, see the following: John Cooper, *Raphael Lemkin and the Struggle for the Genocide Convention* (New York: Palgrave Macmillan, 2007); Steven L. Jacobs, ed., *Lemkin on Genocide* (Lanham, MD: Lexington Books, 2011); Raphael Lemkin, *Totally Unofficial: The Autobiography of Raphael Lemkin*, ed. Donna-Lee Frieze (New Haven, CT: Yale University Press, 2013); and A. Dirk Moses, "Raphael Lemkin, Culture, and the Concept of Genocide," in *The Oxford Handbook of Genocide Studies*, ed. Donald Bloxham and A. Dirk Moses (Oxford: Oxford University Press, 2010), 19–41.

3. Raphael Lemkin, "Genocide," *The American Scholar* 15, no. 2 (1946): 227–30. This article is accessible at: <www.preventgenocide.org/lemkin/americanscholar1946.htm>. See also Raphael Lemkin, "Genocide as a Crime under International Law," *American Journal of International Law* 41, no. 1 (1947): 145–51. This article is accessible at: <www.preventgenocide.org/lemkin/ASIL1947.htm>.

4. The full text of the United Nations Convention on the Prevention and Punishment of the Crime of Genocide is accessible at: <www.un.org/ga/search/view_doc.asp?symbol=a/res/260(III)>.

5. Omer Bartov, "Extreme Violence and the Scholarly Community," *International Social Science Journal* 54, no. 174 (2002): 509.
6. Insightful analyses and important elaborations related to these themes can be found in the following: Susan E. Babbitt and Sue Campbell, eds., *Racism and Philosophy* (Ithaca, NY: Cornell University Press, 1999); Manfred Berg and Simon Wendt, eds., *Racism in the Modern World: Historical Perspectives on Cultural Transfer and Adaptation* (New York: Berghahn Books, 2011); Bernard Boxill, ed., *Race and Racism* (Oxford: Oxford University Press, 2001); David Theo Goldberg, *Racist Culture: Philosophy and the Politics of Meaning* (Oxford: Blackwell, 1993); Peter K. J. Park, *Africa, Asia, and the History of Philosophy: Racism in the Formation of the Philosophical Canon, 1780–1830* (Albany, NY: State University of New York Press, 2013); Roth, ed., *Genocide and Human Rights*; Martin Shuster, "Philosophy and Genocide," in *The Oxford Handbook of Genocide Studies*, 217–35; David Livingston Smith, *Less Than Human: Why We Demean, Enslave, and Exterminate Others* (New York: St. Martin's Press, 2011); and Andrew Valls, ed., *Race and Racism in Modern Philosophy* (Ithaca, NY: Cornell University Press, 2005). In various ways, these sources show that philosophy and philosophers have often contributed to what Robert Bernasconi calls "the formation of a culture of genocide that has by no means been eradicated and that we need to understand better if we are to combat it successfully." See Robert Bernasconi, "Why Do the Happy Inhabitants of Tahiti Bother to Exist at All?" in *Genocide and Human Rights*, 140.
7. For more on this topic, see Richard L. Rubenstein and John K. Roth, *Approaches to Auschwitz: The Holocaust and Its Legacy*, rev. edn. (Louisville, KY: Westminster John Knox Press, 2003).
8. Several of the following paragraphs, including my discussion of Heidegger, are adapted from my contributions to Dinah L. Shelton, ed., *The Encyclopedia of Genocide and Crimes against Humanity* (Detroit, MI: Macmillan Reference, 2004).
9. In books and articles, numerous philosophers have taken Heidegger to task. One of the best accounts is provided by Hans Sluga, *Heidegger's Crisis: Philosophy and Politics in Nazi Germany* (Cambridge, MA: Harvard University Press, 1993), which places Heidegger in the context of German philosophy during the Third Reich and argues that Heidegger was the most prominent example of a large number of German philosophers who were willing and eager to cooperate with the Nazi regime. More recent studies critical of Heidegger include: Emmanuel Faye, *Heidegger: The Introduction of Nazism into Philosophy in Light of the Unpublished Seminars of 1933–1935* (New Haven, CT: Yale University Press, 2009) and Yvonne Sheratt, *Hitler's Philosophers* (New Haven, CT: Yale University Press, 2013). Further developments unfavorable to Heidegger involve the

appearance of previously unpublished notebooks. See Jennifer Schleusser, "Heidegger's Notebooks Renew Focus on Anti-Semitism," *New York Times*, March 31, 2014, C1, and Peter E. Gordon, "Heidegger in Black," *New York Review of Books*, October 9, 2014. Schleusser's article is accessible at: <www.nytimes.com/2014/03/31/books/heideggers-note books-renew-focus-on-anti-semitism.html>. Gordon's essay is accessible at: <www.nybooks.com/articles/archives/2014/oct/09/heidegger-in-black/?insrc=hpma>.

10. Bartov, "Extreme Violence and the Scholarly Community," 511.
11. Primo Levi, *Survival in Auschwitz: The Nazi Assault on Humanity*, trans. Stuart Woolf (New York: Simon & Schuster, 1996), 90.
12. Giorgio Agamben, *Remnants of Auschwitz: The Witness and the Archive*, trans. Daniel Heller-Roazen (New York: Zone Books, 1999), 55.
13. Agamben, *Remnants of Auschwitz*, 63, 69.
14. Agamben, *Remnants of Auschwitz*, 14.
15. Levinas explores and develops this theme in many of his books, essays, and interviews. Among the most accessible is *Ethics and Infinity: Conversations with Philippe Nemo*, trans. Richard A. Cohen (Pittsburgh, PA: Duquesne University Press, 1985).
16. In addition to Rawls's *A Theory of Justice* (Cambridge, MA: Harvard University Press, 1971), see his *Justice as Fairness: A Restatement*, ed. Erin Kelly (Cambridge, MA: Harvard University Press, 2001) and *The Law of Peoples* (Cambridge, MA: Harvard University Press, 1999).
17. For compact and reliable accounts of the history and meanings of racism, see George M. Fredrickson, *Racism: A Short History* (Princeton, NJ: Princeton University Press, 2002) and Ali Rattansi, *Racism: A Very Short Introduction* (Oxford: Oxford University Press, 2007). In this chapter, I use the term "*logic*" primarily to signify a conceptual web or configuration, not a series of deductions from principles or a set of inferences from empirical data. The "logic" of racism—and the "logic" of genocide too—may include elements of both kinds, but as used here "*logic*" connotes a pattern of thinking and planning, a mapping of relationships among ideas and policies that associate congenially with each other. Entailments and implications exist in these patterns and relationships. One idea, one policy, does lead to another, but the relationships are more organic and dialectical than linear and one-directional. My use of scare quotes around the term "*logic*" is not intended to minimize the power or authority that these patterns of thought can have. They both can be immense. But I use the scare quotes to make clear that the "logic" of racism and genocide is less than fully rational, disguised as rational though it may be.

With regard to my claim that the term *race* has done far more harm than good, I find significant support in the instructive series of articles on race that appeared in *Daedalus* 134, no. 1 (2005): 5–116. Especially pertinent are the contributions by Kenneth Prewitt, Jennifer L. Hochschild, George M. Fredrickson, and the philosopher Ian Hacking. Harmful though the very concept of race has been, one cannot—as this chapter shows—be rid of it altogether, because the idea has to be invoked to deconstruct and subvert it and to protest the harm it has done. Hacking's essay "Why Race Still Matters" (102–16) is particularly important. Noting research that seems to link certain diseases and some medical treatments with racially identifiable populations, Hacking warns that such statistical correlations, helpful though they may prove to be, are neither equivalent to, nor sufficient for, claims that "races are real kinds, denoting essentially different kinds of people." Nevertheless, he adds, the recent scientific and medical findings may provide opportunities in which "racists will try to exploit the racial difference" (109). Thus, race still matters because the concept must continue to be very carefully watched and examined as inquiry proceeds.

18. On these points, see, for example, Götz Aly, *Why the Germans? Why the Jews: Envy Race Hatred, and the Prehistory of the Holocaust*, trans. Jefferson Chase (New York: Metropolitan Books, 2014); Eric Ehrenreich, *The Nazi Ancestral Proof: Genealogy, Racial Science, and the Final Solution* (Bloomington, IN: Indiana University Press, 2007); and Alan E. Steinweis, *Studying the Jew: Scholarly Antisemitism in Nazi Germany* (Cambridge, MA: Harvard University Press, 2006).

19. Danilo Kiš, *Garden, Ashes*, trans. William J. Hannaker (Chicago, IL: Dalkey Archive Press, 2003), 34, 37, 39. The discussion of *Garden, Ashes* draws on my contributions to David Patterson and John K. Roth, eds., *Fire in the Ashes: God, Evil, and the Holocaust* (Seattle, WA: University of Washington Press, 2005).

20. Kiš, *Garden, Ashes*, 169.

21. Excerpts from Himmler's speech are reprinted in Paul Mendes-Flohr and Yehuda Reinharz, eds., *The Jew in the Modern World: A Documentary History*, 2nd edn. (New York: Oxford University Press, 1995), 684–5.

22. Linda Melvern, "Identifying Genocide," in *Will Genocide Ever End?*, ed. Carol Rittner, John K. Roth, and James M. Smith (St. Paul, MN: Paragon House, 2002), 101.

23. Further information on the UN's commemoration of the twentieth anniversary, including the link to a video of Colin Keating's full remarks on the occasion, is available at: <www.un.org/apps/news/story.asp?NewsID=47596#.U1L3UWdOWUl>.

24. For the quotations that follow, see Kiš, *Garden, Ashes*, 168–70.

CHAPTER 4

1. Albert Camus, *The Rebel: An Essay on Man in Revolt*, trans. Anthony Bower (New York: Vintage Books, 1956), 4–5.

2. See Samuel Bak, "Facing My Own History and My Story with *Facing History and Ourselves*," in *Illuminations: The Art of Samuel Bak* (Brookline, MA: Facing History and Ourselves, 2010), 2–4.

3. To view the Bak painting online and for Lawrence L. Langer's commentary about it, two links from Facing History and Ourselves are helpful. The painting is accessible at: <www.facinghistory.org/chunk/478?back link=for-educators/educator-resources/resource-collections/illuminations/ samuel-bak-paintings>. Langer's commentary can be found at: <www. facinghistory.org/For-Educators/Educator-Resources/Resource-Collec tions/Illuminations/Introduction-Professor-Lawrence-L-Langer>.

4. Different traditions number the Ten Commandments differently. Jews and many Protestant Christians, for example, take "You shall not murder" to be the Sixth Commandment. For Catholics and Lutherans, that injunction is the Fifth Commandment.

5. The paragraphs that follow in this section are adapted from my chapter, "What Have You Done?" in *The Ten Commandments for Jews, Christians, and Others*, ed. Roger E. Van Harn (Grand Rapids, MI: William B. Eerdmans Publishing Company, 2007).

6. Philip Paul Hallie, "Cruelty: The Empirical Evil," in *Facing Evil: Light at the Core of Darkness*, ed. Paul Woodruff and Harry A. Wilmer (LaSalle, IL: Open Court, 1988), 128.

7. Thomas Hobbes, *Leviathan* (Indianapolis, IN: Bobbs-Merrill, 1958), 106–7. To a considerable degree, human existence is perpetually in the state of war that Hobbes identified. The reason has much to do with humankind's repeated and escalating violations of the Sixth Commandment.

8. Stephen T. Davis, "Genocide, Despair, and Religious Hope: An Essay on Human Nature," in *Genocide and Human Rights: A Philosophical Guide*, ed. John K. Roth (New York: Palgrave Macmillan, 2005), 38.

9. Richard Rhodes, *Masters of Death: The SS-Einsatzgruppen and the Invention of the Holocaust* (New York: Alfred A. Knopf, 2002), 121.

10. Rhodes, *Masters of Death*, 140.

11. On this point, see Claudia Koonz, *The Nazi Conscience* (Cambridge, MA: Harvard University Press, 2003).

12. R. J. Rummel, *Death by Government* (New Brunswick, NJ: Transaction Publishers, 1997), 13, 31. Observations about Rummel's data by the Holocaust historian Yehuda Bauer are worth noting: "Rummel has been criticized for exaggerating the losses. Even if the criticisms were valid, a figure lower by 10 or 20 or even 30 percent would make

absolutely no difference to the general conclusions that Rummel draws." See Yehuda Bauer, *Rethinking the Holocaust* (New Haven, CT: Yale University Press, 2001), 12–13, 277, n.17.

13. Rummel, *Death by Government*, 13, 31.

14. Rummel, *Death by Government*, 28.

15. Elie Wiesel, *Legends of Our Time* (New York: Holt, Rinehart and Winston, 1968), 190.

16. See Alon Confino, *A World without Jews: The Nazi Imagination from Persecution to Genocide* (New Haven, CN: Yale University Press, 2014), 115–22.

17. The episode and quotations are found in Confino, *A World without Jews*, 134–5.

18. See Confino, *A World without Jews*, 130–3. See also Susannah Heschel, *The Aryan Jesus: Christian Theologians and the Bible in Nazi Germany* (Princeton, NJ: Princeton University Press, 2008), esp. 9–10, which is Confino's source for the quotation from Leffler. Also significant in this context is David Patterson, *Anti-Semitism and Its Metaphysical Origins* (Cambridge, UK: Cambridge University Press, 2015).

19. For further information about this trialogue and some of its results, see Leonard Grob and John K. Roth, eds., *Encountering the Stranger: A Jewish-Christian-Muslim Trialogue* (Seattle, WA: University of Washington Press, 2012). Also relevant are the articles in the *Journal of Inter-Religious Studies* (June 2014). Edited by Victoria Barnett, director of programs on ethics, religion, and the Holocaust at USHMM, this issue concentrates on "The Holocaust and Its Implications for Contemporary Interreligious Studies." Contributors to the issue include participants in the 2007 trialogue. The journal issue is available at: <http://irdialogue.org/2014/06/>. For insightful discussion about the significance of the Torah ark at USHMM, which helped to inform my reflections, see Henry F. Knight, "Before Whom Do We Stand?" *Shofar* 28, no. 3 (2010): 116–34. One of the contributors to *Encountering the Stranger*, Knight particularly called attention to the Torah ark at USHMM when our trialogue took place there.

20. David Flusser, "The Decalogue in the New Testament," in *The Ten Commandments in History and Tradition*, ed. Ben-Zion Segal and Gershon Levi (Jerusalem: Magnes Press, Hebrew University of Jerusalem, 1990), 221.

21. The quotations from the Qur'an are from N. J. Dawood's translation, *The Koran: With Parallel Arabic Text* (New York: Penguin Books, 1990).

22. See Michael Gerson, "Iran's Incitement to Genocide," which appeared in the *Washington Post* on April 4, 2013 and is accessible at: <www.washingtonpost.com/opinions/michael-gerson-irans-hate-speech-is-an-incitement-to-genocide/2013/04/04/2686e7a8-9ca1-11e2-9a79-

eb5280c81c63_story.html>. This article provides links to document the uses of language that Gerson identifies as incitements to genocide. Under the United Nations 1948 Convention on the Prevention and Punishment of the Crime of Genocide, "direct and public incitement to commit genocide" is a punishable act. Also pertinent in this context is Alvin H. Rosenfeld, ed., *Resurgent Antisemitism: Global Perspectives* (Bloomington, IN: Indiana University Press, 2013). This 500-page volume documents multiple sources and ways in which anti-Jewish and anti-Israeli hostility remains relentless and virulent in the twenty-first century.

23. For helpful essays on these matters, see Steven Leonard Jacobs, ed., *Confronting Genocide: Judaism, Christianity, Islam* (Lanham, MD: Lexington Books, 2009). Also relevant are Alan L. Berger, ed., *Trialogue and Terror: Judaism, Christianity, and Islam after 9/11* (Eugene, OR: Cascade Books, 2012), David Patterson, *Genocide in Jewish Thought* (Cambridge, UK: Cambridge University Press, 2012), and Richard L. Rubenstein, *Jihad and Genocide* (Lanham, MD: Rowman & Littlefield, 2010).

24. See the catalog for the exhibition at the Pucker Gallery in Boston, which is accessible at: <www.puckergallery.com/pdf/Bak_HOPE_Catalogue_2014_FINAL.pdf>. The quotations are from 3–4. The painting called "Helping Hands," referenced below, is on 37.

25. If there is life beyond death, God's judgment may provide sanctions that condemn murder beyond all doubt and without remainder. Unfortunately, that result comes too late to be effective in history, for neither the murdered nor their murderers have returned to tell what God may have done with them. Nor has God made that situation crystal clear. Meanwhile, within history, murder is sometimes punished but not with sufficiently credible deterring impact. History's mounds of murdered dead grow larger and larger.

26. For helpful insight related to this point, see Alex J. Bellamy, *Massacres and Morality: Mass Atrocities in an Age of Civilian Immunity* (Oxford: Oxford University Press, 2012).

27. For more detail on Tommy Sands, see his autobiography, *The Songman: A Journey in Irish Music* (Dublin: Lilliput Press, 2005). See 252–7 for Sands's commentary on the lyric quoted here.

28. See Sands, *The Songman*, 256.

29. Although Sands indicates that he did not record "Let the Circle Be Wide" until 2009, he notes that he has sung this "song of welcome" repeatedly and around the world. See the comments by Sands that accompany his album *Let the Circle Be Wide* (West Chester, PA: Appleseed Recordings, 2009).

30. The quotation is from Sands's "Let the Circle Be Wide."

CHAPTER 5

1. Cited by Albert Camus in *The Rebel: An Essay on Man in Revolt*, trans. Anthony Bower (New York: Vintage Books, 1956), 67.
2. Arguably, no Holocaust-related book has had more widespread influence than *Night*, but controversy has swirled around the differences between the Yiddish, French, and English versions of that memoir. At the controversy's epicenter is Naomi Seidman, "Elie Wiesel and the Scandal of Jewish Rage," *Jewish Social Studies* 3, no. 1 (1996), 1–19. Seidman argued that the Yiddish and French versions are substantially different accounts and that Wiesel toned down the anger in the former to make the latter more palatable to non-Jewish readers. In addition, see Naomi Seidman, *Faithful Renderings: Jewish–Christian Difference and the Politics of Translation* (Chicago, IL: University of Chicago Press, 2006), especially 199–242. In his preface to the 2006 English edition of *Night*, translated by Marion Wiesel from the French, Wiesel discusses some of the differences among the versions of *Night*. See Elie Wiesel, *Night*, trans. Marion Wiesel (New York: Hill and Wang, 2006), vii–xv. On these topics, see also Harold Bloom, ed., *Elie Wiesel's "Night,"* new edn. (New York: Infobase Publishing, 2010); Steven T. Katz and Alan Rosen, eds., *Elie Wiesel: Jewish, Literary, and Moral Perspectives* (Bloomington, IN: Indiana University Press, 2013); Peter Manseau, "Revising *Night*: Elie Wiesel and the Hazards of Holocaust Theology," *Crosscurrents* 56, no. 3 (2006), 387–99; Alan Rosen, ed., *Approaches to Teaching Wiesel's "Night"* (New York: Modern Language Association of America, 2007); Edward Wyatt, "The Translation of Wiesel's 'Night' Is New, but Old Questions Are Raised," *New York Times*, January 19, 2006, and accessible at: <www.nytimes.com/2006/01/19/books/19nigh.html>.
3. Wiesel, *Night*, 67.
4. Wiesel, *Night*, 67. An earlier translation of *Night* nuances this quotation by referring to "the meaning beneath the words." See Elie Wiesel, *Night*, trans. Stella Rodway (New York: Bantam Books, 1982), 64.
5. Sarah Kofman, *Smothered Words*, trans. Madeleine Dobie (Evanston, IL: Northwestern University Press, 1998), 39.
6. Kofman, *Smothered Words*, 38–9.
7. Important reflections on, and examples of, liturgical responses to the Holocaust can be found in Marcia Sachs Littell and Sharon Weissman Gutman, eds., *Liturgies of the Holocaust: An Interfaith Anthology*, new and revised edn. (Valley Forge, PA: Trinity Press International, 1996). The examples of Holocaust liturgies in this volume come from civic and religious settings. They include texts, ritual acts, and music from the time of the Holocaust itself and from the early postwar years, but the editors

also make the following observation: "In the early 1970s, Yom HaShoah was observed by only a few dozen congregations in America. During the administration of President Jimmy Carter, observance of the Days of Remembrance grew rapidly and marked a permanent day on the calendar. Every American president since that time has supported this endeavor" (1).

8. See, for example, Dan Cohn-Sherbok, ed., *Holocaust Theology: A Reader* (New York: New York University Press, 2002) and Steven T. Katz, Shlomo Biderman, and Gershon Greenberg, eds., *Wrestling with God: Jewish Theological Responses during and after the Holocaust* (Oxford: Oxford University Press, 2007).

9. Emil Fackenheim, "The Holocaust and Philosophy," *The Journal of Philosophy* 82, no. 10 (1985): 505.

10. See, for example, Albert Camus, *The Plague*, trans. Stuart Gilbert (New York: Modern Library, 1948); Karl Jaspers, *The Question of German Guilt*, trans E. B. Ashton (New York: Dial Press, 1948); Hannah Arendt, *The Origins of Totalitarianism* (New York: Harcourt, 1951) and *Eichmann in Jerusalem: A Report on the Banality of Evil* (New York: Viking Press, 1963); Abraham Joshua Heschel, *Man Is Not Alone: A Philosophy of Religion* (New York: Farrar, Straus & Young, 1951); Martin Buber, *Eclipse of God: Studies in the Relation between Religion and Philosophy* (New York: Harper, 1952) and *On Judaism* (New York: Schocken Books, 1967); Theodor Adorno, *Prisms* trans. Samuel and Shierry Weber (London: Neville Spearman, 1967) and *Negative Dialectics*, trans. E. B. Ashton (New York: Seabury Press, 1973); Emmanuel Levinas, *Totality and Infinity: An Essay on Exteriority*, trans. Alphonso Lingis (Pittsburgh, PA: Duquesne University Press, 1969); Emil Fackenheim, *God's Presence in History: Jewish Affirmations and Philosophical Reflections* (New York: New York University Press, 1970); and Jean Améry, *At the Mind's Limits: Contemplations by a Survivor on Auschwitz and Its Realities*, trans. Sidney Rosenfeld and Stella P. Rosenfeld (Bloomington, IN: Indiana University Press, 1980).

11. See Katz, Biderman, and Greenberg, eds., *Wrestling with God*, 11.

12. Cited in Hasia R. Diner, *We Remember with Reverence and Love: American Jews and the Myth of Silence after the Holocaust, 1945–1962* (New York: New York University Press, 2009), 327. For ongoing reflections related to these themes, see Menachem Z. Rosensaft, ed., *God, Faith & Identity from the Ashes: Reflections of Children and Grandchildren of Holocaust Survivors* (Woodstock, VT: Jewish Lights Publishing, 2015).

13. Lawrence Baron helpfully discusses some of these early developments in "The Holocaust and American Public Memory, 1945–1960," *Holocaust and Genocide Studies* 17, no. 1 (2003): 62–88.

14. Rubenstein's essay "The Dean and the Chosen People" depicts these events. See Richard L. Rubenstein, *After Auschwitz: History, Theology, and Contemporary Judaism*, 2nd edn. (Baltimore, MD: Johns Hopkins University Press, 1992), 3–13. See also Richard L. Rubenstein, *Power Struggle* (New York: Scribner, 1974).

15. See Stephen R. Haynes and John K. Roth, eds., *The Death of God Movement and the Holocaust: Radical Theology Encounters the Shoah* (Westport, CT: Greenwood Press, 1999). Also relevant is Daniel J. Peterson and G. Michael Zbaraschuk, eds., *Resurrecting the Death of God: The Origins, Influence, and Return of Radical Theology* (Albany, NY: State University of New York Press, 2014).

16. My discussion of Fackenheim is adapted from Richard L. Rubenstein and John K. Roth, *Approaches to Auschwitz: The Holocaust and Its Legacy*, rev. edn. (Louisville, KY: Westminster John Knox Press, 2003), 348–52.

17. See Emil Fackenheim, *God's Presence in History: Jewish Affirmations and Philosophical Reflections* (Northvale, NJ: Jason Aronson, 1997), 8–14 and *To Mend the World: Foundations of Future Jewish Thought* (New York: Schocken Books, 1982), 9–22.

18. This passage originally appeared in *Judaism* 16, no. 3 (1967), 272–3. The text of Fackenheim's contribution to that journal's symposium on "Jewish Values in the Post-Holocaust Future" is reprinted in Emil L. Fackenheim, *The Jewish Return into History: Reflections in the Age of Auschwitz and a New Jerusalem* (New York: Schocken Books, 1978), 19–24. See also Fackenheim, *God's Presence in History*, 84–98. In the 1997 edition of the latter work, Fackenheim includes a new preface, "No Posthumous Victories for Hitler: After Thirty Years, the '614th Commandment' Reconsidered." Noting that the phrase " 'no posthumous victories for Hitler' became a slogan, often poorly understood, and as such liked by some, disliked by others, mocked by a few," Fackenheim added that "what 'no posthumous victories for Hitler' asked of Jews was, of course, not to spite Hitler, but to carry on *in spite of* him" (xii, Fackenheim's italics).

19. One of the most noteworthy competitors for that distinction would be Irving Greenberg's "working principle," namely, that "no statement, theological or otherwise, should be made that would not be credible in the presence of the burning children." See Greenberg, "Cloud of Smoke, Pillar of Fire: Judaism, Christianity, and Modernity after the Holocaust," in *Auschwitz: Beginning of a New Era? Reflections on the Holocaust*, ed. Eva Fleischner (New York: Ktav, 1977), 23.

20. Fackenheim, *The Jewish Return into History*, 31. Italics added.

21. Fackenheim, *To Mend the World*, 10.

22. For further commentary on Fackenheim's thought, see David Patterson, *Emil L. Fackenheim: A Jewish Philosopher's Response to the Holocaust* (Syracuse, NY: Syracuse University Press, 2008).

23. Prominent among them would be: Robert McAfee Brown, Harry James Cargas, A. Roy and Alice Eckardt, Darrell Fasching, Eva Fleischner, David Gushee, Stephen Haynes, Henry Knight, Elisabeth Maxwell, Johann Baptist Metz, John T. Pawlikowski, Didier Pollefeyt, Carol Rittner, Martin Rumscheidt, Dorothee Soelle, Paul M. van Buren, and Clark Williamson.

24. Bauer's interview with Littell is available online at: <www1.yadvashem. org/odot_pdf/Microsoft%20Word%20-%203725.pdf>.

25. Franklin H. Littell, *The Crucifixion of the Jews* (New York: Harper and Row, 1975), 3.

26. For evidence of Levinas's engagement with Judaism and Jewish tradition, see Emmanuel Levinas, *Difficult Freedom: Essays on Judaism*, trans. Sean Hand (Baltimore, MD: Johns Hopkins University Press, 1990); *Nine Talmudic Readings*, trans. Annette Aronowicz (Bloomington, IN: Indiana University Press, 1990); and *New Talmudic Readings*, trans. Richard Cohen (Pittsburgh, PA: Duquesne University Press, 1999).

27. See Emmanuel Levinas, *Ethics and Infinity*, trans. Richard A. Cohen (Pittsburgh, PA: Duquesne University Press, 1985) and *Entre Nous: On Thinking-of-the-Other*, trans. Michael B. Smith and Barbara Harshav (New York: Columbia University Press, 1998).

28. Emmanuel Levinas, "Useless Suffering," in Entre Nous, 91–101. The quoted passage is on 97.

29. The quotations in this paragraph are from Levinas, "Useless Suffering," 93, 94, and 99.

30. The quotations in this paragraph are from Levinas, "Useless Suffering," 92–4.

31. The quotations in this paragraph are from Levinas, "Useless Suffering," 96–7 and 99–100.

32. Elie Wiesel, "Exile and the Human Condition," in *Against Silence: The Voice and Vision of Elie Wiesel*, ed. Irving Abrahamson (New York: Holocaust Library, 1985), 1:183.

33. Elie Wiesel, "Auschwitz—Another Planet," in *Against Silence*, 2:293.

34. Camus, *The Rebel*, 303.

PART II

1. Henry C. Theriault, "Rethinking Dehumanization in Genocide," in *The Armenian Genocide: Cultural and Ethical Legacies*, ed. Richard Hovannisian (New Brunswick, NJ: Transaction Publishers, 2007), 27.

2. Theriault, "Rethinking Dehumanization in Genocide," 31.

3. George Orwell, *1984* (New York: New American Library, 1983), 220.

CHAPTER 6

1. John K. Roth, "Tears and Elie Wiesel," *Princeton Seminary Bulletin* 65, no. 2 (1972): 42.
2. Elie Wiesel, *A Jew Today*, trans. Marion Wiesel (New York: Random House, 1978), 144.
3. In my early reading of Wiesel's writings, I was particularly taken by his treatment of classical figures from the Hebrew Bible, by the Hasidic masters he introduced to me, and always by the religious questions and spiritual questioning that permeated his fiction. These ingredients kept drawing me deeper and deeper into Wiesel's ways of thinking, which I learned were immersed and anchored in his understanding of Judaism and in his Jewish identity.
4. Wiesel, *A Jew Today*, 3.
5. Wiesel, *A Jew Today*, 4.
6. Wiesel, *A Jew Today*, 4.
7. Wiesel, *A Jew Today*, 11–12.
8. Wiesel, *A Jew Today*, 11.
9. See Elie Wiesel, *All Rivers Run to the Sea: Memoirs* (New York: Alfred A. Knopf, 1995), 23.
10. Wiesel, *All Rivers Run to the Sea*, 68–70. Wiesel mentions Maria briefly in *Night*. See Elie Wiesel, *Night*, trans. Marion Wiesel (New York: Hill & Wang, 2006), 20.
11. Elie Wiesel, *The Fifth Son*, trans. Marion Wiesel (New York: Summit Books, 1985), 184.
12. See Wiesel, *Night*, 14.
13. Books in which Wiesel focuses explicitly on biblical figures include *Five Biblical Portraits* (Notre Dame, IN: University of Notre Dame Press, 1981); *Messengers of God: Biblical Portraits and Legends*, trans. Marion Wiesel (New York: Random House, 1973); *Sages and Dreamers: Biblical, Talmudic, and Hasidic Portraits and Legends* (New York: Summit Books, 1991); and *Wise Men and Their Tales: Portraits of Biblical, Talmudic, and Hasidic Masters* (New York: Schocken Books, 2003).
14. The discussion that follows is adapted from portions of my book, *A Consuming Fire: Encounters with Elie Wiesel and the Holocaust* (Atlanta, GA: John Knox Press, 1979).
15. See Harry James Cargas, *Harry James Cargas in Conversation with Elie Wiesel* (New York: Paulist Press, 1976), 80.
16. Wiesel, *Messengers of God*, 235.
17. Wiesel, *Messengers of God*, 181.
18. Wiesel, *Messengers of God*, 200.
19. Wiesel, *Messengers of God*, 229–30.

20. This passage is from the Jerusalem Bible. See also Wiesel, *Messengers of God*, 231–2.
21. Wiesel, *Messengers of God*, 235.
22. Wiesel, *A Jew Today*, 144–5.
23. For this reminder I am indebted to the historian Victoria Barnett, the staff director for the Committee on Ethics, Religion, and the Holocaust at the United States Holocaust Memorial Museum. Her helpful reading of an earlier version of this chapter led to an email exchange in which she correctly noted that in the United States, "there have been Christian-Jewish partnerships and conversations, including self-critical theological ones, since the 1890s at least." Barnett sees two tracks of Christian-Jewish dialogue in the United States. One emerges directly out of Holocaust studies, but another, of longer standing, continues without the Holocaust at its base. By now, of course, many initiatives in the second track, Barnett acknowledges, "do incorporate Holocaust commemoration."
24. For amplification of these themes, see John K. Roth, *Holocaust Politics* (Louisville, KY: Westminster John Knox Press, 2001), especially 188–96. See also Alan L. Berger, ed., *Post-Holocaust Jewish–Christian Dialogue: After the Flood, before the Rainbow* (Lanham, MD: Lexington Books, 2015).
25. Jorge Mario Bergoglio and Abraham Skorka, *On Heaven and Earth: Pope Francis on Faith, Family, and the Church in the Twenty-first Century*, trans. Alejandro Bermudez and Howard Goodman (New York: Image, 2013), 183.
26. Pope Paul VI, the first pontiff to visit Israel, met a necessary condition for Roman Catholic sainthood with his beatification in October 2014. The relevant text from *Nostra Aetate* can be found at: <www.sacredheart.edu/faithservice/centerforchristianandjewishunderstanding/documentsandstatements/nostraaetateoctober281965vaticaniidocument/>.
27. See Jules Isaac, *The Teaching of Contempt: Christian Roots of Anti-Semitism*, trans. Helen Weaver (New York: Holt Rinehart and Winston, 1964). Isaac's conversations with Pope John XXIII in June 1960 advanced deliberations and reforms reflected in the actions of the Second Vatican Council and *Nostra Aetate*. On the important parts played by US Catholic leaders in support of *Nostra Aetate*, see James A. Rudin, *Cushing, Spellman, O'Conner: The Surprising Story of How Three American Cardinals Transformed Catholic-Jewish Relations* (Grand Rapids, MI: William B. Eerdmans, 2012).
28. As John T. Pawlikowski points out, *Nostra Aetate* entailed that the Jewish people "cannot be seen as exiled from their original covenant with God." It did not resolve, however, two issues that remain contentious: (1) Can Christians affirm both the universal significance of Jesus as the incarnation of God and the continuing validity of the Jewish

covenant with God? (2) Should Christians try to convert Jews? See Pawlikowski's "Fifty Years of Christian-Jewish Dialogue—What Has It Changed?" *Journal of Ecumenical Studies* 49, no. 1 (2014): 99, 102, 105. This article provides a compact and reliable overview of several key moments and developments in Christian-Jewish relations.

29. Sources as diverse as Fox News, the *New York Times*, and the Catholic News Service stressed this point in their early March 2011 stories about the release of Benedict's book. For more information, see the *New York Times* (March 3, 2011), p. A5 and the following websites: <www.foxnews. com/world/2011/03/02/pope-exonerates-jews-jesus-death-new-book/> and <www.catholicnews.com/data/stories/cns/1100846.htm>.

30. Steinberg's statements can be found at the Fox News site identified in note 29.

31. Foxman's statement can be found at: <www.adl.org/press-center/press-releases/interfaith/adl-says-pope-benedicts-exoneration-of-jews-historical. html>.

32. Bergoglio and Skorka, *On Heaven and Earth*, 19.

33. This document is available at: <http://pcinterreligious.org/uploads/pdfs/ DIALOGUE_IN_TRUTH_AND_CHARITY_website-1.pdf>. Page numbers for quotations from it appear in parentheses in the discussion that follows.

34. Earlier in 2009, Pope Benedict XVI found himself embroiled in another controversy that affected Christian-Jewish relations when he lifted the excommunication of four bishops from the ultra-conservative Society of St. Pius X. Apparently, that action's purpose was to open paths for reconciliation that would heal schism, a dreaded reality in Roman Catholicism. A global firestorm ensued when it became clear that one of the rehabilitated bishops, Richard Williamson, has been a Holocaust denier. The Vatican's damage control kept the crisis from spiraling out of control, but Benedict XVI's misstep did nothing to improve Christian-Jewish relations. For insightful commentary by Christians and Jews— many of them Americans—on the Williamson affair, see Carol Rittner and Stephen D. Smith, eds., *No Going Back: Letters to Pope Benedict XVI on the Holocaust, Jewish-Christian Relations & Israel* (London: Quill Press, 2009).

35. The full text of this interview is available at: <www.catholicnewsagency. com/news/pope-francis-interview-with-la-vanguardia---full-text-45430/>. Pope Francis reiterated views of this kind in his interview with Henrique Cymerman on November 28, 2014. The interview is available at: <www. ynetnews.com/articles/0,7340,L-4597267,00.html>.

36. On these points, two books by Michael Phayer are significant. See *The Catholic Church and the Holocaust, 1930–1965* (Bloomington, IN: Indiana University Press, 2000) and *Pius XII, the Holocaust, and the Cold*

War (Bloomington, IN: Indiana University Press, 2008). See also Carol Rittner and John K. Roth, eds., *Pope Pius XII and the Holocaust* (New York: Continuum, 2002) and Paul O'Shea, *A Cross Too Heavy: Pope Pius XII and the Jews of Europe* (New York: Palgrave Macmillan, 2011). The State of Israel came into existence in 1948, during the reign of Pius XII, but the Vatican did not officially recognize the State of Israel until 1993. The posture of Pius XII contributed to that delay. Significantly, during Pope Francis's visit to Israel in the spring of 2014, he laid a wreath at the grave of Theodor Herzl, the father of modern Zionism. That act was widely seen as a decisive repudiation of the position taken by Pope Pius X when he granted Herzl an audience on January 26, 1904. Herzl's diary account of the meeting, which lasted about twenty-five minutes, documented that the pope rebuffed Herzl's effort to obtain papal support for a Jewish state in Palestine: "The Jews have not recognized our Lord," Herzl quoted the pope, "therefore we cannot recognize the Jewish people." Herzl's diary entry about this meeting is available at: <www.ccjr.us/dialogika-resources/primary-texts-from-the-history-of-the-relationship/1253-herzl1904>.

37. For Christian-Jewish dialogue on these matters, see Leonard Grob and John K. Roth, eds., *Anguished Hope: Holocaust Scholars Confront the Palestinian-Israeli Conflict* (Grand Rapids, MI: William B. Eerdmans, 2008).

38. Dated May 9, 2014, Rosner's sobering article, "Kerry's Mideast 'Failure' Was a Success," appeared in the *New York Times* and is available at: <www.nytimes.com/2014/05/10/opinion/rosner-kerrys-mideast-failure-was-a-success.html?action=click&module=Search&region=searchResults&mabReward=relbias%3Ar&url=http%3A%2F%2Fquery.nytimes.com%2Fsearch%2Fsitesearch%2F%3Faction%3Dclick%26region%3DMasthead%26pgtype%3DHomepage%26module%3DSearchSubmit%26contentCollection%3DHomepage%26t%3Dqry321%23%2FShmuel+Rosner>.

39. As Melanie Phillips argues, however, evangelical Christians, especially younger ones, are not immune to supersessionism and demonization of the State of Israel. She maintains that, particularly through their involvement in the "Christ at the Checkpoint" conferences run by the Bethlehem Bible College and Holy Land Trust, significant numbers of younger evangelical Christians have accepted an outlook that stresses Palestinian victimology, sees the State of Israel as a brutal oppressor, and jeopardizes solidarity between Christians and Jews. Those perspectives open the door for a resurgence of Christian supersessionism or replacement theology, outlooks that have done immense harm to Jews and to the integrity of Christianity as well. See her article, "'Jesus Was a Palestinian': The Return of Christian Anti-Semitism," in *Commentary*, June 1, 2014, which is available at: <www.commentarymagazine.com/article/jesus-was-

a-palestinian-the-return-of-christian-anti-semitism>. In this highly critical account, Phillips musters evidence to show that especially "within the Protestant world," many churches and denominations are "deeply hostile to the State of Israel."

40. For further information about my position on these matters, see John K. Roth, "Duped by Morality? Defusing Minefields in the Israeli–Palestinian Struggle," in *Anguished Hope*, ed. Grob and Roth, 30–49.
41. The full text of the open letter is accessible at: <www.pcusa.org/news/2014/6/26/open-letter-pcusa-us-our-american-jewish-partners/>.
42. Gary M. Bretton-Granatoor, "The Presbyterians' Judaism Problem," *Jewish Telegraphic Agency*, June 27, 2014. The full text of the article is accessible at: <www.jta.org/2014/06/27/news-opinion/opinion/op-ed-the-presbyterians-judaism-problem-1?utm_source=Newsletter+subscribers&utm_campaign=ddaff67904-JTA_Daily_Briefing_6_27_2014&utm_medium=email&utm_term=0_2dce5bc6f8-ddaff67904-25357233>.
43. Jane Eisner, "Why Presbyterian Divestment Feels Like Anti-Semitism," *Jewish Daily Forward*, June 25, 2014. The editorial is accessible at: <http://forward.com/articles/200724/why-presbyterian-divestment-feels-like-anti-semiti/?p=all>.
44. Immediately after the PCUSA divestment vote, international media tracked reactions to it. See, for example, Rebecca Shimoni Stoil, "Presbyterian Church Votes in Favor of Divestment," *The Times of Israel*, June 21, 2014, which features a sampling of Jewish commentary. The article is accessible at: <www.timesofisrael.com/presbyterian-church-votes-in-favor-of-divesting-from-israel/>.
45. See *Kairos Palestine: A Moment of Truth* (Louisville, KY: Israel/Palestine Mission Network of the Presbyterian Church (USA), 2010), 14 (2.3.2). In addition to "Kairos Palestine," this booklet contains a three-week congregational study plan, which, along with *A Steadfast Hope: The Palestinian Quest for a Just Peace*, a film in DVD format, received considerable attention, some of it highly critical, in Presbyterian circles. The Israel/Palestine Mission Network (IPMN) of the Presbyterian Church (USA) has identified itself as "a grassroots organization established in 2004 with a mandate from the denomination's General Assembly to advocate for Palestinian rights and bring a deeper understanding to their struggle under military occupation. As part of its mandate, the IPMN speaks *to* the church, not *for* the church."
46. Chris Leighton, "An Open Letter to the Presbyterian Church," February 8, 2014. The letter is accessible at the ICJS website: <www.icjs.org/featured-articles/open-letter-presbyterian-church-0>.
47. Mark Braverman, *Fatal Embrace: Christians, Jews, and the Search for Peace in the Holy Land* (Austin, TX: Synergy Books, 2010), 114. Braverman's critique aims at several American Christian post-Holocaust

thinkers in particular, among them James Carroll, R. Kendall Soulen, Paul van Buren, and Clark Williamson. He counts three other American scholars as key allies: Walter Brueggemann and Rosemary Ruether, both Christians, and the Jewish liberation theologian Marc Ellis.

48. Braverman, *Fatal Embrace*, 188.

49. See Uriel Heilman, "Survey: More Than a Quarter of the World Hates Jews," *Jewish Telegraphic Agency* (JTA), May 13, 2014. The article is accessible at: <www.jta.org/2014/05/13/news-opinion/world/survey-more-than-a-quarter-of-the-world-hates-jews?utm_source=Newsletter+sub scribers&utm_campaign=5963f2bb97-JTA_Daily_Briefing_5_13_2014& utm_medium=email&utm_term=0_2dce5bc6f8-5963f2bb97-25357233>. See also "Int'l Survey Says Anti-Semitic Attitudes Pervasive," Associated Press, May 13, 2014. The article is accessible at: <http://bigstory.ap.org/article/intl-survey-says-anti-semitic-attitudes-pervasive>. Further details are available at the ADL website for the survey: <http://global100.adl.org/#map/americas>.

50. See, for example, Jonathan Sacks, "Europe's Alarming New Anti-Semitism," *Wall Street Journal*, October 3, 2014. The article is accessible at: <http://online.wsj.com/articles/europes-alarming-new-anti-semitism-1412270003>. See also Michael Berenbaum, *Not Your Father's Antisemitism: Hatred of the Jews in the 21ˢᵗ Century* (St. Paul, MN: Paragon House, 2008).

51. Braverman, *Fatal Embrace*, 39.

52. Wiesel, *All Rivers Run to the Sea*, 121, 130. Shushani's students included the philosopher Emmanuel Levinas.

53. Wiesel, *Legends of Our Time* (New York: Holt, Rinehart and Winston, 1968), 93.

CHAPTER 7

1. For more information on this topic, see Alex Alvarez, *Native America and the Question of Genocide* (Lanham, MD: Rowman & Littlefield, 2014) and Carroll P. Kakel, III, *The American West and the Nazi East: A Comparative and Interpretive Perspective* (New York: Palgrave Macmillan, 2011).

2. See, for example, Alan S. Rosenbaum, ed., *Is the Holocaust Unique? Perspectives on Comparative Genocide*, 3rd edn. (Boulder, CO: Westview Press, 2009). For my chapter on "The Ethics of Uniqueness," see 27–38. The first edition of Rosenbaum's book appeared in 1996, the second in 2001.

3. I quote from the typescript that Catherine Filloux generously shared with me in the spring of 2006. Her play is published in William Carden and Pamela Berlin, eds., *HB Playwrights Short Play Festival: 2003 The Subway Plays* (Hanover, NH: Smith and Kraus, 2004). The performance

of *The G Word* takes about fifteen minutes. The scene is a subway car. A ghostly Lemkin confronts the general, convincing the post-traumatically stressed officer not to take his own life but to honor the courageous dead by turning his haunting memory of them into ongoing resistance.

Samantha Power states that "Lemkin proudly brandished the letter from the *Webster's New International Dictionary* that informed him that 'genocide' had been admitted." She does not give the letter's date, nor does she indicate when the word first appeared in *Merriam-Webster's*. Power does note the following: "Genocide was incorporated into the French *Encylopédie Larousse* in 1953 after approval from the French Academy. The *Oxford English Dictionary* first listed 'genocide' as an entry in the 'Addenda and Corrigenda' section of the 1955 update to the third edition."

While Lemkin's term was gradually incorporated into other languages and dictionaries without much modification, this practice was scarcely uniform, and his word was often translated in ways that did not capture his intended meanings. According to Power, the typical German rendering of the term, for example, is *Völkermord*, or "murder of a nation." See Samantha Power, *"A Problem from Hell": America and the Age of Genocide* (New York: Basic Books, 2002), 44, 525 n.44.

Playwrights and performances of their works grow in importance with regard to confronting the Holocaust, genocide, and other mass atrocities. See, for example, Robert Skloot, *The Darkness We Carry: The Drama of the Holocaust* (Madison, WI: University of Wisconsin Press, 1988) and two of Skloot's edited volumes: *The Theatre of the Holocaust*, 2 vols. (Madison, WI: University of Wisconsin Press, 1982–99) and *The Theatre of Genocide: Four Plays about Mass Murder in Rwanda, Bosnia, Cambodia, and Armenia* (Madison, WI: University of Wisconsin Press, 2008).

4. My account is indebted to Steven Leonard Jacobs, "Genesis of the Concept of Genocide According to Its Author from the Original Sources," *Human Rights Review* 3, no. 2 (2002): 99.

5. For further information, see <www.merriam-webster.com/dictionary/genocide>.

6. For further information, see <www.merriam-webster.com/top-ten-lists/top-10-most-frequently-looked-up-words/affect-effect.html>. For the distinction between *effect* and *affect*, my inquiry included the "Glossary of Problematic Words and Phrases" in *The Chicago Manual of Style*, 16th edn. (Chicago: University of Chicago Press, 2010), 264.

7. See Samuel Totten and William S. Parsons, eds., *Centuries of Genocide: Critical Essays and Eyewitness Accounts*, 4th edn. (New York: Routledge, 2013).

8. Raphael Lemkin, *Axis Rule in Occupied Europe: Laws of Occupation, Analysis of Government, Proposals for Redress* (Washington, DC: Carnegie Endowment for International Peace, 1944), 79.

9. Kurt Jonassohn, "The Sociology of Genocide," in *Encyclopedia of Genocide*, ed. Israel W. Charny, 2 vols. (Santa Barbara, CA: ABC-CLIO, 1999), 518.

10. Nicholas Wade, *Before the Dawn: Recovering the Lost History of Our Ancestors* (New York: Penguin Books, 2006), 151, 85. See also Ben Kiernan, *Blood and Soil: A World History of Genocide and Extermination from Sparta to Darfur* (New Haven, CT: Yale University Press, 2007), 1–9.

11. Biblical references pointing to cases that, arguably, could be considered instances of genocide—figurative or literal—include: Deuteronomy 2:31–4, 3:1–7; Joshua 6:20–1, 8:1–29; 1 Samuel 30:1–19; and Judges 20.

12. Frank Chalk and Kurt Jonassohn, *The History and Sociology of Genocide: Analyses and Case Studies* (New Haven, CT: Yale University Press, 1990), 29.

13. See Adam Jones, *Genocide: A Comprehensive Introduction*, 2nd edn. (New York: Routledge, 2006), 16–20.

14. Scott Straus, "Contested Meanings and Conflicting Imperatives: A Conceptual Analysis of Genocide," *Journal of Genocide Research* 3, no. 3 (2001): 359. Also helpful is Martin Shaw, *What Is Genocide?* (Cambridge, UK: Polity Press, 2007).

15. Benjamin A. Valentino, *Final Solutions: Mass Killing and Genocide in the Twentieth Century* (Ithaca, NY: Cornell University Press, 2004), 10. See 11–12 for the subsequent quotations in this paragraph.

16. For more detail on this point and those that follow, see my essay, "The Politics of Definition," in *Will Genocide Ever End?*, ed. Carol Rittner, John K. Roth, and James M. Smith (St. Paul, MN: Paragon House, 2002), 23–9.

17. Primo Levi, *The Drowned and the Saved*, trans. Raymond Rosenthal (New York: Summit Books, 1986), 200.

18. Raul Hilberg, *The Destruction of the European Jews*, 3rd edn. (New Haven, CT: Yale University Press, 2003), 3:1090.

19. Shaw, *What Is Genocide?*, 154.

20. For the source of the quotations in this paragraph, see Levi, *The Drowned and the Saved*, 106, 109, 111, 119, and 126.

21. Primo Levi, *Survival in Auschwitz: The Nazi Assault on Humanity*, trans. Stuart Woolf (New York: Simon & Schuster, 1996), 29.

22. Sarah Kofman, *Smothered Words*, trans. Madeleine Dobie (Evanston, IL: Northwestern University Press, 1998), 70.

23. See Raul Hilberg, ed., *Documents of Destruction: Germany and Jewry 1933–1945* (Chicago, IL: Quadrangle Books, 1971), vi.

24. For an instructive source on this point, see Leon Goldensohn, *The Nuremberg Interviews: An American Psychiatrist's Conversations with Defendants and Witnesses*, ed. Robert Gellately (New York: Alfred A. Knopf, 2004). Goldensohn monitored the mental health of the Nazi

defendants who stood trial before the International Military Tribunal in Nuremberg in 1945–6. He also interviewed Nazis who were witnesses in those trials, including Rudolf Höss, the former SS commandant of Auschwitz, and Otto Ohlendorf, the SS general who commanded *Einsatzgruppe* D on the eastern front, a shooting squadron responsible for some 90,000 Jewish deaths. Goldensohn's interviews show these men to be largely devoid of anything resembling guilt, remorse, or repentance for their actions.

25. Hilberg, *The Destruction of the European Jews*, 3:1059, 1084.
26. See Hilberg, *The Destruction of the European Jews*, 3:1080–104.
27. Jean Hatzfeld, *The Antelope's Strategy: Living in Rwanda after the Genocide*, trans. Linda Coverdale (New York: Farrar, Straus and Giroux, 2009), 37. A former sports reporter, Hatzfeld was born in Madagascar in 1949. Fleeing from the Nazis, his Jewish parents went there in 1942.
28. Hatzfeld, *The Antelope's Strategy*, 38.
29. Hatzfeld, *The Antelope's Strategy*, 37.
30. Hatzfeld, *The Antelope's Strategy*, 37.
31. Hatzfeld, *The Antelope's Strategy*, 41.
32. Hatzfeld, *The Antelope's Strategy*, 42.
33. Hatzfeld, *The Antelope's Strategy*, 38.
34. Hatzfeld, *The Antelope's Strategy*, 44, 46.
35. Hatzfeld, *The Antelope's Strategy*, 57.
36. Hatzfeld, *The Antelope's Strategy*, 45, 111.
37. Hatzfeld, *The Antelope's Strategy*, 130.
38. Hatzfeld, *The Antelope's Strategy*, 18.
39. Hatzfeld, *The Antelope's Strategy*, 79.
40. Hatzfeld, *The Antelope's Strategy*, 4, 153.
41. Hatzfeld, *The Antelope's Strategy*, 228–9.
42. See Power, *"A Problem from Hell,"* 40–5.

CHAPTER 8

1. Franz-Josef Brüggemeier, Mark Cioc, and Thomas Zeller, eds., *How Green Were the Nazis? Nature, Environment, and Nation in the Third Reich* (Athens, OH: Ohio University Press, 2005), iv. The photo can be seen at: <www.amazon.com/How-Green-Were-Nazis-Environment/dp/0821416472/ref=sr_sp-atf_title_1_1?s=books&ie=UTF8&qid=1401752447&sr=1-1&keywords=how+green+were+the+nazis>.
2. When the Germans occupied Hungarian territory in March 1944, Khust fell under German jurisdiction. According to the *Encyclopedia Judaica*'s entry for Khust (2008), "in March 1944 there were 5,351 Jews in Khust, and a ghetto and a Judenrat were set up. Another 5,000 Jews from the area were brought into the ghetto. In late May and early June, all ghetto

inhabitants were deported in four transports to Auschwitz, where most of them were sent to gas chambers." Some of the Jews deported from Khust—probably Berk among them—were transferred from Auschwitz to Buchenwald and Mauthausen.

3. The quotations in this paragraph are from Raul Hilberg, *Sources of Holocaust Research: An Analysis* (Chicago, IL: Ivan R. Dee, 2001), 204.

4. Timothy Snyder, *Bloodlands: Europe between Hitler and Stalin* (New York: Basic Books, 2010). Snyder calls his path-breaking book "a history of political mass murder" (x). Emphasizing that "in the middle of Europe in the middle of the twentieth century, the Nazi and Soviet regimes murdered some fourteen million people," his multifaceted contribution to Holocaust and genocide studies shows that sound understanding of the Holocaust depends on properly situating that catastrophe geographically and comparatively with regard to the ways in which the German and Soviet atrocities in the bloodlands "shared a place, and . . . shared a time" (vii, 380).

5. For more detail on the findings from the contributors discussed below, see Peter Hayes and John K. Roth, eds., *The Oxford Handbook of Holocaust Studies* (Oxford: Oxford University Press, 2010), 128–41, 218–32, 310–25, 340–53, 354–63, 381–96, 478–89, and 490–506.

6. Elie Wiesel, *Night*, trans. Marion Wiesel (New York: Hill and Wang, 2006), 8, 10, 12, 15, 17, 23, 37, 40, 68, 77, 85, 96.

7. Wiesel, *Night*, 34.

8. Wiesel, *Night*, 34.

9. For further insights on this theme, see Didier Pollefeyt, ed., *Holocaust and Nature* (Berlin: LIT Verlag, 2013).

10. A Holocaust-related point requires the qualification in this sentence. At least before the hell of World War II and the Holocaust broke out in all of its fury, environmental concerns got some attention in Nazi Germany. Debates continue about "how green were the Nazis?" but their conservation and ecological interests were neither unified nor unifying. Nazi plans for the protection of nature were more sporadic than sustained, and they reflected infighting more than coherence. Far from being global, Nazi environmentalism also tended to be "local, regional, or state-centered." See Brüggemeier, Cioc, and Zeller, eds., *How Green Were the Nazis?*, esp. 2 for the quoted phrase from the editors' introduction. Also helpful is Frank Uekoetter, *The Green and the Brown: A History of Conservation in Nazi Germany* (Cambridge: Cambridge University Press, 2006). I continue to believe that a fully fledged, global caring for the natural world would be utterly inconsistent with—indeed in determined opposition to—genocide and the destructive warfare that so often abets it. Some caution, however, remains appropriate. As the Nazi example shows, by no means is every form of environmental

concern incompatible with massive human rights abuses and even genocide itself.

11. On these points, see, for example, the findings of the US government's 2014 National Climate Assessment. Its report is available at <www. globalchange.gov/>. See also the website for the work being done by the environmental activist Bill McKibben and his international network: <http://350.org/>.

12. Issues related to this theme are explored in Jürgen Zimmerer, ed., "Climate Change, Environmental Violence and Genocide," a special issue of *The International Journal of Human Rights* 18, no. 3 (2014).

13. Michael Imort, "'Eternal Forest—Eternal *Volk*': The Rhetoric and Reality of National Socialist Forest Policy," in *How Green Were the Nazis?*, 43, 45, 52, 53, 54.

14. The quotations are taken from the Anne Frank House website at: <www. annefrank.org/en/News/Anne-Frank-Tree/>. This site contains much information about the history of the Anne Frank Tree.

15. See Philip Hallie, "Cruelty: The Empirical Evil," in *Facing Evil: Light at the Core of Darkness*, ed. Paul Woodruff and Harry A. Wilmer (La Salle, IL: Open Court, 1994), 128–30. Also relevant is Hallie's *Tales of Good and Evil, Help and Harm* (New York: HarperCollins, 1997).

CHAPTER 9

1. See Joseph Freeman, *The Road to Hell: Recollections of the Nazi Death March* (St. Paul, MN: Paragon House, 1998). Freeman's other books are *Job: The Story of a Holocaust Survivor* (Westport, CN: Praeger, 1996) and *Kingdom of Night: The Saga of a Woman's Struggle for Survival* (Lanham, MD: University Press of America, 2006). The latter is about his spouse, Helen.

2. See James E. Young, *The Texture of Memory: Holocaust Memorials and Meaning* (New Haven, CN: Yale University Press, 1993).

3. Philip Hallie, *Tales of Good and Evil, Help and Harm* (New York: HarperCollins, 1997), 22.

4. Raul Hilberg, *Sources of Holocaust Research: An Analysis* (Chicago, IL: Ivan R. Dee, 2001), 7–8.

5. Hilberg, *Sources of Holocaust Research*, 44.

6. Hilberg, *Sources of Holocaust Research*, 48–9.

7. Hilberg, *Sources of Holocaust Research*, 49.

8. Timothy Snyder, *Bloodlands: Europe between Hitler and Stalin* (New York: Basic Books, 2010), viii, xvii, 383.

9. Greenspan has published extensively on his intensive relationships with Holocaust survivors. See, for example, his *On Listening to Holocaust Survivors: Beyond Testimony*, 2nd edn. (St. Paul, MN: Paragon House,

2010) and also his dialogue with Holocaust survivor Agi Rubin, which has been published as Agi Rubin and Henry Greenspan, *Reflections: Auschwitz, Memory, and a Life Recreated* (St. Paul, MN: Paragon House, 2006). For an overview of Greenspan's perspectives, see his chapter on "Survivor Accounts," in *The Oxford Handbook of Holocaust Studies*, ed. Peter Hayes and John K. Roth (Oxford: Oxford University Press, 2010, 414–27. The quoted phrase is from this article, 414.

10. Henry Greenspan, "The Unsaid, the Incommunicable, the Unbearable, and the Irretrievable," *Oral History Review* 41, no. 2 (2014): 229–43.

11. Especially relevant in this regard is Lawrence L. Langer, *Holocaust Testimonies: The Ruins of Memory* (New Haven, CT: Yale University Press, 1991).

12. Lawrence L. Langer, *Preempting the Holocaust* (New Haven, CT: Yale University Press, 1998), 10.

13. The discussion that follows, including the excerpt of trial testimony, is indebted to Tazreena Sajjad's chapter, "Rape on Trial: Promises of International Jurisprudence, Perils of Retributive Justice, and the Realities of Impunity," in *Rape: Weapon of War and Genocide*, ed. Carol Rittner and John K. Roth (St. Paul, MN: Paragon House, 2012), 61–81. The full transcript of the Foča trial case, which is named and numbered as Kunarac et al. (IT-96-23) is available at: <www.icty.org/x/cases/kunarac/trans/en/000329ed.htm>. See especially pages 1241–2 and 1261–4.

14. On this topic, see Janine Natalya Clark, *International Trials and Reconciliation: Assessing the Impact of the International Criminal Tribunal for the Former Yugoslavia* (New York: Routledge, 2014).

15. Jan Tomasz Gross with Irena Grudzińska Gross, *Golden Harvest: Events at the Periphery of the Holocaust* (Oxford: Oxford University Press, 2012), xiii. The photograph is reproduced in the book's front matter, ii–iii.

16. Gross, *Golden Harvest*, xiii.

17. *Golden Harvest* is not the only book in which Gross has raised important questions and documented findings that renew tensions about Polish-Jewish relationships during and after the Holocaust. See, for example, his books *Neighbors: The Destruction of the Jewish Community in Jedwabne, Poland* (Princeton, NJ: Princeton University Press, 2001) and *Fear: Anti-Semitism in Poland after Auschwitz: An Essay in Historical Interpretation* (New York: Random House, 2006).

18. Gross, *Golden Harvest*, 77.

19. Primo Levi, *Survival in Auschwitz: The Nazi Assault on Humanity*, trans. Stuart Woolf (New York: Simon & Schuster, 1996), 121.

20. Primo Levi, *Moments of Reprieve: A Memoir of Auschwitz*, trans. Ruth Feldman (New York: Penguin Books, 1987), 160.

CHAPTER 10

1. Christopher R. Browning, *Nazi Policy, Jewish Workers, German Killers* (Cambridge, UK: Cambridge University Press, 2000), 167. Subsequent quotations in this paragraph can be found on the following pages of Browning's book: 166, 169, and 175.

2. Supported by the European Research Council, "Corpses of Mass Violence and Genocide," an important four-year research and publication initiative, began in February 2012 under the direction of Élisabeth Anstett and Jean-Marc Dreyfus. This project, the first of its kind, explores and documents how societies have coped with the vast accumulation of human remains produced by mass atrocity crimes. The first book in a planned series is Élisabeth Anstett and Jean-Marc Dreyfus, eds., *Destruction and Human Remains: Disposal and Concealment in Genocide and Mass Violence* (Manchester, UK: Manchester University Press, 2014).

3. The letter is undated, but it reached me in early March 2012.

4. Charlotte Delbo, *Auschwitz and After*, trans. Rosette C. Lamont (New Haven, CT: Yale University Press, 1995), 138. The quotation is from *Useless Knowledge*, the second part of the trilogy called *Auschwitz and After*.

5. The statement attributed to Shalev is found in Ethan Bronner, "From Overseas Visitors, a Growing Demand to Study the Holocaust," *New York Times*, February 14, 2012. Available online at: <www.nytimes.com/2012/02/15/world/middleeast/lessons-from-the-holocaust-are-widespread-and-varied.html?_r=1&pagewanted=all>.

6. Browning, *Nazi Policy, Jewish Workers, German Killers*, 32.

7. Jean Améry, *At the Mind's Limits: Contemplations by a Survivor of Auschwitz and Its Realities*, trans. Sidney Rosenfeld and Stella P. Rosenfeld (Bloomington, IN: Indiana University Press, 1980), xi.

8. Améry, *At the Mind's Limits*, 70.

9. Améry, *At the Mind's Limits*, 79.

10. The editorial, "Preserve the Memory," by Fr. Federico Lombardi, is available online at: <www.news.va/en/news/fr-lombardi-editorial-preserve-the-memory>.

11. Elie Wiesel, *Legends of Our Time* (New York: Holt, Rinehart and Winston, 1968), 162.

12. Delbo, *Auschwitz and After*, 84.

13. See Alan Weisman, *The World Without Us* (New York: St. Martin's Press, 2007).

14. Drawing on recent research in evolution, genetics, archaeology, and more, Nicholas Wade indicates that "the earliest starting point in the human narrative" took place about 5 million years ago. The initial evidence of identifiable human behavior, what Wade calls the beginning

of "the modern human story," is about 50,000 years old. Written records of human experience are not more than 5,000 years old. See Nicholas Wade, *Before the Dawn: Recovering the Lost History of Our Ancestors* (New York: Penguin Books, 2006), 1.

Adding to the sense of "deep time" in which human existence barely flickers, the earth is reliably estimated to be roughly 4.5 billion years old, a mind-boggling number. Accordingly, John McPhee measures the extent of human history as follows: "Consider the earth's history as the old measure of the English yard, the distance from the king's nose to the tip of his outstretched hand. One stroke of a nail file on his middle finger erases human history." See John McPhee, *Basin and Range* (1981) in *Annals of the Former World* (New York: Farrar, Straus and Giroux, 1998), 77.

15. Delbo, *Auschwitz and After*, 241.
16. Delbo, *Auschwitz and After*, 258.
17. After the Holocaust, Delbo gathered as much information as she could about the women who were on her Auschwitz transport. Their stories are told in Charlotte Delbo, *Convoy to Auschwitz: Women of the French Resistance*, trans. Carol Cosman (Boston, MA: Northeastern University Press, 1977).
18. Charlotte Delbo, *Days and Memory*, trans. Rosette C. Lamont (Marlboro, VT: Marlboro Press, 1990), 2.
19. Delbo, *Auschwitz and After*, 145.
20. Delbo, *Auschwitz and After*, 142, 144.
21. For elaboration on this theme, see David Patterson and John K. Roth, eds., *After-Words: Post-Holocaust Struggles with Forgiveness, Reconciliation, Justice* (Seattle, WA: University of Washington Press, 2004).
22. Albert Camus, *The Myth of Sisyphus and Other Essays*, trans. Justin O'Brien (New York: Vintage Books, 1955), 90. *The Myth of Sisyphus* was written, according to Camus, "in 1940, amid the French and European disaster," and originally published in France in 1942. See iv and v.
23. See Philip Hallie, *Lest Innocent Blood Be Shed: The Story of the Village of Le Chambon and How Goodness Happened There* (New York: HarperPerennial, 1994).
24. Philip Hallie, "Camus's Hug," in *The American Scholar* 64, no. 3 (1995): 428–35.
25. Hallie, "Camus's Hug," 434–5.
26. Philip Hallie, "Cruelty: The Empirical Evil," in *Facing Evil: Light at the Core of Darkness*, ed. Paul Woodruff and Harry A. Wilmer (LaSalle, IL: Open Court, 1994), 129. See also Hallie's contributions to *Facing Evil*, a DVD (Princeton, NJ: Films for the Humanities & Sciences, 2005).
27. Hallie, "Cruelty: The Empirical Evil," 129.
28. Philip Hallie, *Tales of Good and Evil, Help and Harm* (New York: HarperCollins, 1997), 173.

29. The quotation is from Stella Rodway's translation of *Night*. Marion Wiesel's later translation says "we were forced to look at him at close range." Rodway's wording fits better with the themes in this essay. See Elie Wiesel, *Night*, trans. Stella Rodway (New York: Bantam Books, 1982), 62. For comparison, see Elie Wiesel, *Night*, trans. Marion Wiesel (New York: Hill and Wang, 2006), 65.
30. Wiesel, *Night* (2006, Marion Wiesel's translation), 115.
31. Delbo, *Auschwitz and After*, 267.
32. Elie Wiesel, *Open Heart*, trans. Marion Wiesel (New York: Alfred A. Knopf, 2012), 73.
33. Delbo, *Auschwitz and After*, 230.

EPILOGUE

1. Paul Hunter, *Ripening* (Eugene, OR: Silverfish Review Press, 2007), 37.
2. Kay Ryan, *The Niagara River* (New York: Grove Press, 2005), 35.
3. Obama's speech is accessible at: <www.whitehouse.gov/the-press-office/2014/09/24/remarks-president-obama-address-united-nations-general-assembly>.
4. King's speech is accessible at: <http://mlk-kpp01.stanford.edu/index.php/encyclopedia/documentsentry/where_do_we_go_from_here_delivered_at_the_11th_annual_sclc_convention/>.
5. G. W. F. Hegel, *Introduction to the Philosophy of History*, trans. Leo Rauch (Indianapolis, IN: Hackett Publishing Company, 1988), 24.

Bibliography

Abrahamson, Irving, ed. *Against Silence: The Voice and Vision of Elie Wiesel.* 3 vols. New York: Holocaust Library, 1985.

Adorno, Theodor. *Prisms.* Translated by Samuel and Shierry Weber. London: Neville Spearman, 1967.

Adorno, Theodor. *Negative Dialectics.* Translated by E. B. Ashton. New York: Seabury Press, 1973.

Agamben, Giorgio. *Remnants of Auschwitz: The Witness and the Archive.* Translated by Daniel Heller-Roazen. New York: Zone Books, 1999.

Alexander, Jeffrey C., Martin Jay, Bernhard Giesen, Michael Rothberg, Robert Manne, Nathan Glazar, Elihu Katz, and Ruth Katz. *Remembering the Holocaust: A Debate.* Oxford: Oxford University Press, 2009.

Alvarez, Alex. *Native America and the Question of Genocide.* Lanham, MD: Rowman & Littlefield, 2014.

Aly, Götz. *Why the Germans? Why the Jews? Envy, Race Hatred, and the Prehistory of the Holocaust.* Translated by Jefferson Chase. New York: Metropolitan Books, 2014.

Améry, Jean. *At the Mind's Limits: Contemplations by a Survivor on Auschwitz and Its Realities.* Translated by Sidney Rosenfeld and Stella P. Rosenfeld. Bloomington, IN: Indiana University Press, 1980.

Anstett, Élisabeth, and Jean-Marc Dreyfus, eds. *Destruction and Human Remains: Disposal and Concealment in Genocide and Mass Violence.* Manchester, UK: Manchester University Press, 2014.

Arendt, Hannah. *Eichmann in Jerusalem: A Report on the Banality of Evil.* New York: Viking Press, 1963.

Arendt, Hannah. *The Origins of Totalitarianism.* New York: Harcourt, 1951.

Babbitt, Susan E., and Sue Campbell, eds. *Racism and Philosophy.* Ithaca, NY: Cornell University Press, 1999.

Bak, Samuel. *Illuminations: The Art of Samuel Bak.* Brookline, MA: Facing History and Ourselves, 2010.

Barnett, Victoria J. *Bystanders: Conscience and Complicity During the Holocaust.* Westport, CT: Praeger Publishers, 2000.

Baron, Lawrence. "The Holocaust and American Public Memory, 1945–1960." *Holocaust and Genocide Studies* 17, no. 1 (2003): 62–88.

Bartov, Omer. "Extreme Violence and the Scholarly Community." *International Social Science Journal* 54, no. 174 (2002): 509–18.

Bartov, Omer, ed. *The Holocaust: Origins, Implementation, Aftermath.* New York: Routledge, 2000.

Bartrop, Paul. *Genocide: The Basics*. New York: Routledge, 2014.

Bauer, Yehuda. *Rethinking the Holocaust*. New Haven, CT: Yale University Press, 2001.

Bellamy, Alex J. *Responsibility to Protect: The Global Effort to End Mass Atrocities*. Cambridge, UK: Polity Press, 2009.

Bellamy, Alex J. "Military Intervention." In *The Oxford Handbook of Genocide Studies*, edited by Donald Bloxham and A. Dirk Moses, 597–616. Oxford: Oxford University Press, 2010.

Bellamy, Alex J. *Global Politics and the Responsibility to Protect: From Words to Deeds*. New York: Routledge, 2011.

Bellamy, Alex J. *Massacres and Morality: Mass Atrocities in an Age of Civilian Immunity*. Oxford: Oxford University Press, 2012.

Bellamy, Alex J. *The Responsibility to Protect: A Defense*. Oxford: Oxford University Press, 2015.

Berenbaum, Michael. "Who Owns the Holocaust?" *Moment* 25, no. 6 (2000): 60.

Berenbaum, Michael, ed. *Not Your Father's Antisemitism: Hatred of the Jews in the 21ˢᵗ Century*. St. Paul, MN: Paragon House, 2008.

Berg, Manfred, and Simon Wendt, eds. *Racism in the Modern World: Historical Perspectives on Cultural Transfer and Adaptation*. New York: Berghahn Books, 2011.

Berger, Alan L., ed. *Trialogue and Terror: Judaism, Christianity, and Islam after 9/11*. Eugene, OR: Cascade Books, 2012.

Berger, Alan L., ed. *Post-Holocaust Jewish–Christian Dialogue: After the Flood, before the Rainbow*. Lanham, MD: Lexington Books, 2015.

Bergoglio, Jorge Mario [Pope Francis], and Abraham Skorka. *On Heaven and Earth: Pope Francis on Faith, Family, and the Church in the Twenty-first Century*. Translated by Alejandro Bermudez and Howard Goodman. New York: Image, 2013.

Bernasconi, Robert. "Why Do the Happy Inhabitants of Tahiti Bother to Exist at All?" In *Genocide and Human Rights: A Philosophical Guide*, edited by John K. Roth, 139–48. New York: Palgrave Macmillan, 2005.

Bloom, Harold, ed. *Elie Wiesel's "Night."* New edn. New York: Infobase Publishing, 2010.

Bloxham, Donald, and A. Dirk Moses, eds. *The Oxford Handbook of Genocide Studies*. Oxford: Oxford University Press, 2010.

Boder, David P. *I Did Not Interview the Dead*. Urbana, IL: University of Illinois Press, 1949.

Boxill, Bernard, ed. *Race and Racism*. Oxford: Oxford University Press, 2001.

Braverman, Mark. *Fatal Embrace: Christians, Jews, and the Search for Peace in the Holy Land*. Austin, TX: Synergy Books, 2010.

Bretton-Granatoor, Gary M. "Op-Ed: The Presbyterians' Judaism Problem." *Jewish Telegraphic Agency*, June 27, 2014.

Brombert, Victor. *Musings on Mortality: From Tolstoy to Primo Levi*. Chicago, IL: University of Chicago Press, 2013.

Browning, Christopher R. *Nazi Policy, Jewish Workers, German Killers*. Cambridge, UK: Cambridge University Press, 2000.

Brudholm, Thomas, and Thomas Cushman, eds. *The Religious in Responses to Mass Atrocity: Interdisciplinary Perspectives*. Cambridge, UK: Cambridge University Press, 2009.

Brüggemeier, Franz-Josef, Mark Cioc, and Thomas Zeller, eds. *How Green Were the Nazis? Nature, Environment, and Nation in the Third Reich*. Athens, OH: Ohio University Press, 2005.

Buber, Martin. *Eclipse of God: Studies in the Relation between Religion and Philosophy*. New York: Harper, 1952.

Buber, Martin. *On Judaism*. New York: Schocken Books, 1967.

Burleigh, Michael. *Moral Combat: Good and Evil in World War II*. New York: HarperPerennial, 2012.

Camus, Albert. *The Plague*. Translated by Stuart Gilbert. New York: Modern Library, 1948.

Camus, Albert. *The Myth of Sisyphus and Other Essays*. Translated by Justin O'Brien. New York: Vintage Books, 1955.

Camus, Albert. *The Rebel: An Essay on Man in Revolt*. Translated by Anthony Bower. New York: Vintage Books, 1956.

Card, Claudia. *Confronting Evils: Terror, Torture, Genocide*. Cambridge, UK: Cambridge University Press, 2010.

Carden, William, and Pamela Berlin, eds. *HB Playwrights Short Play Festival: 2003 The Subway Plays*. Hanover, NH: Smith and Kraus, 2004.

Cargas, Harry James. *Harry James Cargas in Conversation with Elie Wiesel*. New York: Paulist Press, 1976.

Chalk, Frank, and Kurt Jonassohn. *The History and Sociology of Genocide: Analyses and Case Studies*. New Haven, CT: Yale University Press, 1990.

Charny, Israel W., ed. *Encyclopedia of Genocide*. 2 vols. Santa Barbara, CA: ABC-CLIO, 1999.

Clapham, Andrew, and Paola Gaeta, eds. *The Oxford Handbook of International Law in Armed Conflict*. Oxford: Oxford University Press, 2014.

Clark, Janine Natalya. *International Trials and Reconciliation: Assessing the Impact of the International Criminal Tribunal for the Former Yugoslavia*. New York: Routledge, 2014.

Cohn-Sherbok, Dan, ed. *Holocaust Theology: A Reader*. New York: New York University Press, 2002.

Confino, Alon. *A World without Jews: The Nazi Imagination from Persecution to Genocide*. New Haven, CT: Yale University Press, 2014.

Cooper, John. *Raphael Lemkin and the Struggle for the Genocide Convention*. New York: Palgrave Macmillan, 2007.

Crowe, David M. *War Crimes, Genocide, and Justice: A Global History*. New York: Palgrave Macmillan, 2014.

Davis, Stephen T. "Genocide, Despair, and Religious Hope: An Essay on Human Nature." In *Genocide and Human Rights: A Philosophical Guide*, edited by John K. Roth, 35–45. New York: Palgrave Macmillan, 2005.

Dean, Carolyn J. *The Fragility of Empathy after the Holocaust*. Ithaca, NY: Cornell University Press, 2004.

Delbo, Charlotte. *Convoy to Auschwitz: Women of the French Resistance*. Translated by Carol Cosman. Boston, MA: Northeastern University Press, 1977.

Delbo, Charlotte. *Days and Memory*. Translated by Rosette C. Lamont. Marlboro, VT: Marlboro Press, 1990.

Delbo, Charlotte. *Auschwitz and After*. Translated by Rosette C. Lamont. New Haven, CT: Yale University Press, 1995.

Desbois, Patrick. *The Holocaust by Bullets*. New York: Palgrave Macmillan, 2008.

Diner, Hasia R. *We Remember with Reverence and Love: American Jews and the Myth of Silence after the Holocaust, 1945–1962*. New York: New York University Press, 2009.

Ehrenreich, Eric. *The Nazi Ancestral Proof: Genealogy, Racial Science, and the Final Solution*. Bloomington, IN: Indiana University Press, 2007.

Eisner, Jane. "Why Presbyterian Divestment Feels Like Anti-Semitism." *Jewish Daily Forward*, June 25, 2014.

Evans, Gareth. *The Responsibility to Protect: Ending Mass Atrocity Crimes Once and For All*. Washington, DC: Brookings Institution Press, 2008.

Fackenheim, Emil. *God's Presence in History: Jewish Affirmations and Philosophical Reflections*. New York: New York University Press, 1970.

Fackenheim, Emil. *The Jewish Return into History: Reflections in the Age of Auschwitz and a New Jerusalem*. New York: Schocken Books, 1978.

Fackenheim, Emil. *To Mend the World: Foundations of Future Jewish Thought*. New York: Schocken Books, 1982.

Fackenheim, Emil. "The Holocaust and Philosophy." *The Journal of Philosophy* 82, no. 10 (1985): 505–14.

Faye, Emmanuel. *Heidegger: The Introduction of Nazism into Philosophy in Light of the Unpublished Seminars of 1933–1935*. New Haven, CT: Yale University Press, 2009.

Feltham, Colin. *Failure*. New York: Routledge, 2014.

Flusser, David. "The Decalogue in the New Testament." In *The Ten Commandments in History and Tradition*, edited by Ben-Zion Segal and Gershon Levi, 221–43. Jerusalem: Magnes Press, Hebrew University of Jerusalem: 1990.

Fredrickson, George M. *Racism: A Short History*. Princeton, NJ: Princeton University Press, 2002.

Freeman, Joseph. *Job: The Story of a Holocaust Survivor*. Westport, CN: Praeger, 1996.

Freeman, Joseph. *The Road to Hell: Recollections of the Nazi Death March*. St. Paul, MN: Paragon House, 1998.

Freeman, Joseph. *Kingdom of Night: The Saga of a Woman's Struggle for Survival*. Lanham, MD: University Press of America, 2006.

Freud, Sigmund. "The Disillusionment of the War." Translated by E. C. Mayne. In *The Standard Edition of the Complete Works of Sigmund Freud*, vol. XIV, edited by James Strachey, 275–88. London: Hogarth Press, 1957.

Gerson, Michael. "Iran's Incitement to Genocide." *Washington Post*, April 4, 2013.

Glanville, Luke. *Sovereignty and the Responsibility to Protect: A New History*. Chicago, IL: University of Chicago Press, 2014.

Goldberg, David Theo. *Racist Culture: Philosophy and the Politics of Meaning*. Oxford: Blackwell, 1993.

Goldenberg, Myrna, and Amy H. Shapiro, eds. *Different Horrors, Same Hell: Gender and the Holocaust*. Seattle, WA: University of Washington Press, 2013.

Goldensohn, Leon. *The Nuremberg Interviews: An American Psychiatrist's Conversations with Defendants and Witnesses*, edited by Robert Gellately. New York: Alfred A. Knopf, 2004.

Goldhagen, Daniel Jonah. *Hitler's Willing Executioners: Ordinary Germans and the Holocaust*. New York: Alfred A. Knopf, 1996.

Goldhagen, Daniel Jonah. *Worse Than War: Genocide, Eliminationism, and the Ongoing Assault on Humanity*. New York: PublicAffairs, 2009.

Gordon, Peter E. "Heidegger in Black." *New York Review of Books*, October 9, 2014.

Gray, Michael. *Contemporary Debates in Holocaust Education*. New York: Palgrave Macmillan, 2014.

Greenberg, Irving. "Cloud of Smoke, Pillar of Fire: Judaism, Christianity, and Modernity after the Holocaust." In *Auschwitz: Beginning of a New Era? Reflections on the Holocaust*, edited by Eva Fleischner, 7–55. New York: Ktav, 1977.

Greenspan, Henry. *On Listening to Holocaust Survivors: Beyond Testimony*. 2nd edn. St. Paul, MN: Paragon House, 2010.

Greenspan, Henry. "Survivor Accounts." In *The Oxford Handbook of Holocaust Studies*, edited by Peter Hayes and John K. Roth, 414–27. Oxford: Oxford University Press, 2010.

Greenspan, Henry. "The Unsaid, the Incommunicable, the Unbearable, and the Irretrievable." *Oral History Review* 41, no. 2 (2014): 229–43.

Grob, Leonard, and John K. Roth, eds. *Anguished Hope: Holocaust Scholars Confront the Palestinian–Israeli Conflict*. Grand Rapids, MI: William B. Eerdmans, 2008.

Grob, Leonard, and John K. Roth, eds. *Encountering the Stranger: A Jewish–Christian–Muslim Trialogue*. Seattle, WA: University of Washington Press, 2012.

Gross, Jan Tomasz. *Neighbors: The Destruction of the Jewish Community in Jedwabne, Poland*. Princeton, NJ: Princeton University Press, 2001.

Gross, Jan Tomasz. *Fear: Anti-Semitism in Poland after Auschwitz: An Essay in Historical Interpretation*. New York: Random House, 2006.

Gross, Jan Tomasz, with Irena Grudzińska Gross. *Golden Harvest: Events at the Periphery of the Holocaust*. Oxford: Oxford University Press, 2012.

Gushee, David. *Righteous Gentiles of the Holocaust: Genocide and Moral Obligation*. 2nd edn. St. Paul, MN: Paragon House, 2003.

Haas, Peter J. *Morality after Auschwitz: The Radical Challenge of the Nazi Ethic*. Philadelphia, PA: Fortress Press, 1988.

Hacking, Ian. "Why Race Still Matters." *Daedelus* 134, no. 1 (2005): 102–16.

Hallie, Philip. "Cruelty: The Empirical Evil." In *Facing Evil: Light at the Core of Darkness*, edited by Paul Woodruff and Harry A. Wilmer, 118–37. LaSalle, IL: Open Court, 1988.

Hallie, Philip. *Lest Innocent Blood Be Shed: The Story of the Village of Le Chambon and How Goodness Happened There*. New York: HarperPerennial, 1994.

Hallie, Philip. "Camus's Hug." *The American Scholar* 64, no. 3 (1995): 428–35.

Hallie, Philip. *Tales of Good and Evil, Help and Harm*. New York: HarperCollins, 1997.

Harrison, Robert Pogue. *The Dominion of the Dead*. Chicago, IL: University of Chicago Press, 2003.

Hatzfeld, Jean. *Machete Season: The Killers in Rwanda Speak*. Translated by Linda Coverdale. New York: Farrar, Straus and Giroux, 2005.

Hatzfeld, Jean. *The Antelope's Strategy: Living in Rwanda after the Genocide*. Translated by Linda Coverdale. New York: Farrar, Straus and Giroux, 2009.

Hayes, Peter. "Ethics and Corporate History in Nazi Germany." In *Lessons and Legacies IX: Memory, History, and Responsibility; Reassessments of the Holocaust, Implications for the Future*, edited by Jonathan Petropoulos, Lynn Rapaport, and John K. Roth, 300–3. Evanston, IL: Northwestern University Press, 2010.

Hayes, Peter, and John K. Roth, eds. *The Oxford Handbook of Holocaust Studies*. Oxford: Oxford University Press, 2010.

Haynes, Stephen R., and John K. Roth, eds. *The Death of God Movement and the Holocaust: Radical Theology Encounters the Shoah*. Westport, CT: Greenwood Press, 1999.

Hedgepath, Sonja M., and Rochelle G. Saidel, eds. *Sexual Violence against Jewish Women during the Holocaust*. Waltham, MA: Brandeis University Press, 2010.

Hegel, G. W. F. *Introduction to the Philosophy of History*. Translated by Leo Rauch. Indianapolis, IN: Hackett Publishing Company, 1988.

Hehir, Aidan. *The Responsibility to Protect: Rhetoric, Reality, and the Future of Humanitarian Intervention*. New York: Palgrave Macmillan, 2012.

Heilman, Uriel. "Survey: More Than a Quarter of the World Hates Jews." *Jewish Telegraphic Agency*, May 13, 2014.

Herr, Alexis. "Fossoli di Carpi: The History and Memory of the Holocaust in Italy." PhD diss., Clark University, 2014.

Heschel, Abraham Joshua. *Man Is Not Alone: A Philosophy of Religion*. New York: Farrar, Straus & Young, 1951.

Heschel, Susannah. *The Aryan Jesus: Christian Theologians and the Bible in Nazi Germany*. Princeton, NJ: Princeton University Press, 2008.

Hilberg, Raul. *Sources of Holocaust Research: An Analysis*. Chicago, IL: Ivan R. Dee, 2001.

Hilberg, Raul. *The Destruction of the European Jews*. 3rd edn. 3 vols. New Haven, CT: Yale University Press, 2003.

Hilberg, Raul. "Incompleteness in Holocaust Historiography." In *Gray Zones: Ambiguity and Compromise in the Holocaust and Its Aftermath*, edited by Jonathan Petropoulos and John K. Roth, 81–92. New York: Berghahn Books, 2005.

Hilberg, Raul, ed. *Documents of Destruction: Germany and Jewry 1933–1945*. Chicago, IL: Quadrangle Books, 1971.

Hobbes, Thomas. *Leviathan*. Indianapolis, IN: Bobbs-Merrill, 1958.

Hunter, Paul. *Ripening*. Eugene, OR: Silverfish Review Press, 2007.

Imort, Michael. "'Eternal Forest—Eternal *Volk*': The Rhetoric and Reality of National Socialist Forest Policy." In *How Green Were the Nazis? Nature, Environment, and Nation in the Third Reich*, edited by Franz-Josef Brüggemeier, Mark Cioc, and Thomas Zeller, 43–72. Athens, OH: Ohio University Press, 2005.

Ingrao, Christian. *Believe and Destroy: Intellectuals in the SS War Machine*. Translated by Andrew Brown. Cambridge, UK: Polity Press, 2013.

International Commission on Intervention and State Sovereignty. *The Responsibility to Protect: Report of the International Commission on Intervention and State Sovereignty*. Ottawa, ON: International Development Research Centre, 2001.

Isaac, Jules. *The Teaching of Contempt: Christian Roots of Anti-Semitism*. Translated by Helen Weaver. New York: Holt, Rinehart and Winston, 1964.

Jacobs, Steven Leonard, ed. *Confronting Genocide: Judaism, Christianity, Islam*. Lanham, MD: Lexington Books, 2009.

Jacobs, Steven Leonard. "Genesis of the Concept of Genocide According to Its Author from the Original Sources." *Human Rights Review* 3, no. 2 (2002): 98–103.

Jacobs, Steven Leonard, ed. *Lemkin on Genocide*. Lanham, MD: Lexington Books, 2011.

Jaspers, Karl. *The Question of German Guilt*. Translated by E. B. Ashton. New York: Dial Press, 1948.

Jonassohn, Kurt. "The Sociology of Genocide." In *Encyclopedia of Genocide*, 2 vols., edited by Israel W. Charny, 518–20. Santa Barbara, CA: ABC-CLIO, 1999.

Jones, Adam. *Genocide: A Comprehensive Introduction*. 2nd edn. New York: Routledge, 2006.

Kakel, Carroll P., III. *The American West and the Nazi East: A Comparative and Interpretive Perspective*. New York: Palgrave Macmillan, 2011.

Katz, Steven T., Shlomo Biderman, and Gershon Greenberg, eds. *Wrestling with God: Jewish Theological Responses during and after the Holocaust*. New York: Oxford University Press, 2007.

Katz, Steven T., and Alan Rosen, eds. *Elie Wiesel: Jewish, Literary, and Moral Perspectives*. Bloomington, IN: Indiana University Press, 2013.

Keegan, John. *The First World War*. New York: Vintage Books, 2000.

Kellenbach, Katharina von. *The Mark of Cain: Guilt and Denial in the Post-war Lives of Nazi Perpetrators*. Oxford: Oxford University Press, 2013.

Kiernan, Ben. *Blood and Soil: A World History of Genocide and Extermination from Sparta to Darfur*. New Haven, CT: Yale University Press, 2007.

Kiš, Danilo. *Garden, Ashes*. Translated by William J. Hannaker. Chicago, IL: Dalkey Archive Press, 2003.

Knight, Henry F. "Before Whom Do We Stand?" *Shofar* 28, no. 3 (2010): 116–34.

Knight, W. Andy, and Frazer Egerton, eds. *The Routledge Handbook of the Responsibility to Protect*. New York: Routledge, 2012.

Kofman, Sarah. *Smothered Words*. Translated by Madeleine Dobie. Evanston, IL: Northwestern University Press, 1998.

Koonz, Claudia. *The Nazi Conscience*. Cambridge, MA: Harvard University Press, 2003.

Kristof, Nicholas D. "The Grotesque Vocabulary in Congo," *New York Times*, February 11, 2010, A33.

Kristof, Nicholas D. "The World Capital of Killing." *New York Times*, February 7, 2010, WK12.

Kristof, Nicholas D. "A Policy of Rape Continues." *New York Times*, July 25, 2013, A27.

Kristof, Nicholas D., and Sheryl WuDunn. *Half the Sky: Turning Oppression into Opportunity for Women Worldwide*. New York: Alfred A. Knopf, 2009.

Kristof, Nicholas D., and Sheryl WuDunn. *A Path Appears: Transforming Lives, Creating Opportunity*. New York: Alfred A. Knopf, 2014.

Kühne, Thomas. *Belonging and Genocide: Hitler's Community*. New Haven, CT: Yale University Press, 2010.

Langer, Lawrence L. *Versions of Survival: The Holocaust and the Human Spirit*. Albany, NY: State University of New York Press, 1982.

Langer, Lawrence L. "The Dilemma of Choice in the Deathcamps." In *Holocaust: Religious and Philosophical Implications*, edited by John K. Roth and Michael Berenbaum, 222–31. St. Paul, MN: Paragon House, 1989.

Langer, Lawrence L. *Holocaust Testimonies: The Ruins of Memory*. New Haven, CT: Yale University Press, 1991.

Langer, Lawrence L. *Preempting the Holocaust*. New Haven, CT: Yale University Press, 1998.

Lemkin, Raphael. *Axis Rule in Occupied Europe: Laws of Occupation, Analysis of Government, Proposals for Redress*. Washington, DC: Carnegie Endowment for International Peace, 1944.

Lemkin, Raphael. "Genocide." *The American Scholar* 15, no. 2 (1946): 227–30.

Lemkin, Raphael. "Genocide as a Crime under International Law." *American Journal of International Law* 41, no. 1 (1947): 145–51.

Lemkin, Raphael. *Totally Unofficial: The Autobiography of Raphael Lemkin*, edited by Donna-Lee Frieze. New Haven, CT: Yale University Press, 2013.

Levi, Primo. *The Drowned and the Saved*. Translated by Raymond Rosenthal. New York: Summit Books, 1988.

Levi, Primo. *Moments of Reprieve: A Memoir of Auschwitz*. Translated by Ruth Feldman. New York: Penguin Books, 1987.

Levi, Primo. *Other People's Trades*. Translated by Raymond Rosenthal. New York: Summit Books, 1989.

Levi, Primo. *Survival in Auschwitz: The Nazi Assault on Humanity*. Translated by Stuart Woolf. New York: Simon & Schuster, 1996.

Levi, Primo. *The Voice of Memory: Interviews, 1961–1987*. Edited by Marco Belpoliti and Robert Gordon. Translated by Robert Gordon. New York: The New Press, 2001.

Levinas, Emmanuel. *Totality and Infinity: An Essay on Exteriority*. Translated by Alphonso Lingis. Pittsburgh, PA: Duquesne University Press, 1969.

Levinas, Emmanuel. *Ethics and Infinity: Conversations with Philippe Nemo*. Translated by Richard A. Cohen. Pittsburgh, PA: Duquesne University Press, 1985.

Levinas, Emmanuel. *Difficult Freedom: Essays on Judaism*. Translated by Sean Hand. Baltimore, MD: Johns Hopkins University Press, 1990.

Levinas, Emmanuel. *Nine Talmudic Readings*. Translated by Annette Aronowicz. Bloomington, IN: Indiana University Press, 1990.

Levinas, Emmanuel. *Entre Nous: On Thinking-of-the-Other*. Translated by Michael B. Smith and Barbara Harshav. New York: Columbia University Press, 1998.

Levinas, Emmanuel. *New Talmudic Readings*. Translated by Richard Cohen. Pittsburgh, PA: Duquesne University Press, 1999.

Levinas, Emmanuel. *Is It Righteous to Be? Interviews with Emmanuel Levinas*. Edited by Jill Robbins. Translated by Maureen V. Gedney. Stanford, CA: Stanford University Press, 2001.

Levine, Paul A. "On-lookers." In *The Oxford Handbook of Holocaust Studies*, edited by Peter Hayes and John K. Roth, 156–69. Oxford: Oxford University Press, 2010.

Lichtblau, Eric. *The Nazis Next Door: How America Became a Safe Haven for Hitler's Men*. Boston, MA: Houghton Mifflin Harcourt, 2014.

Littell, Franklin H. *The Crucifixion of the Jews*. New York: Harper and Row, 1975.

Littell, Marcia Sachs, and Sharon Weissman Gutman, eds. *Liturgies of the Holocaust: An Interfaith Anthology*. New and revised edn. Valley Forge, PA: Trinity Press International, 1996.

Lower, Wendy. *Hitler's Furies: German Women in the Nazi Killing Fields*. Boston: Houghton Mifflin Harcourt, 2013.

Manseau, Peter. "Revising *Night*: Elie Wiesel and the Hazards of Holocaust Theology." *Crosscurrents* 56, no. 3 (2006): 387–99.

Martin, Adrienne. *How We Hope: A Moral Psychology*. Princeton, NJ: Princeton University Press, 2013.

May, Larry. *Genocide: A Normative Account*. Cambridge, UK: Cambridge University Press, 2010.

McKale, Donald M. *Nazis After Hitler: How Perpetrators of the Holocaust Cheated Justice and Truth*. Lanham, MD: Rowman & Littlefield, 2012.

McMillan, Dan. *How Could This Happen: Explaining the Holocaust*. New York: Basic Books, 2014.

McPhee, John. *Basin and Range* (1981) in *Annals of the Former World*. New York: Farrar, Straus and Giroux, 1998.

Meierhenrich, Jens, ed. *Genocide: A Reader*. Oxford: Oxford University Press, 2014.

Melvern, Linda. "Identifying Genocide." In *Will Genocide Ever End?*, edited by Carol Rittner, John K. Roth, and James M. Smith, 99–103. St. Paul, MN: Paragon House, 2002.

Mendes-Flohr, Paul, and Yehuda Reinharz, eds. *The Jew in the Modern World: A Documentary History*. 2nd edn. Oxford: Oxford University Press, 1995.

Mibenge, Chiseche Salome. *Sex and International Tribunals: The Erasure of Gender from the War Narrative*. Philadelphia, PA: University of Pennsylvania Press, 2013.

Monroe, Kristen Renwick. *Ethics in an Age of Terror and Genocide: Identity and Moral Choice*. Princeton, NJ: Princeton University Press, 2012.

Moses, A. Dirk. "Raphael Lemkin, Culture, and the Concept of Genocide." In *The Oxford Handbook of Genocide Studies*, edited by Donald Bloxham and A. Dirk Moses, 19–41. Oxford: Oxford University Press, 2010.

Moyn, Samuel. *The Last Utopia: Human Rights in History*. Cambridge, MA: Harvard University Press, 2010.

Orford, Anne. *International Authority and the Responsibility to Protect*. Cambridge, UK: Cambridge University Press, 2011.

Orwell, George. *1984*. New York: New American Library, 1983.

O'Shea, Paul. *A Cross Too Heavy: Pope Pius XII and the Jews of Europe*. New York: Palgrave Macmillan, 2011.

Park, Peter K. J. *Africa, Asia, and the History of Philosophy: Racism in the Formation of the Philosophical Canon, 1780–1830*. Albany, NY: State University of New York Press, 2013.

Patterson, David. *Emil L. Fackenheim: A Jewish Philosopher's Response to the Holocaust*. Syracuse, NY: Syracuse University Press, 2008.

Patterson, David. *Genocide in Jewish Thought*. Cambridge, UK: Cambridge University Press, 2012.

Patterson, David. *Anti-Semitism and Its Metaphysical Origins*. Cambridge, UK: Cambridge University Press, 2015.

Patterson, David, and John K. Roth, eds. *After-Words: Post-Holocaust Struggles with Forgiveness, Reconciliation, Justice*. Seattle, WA: University of Washington Press, 2004.

Patterson, David, and John K. Roth, eds. *Fire in the Ashes: God, Evil, and the Holocaust*. Seattle, WA: University of Washington Press, 2005.

Pawlikowski, John T. "Fifty Years of Christian-Jewish Dialogue—What Has It Changed?" *Journal of Ecumenical Studies* 49, no. 1 (2014): 99–106.

Peterson, Daniel J., and G. Michael Zbaraschuk, eds. *Resurrecting the Death of God: The Origins, Influence, and Return of Radical Theology*. Albany, NY: State University of New York Press, 2014.

Petropoulos, Jonathan, and John K. Roth, eds. *Gray Zones: Ambiguity and Compromise in the Holocaust and Its Aftermath*. New York: Berghahn Books, 2005.

Phayer, Michael. *The Catholic Church and the Holocaust, 1930–1965*. Bloomington, IN: Indiana University Press, 2000.

Phayer, Michael. *Pius XII, the Holocaust, and the Cold War*. Bloomington, IN: Indiana University Press, 2008.

Phillips, Melanie. "'Jesus Was a Palestinian': The Return of Christian Anti-Semitism." *Commentary*, June 1, 2014.

Pollefeyt, Didier, ed. *Holocaust and Nature*. Berlin: LIT Verlag, 2013.

Power, Samantha. *"A Problem from Hell": America and the Age of Genocide*. New York: Basic Books, 2002.

Rattansi, Ali. *Racism: A Very Short Introduction.* Oxford: Oxford University Press, 2007.

Rawls, John. *A Theory of Justice.* Cambridge, MA: Harvard University Press, 1971.

Rawls, John. *The Law of Peoples.* Cambridge, MA: Harvard University Press, 1999.

Rawls, John. *Justice as Fairness: A Restatement,* edited by Erin Kelly. Cambridge, MA: Harvard University Press, 2001.

Rhodes, Richard. *Masters of Death: The SS-Einsatzgruppen and the Invention of the Holocaust.* New York: Alfred A. Knopf, 2002.

Rittner, Carol, and John K. Roth, eds. *Different Voices: Women and the Holocaust.* St. Paul, MN: Paragon House, 1993.

Rittner, Carol, and John K. Roth, eds. *Pope Pius XII and the Holocaust.* New York: Continuum, 2002.

Rittner, Carol, and John K. Roth, eds. *Rape: Weapon of War and Genocide.* St. Paul, MN: Paragon House, 2012.

Rittner, Carol, John K. Roth, and James M. Smith, eds. *Will Genocide Ever End?* St. Paul, MN: Paragon House, 2002.

Rittner, Carol, and Stephen D. Smith, eds. *No Going Back: Letters to Pope Benedict XVI on the Holocaust, Jewish–Christian Relations & Israel.* London: Quill Press, 2009.

Rosen, Alan, ed. *Approaches to Teaching Wiesel's "Night."* New York: Modern Language Association of America, 2007.

Rosen, Alan. *The Wonder of Their Voices: The 1946 Holocaust Interviews of David Boder.* Oxford: Oxford University Press, 2010.

Rosenbaum, Alan S., ed. *Is the Holocaust Unique? Perspectives on Comparative Genocide.* 3rd edn. Boulder, CO: Westview Press, 2009.

Rosenfeld, Alvin H., ed. *Resurgent Antisemitism: Global Perspectives.* Bloomington, IN: Indiana University Press, 2013.

Rosensaft, Menachem Z., ed. *God, Faith & Identity from the Ashes: Reflections of Children and Grandchildren of Holocaust Survivors.* Woodstock, VT: Jewish Lights Publishing, 2015.

Rosner, Shmuel. "Kerry's Mideast 'Failure' Was a Success." *New York Times,* May 9, 2014.

Roth, John K. "Tears and Elie Wiesel." *Princeton Seminary Bulletin* 65, no. 2 (1972): 42–8.

Roth, John K. *A Consuming Fire: Encounters with Elie Wiesel and the Holocaust.* Atlanta, GA: John Knox Press, 1979.

Roth, John K. *Holocaust Politics.* Louisville, KY: Westminster John Knox Press, 2001.

Roth, John K. "The Politics of Definition." In *Will Genocide Ever End?,* edited by Carol Rittner, John K. Roth, and James M. Smith, 23–9. St. Paul, MN: Paragon House, 2002.

Roth, John K. *Ethics During and After the Holocaust: In the Shadow of Birkenau.* New York: Palgrave Macmillan, 2005.

Roth, John K., ed. *Genocide and Human Rights: A Philosophical Guide.* New York: Palgrave Macmillan, 2005.

Roth, John K. "Duped by Morality? Defusing Minefields in the Israeli–Palestinian Struggle." In *Anguished Hope: Holocaust Scholars Confront the Palestinian–Israeli Conflict,* edited by Leonard Grob and John K. Roth, 30–49. Grand Rapids, MI: William B. Eerdmans, 2008.

Roth, John K, and Michael Berenbaum, eds. *Holocaust: Religious and Philosophical Implications.* St. Paul, MN: Paragon House, 1989.

Rubenstein, Richard L. *Power Struggle.* New York: Scribner, 1974.

Rubenstein, Richard L. *After Auschwitz: History, Theology, and Contemporary Judaism.* 2nd edn. Baltimore, MD: Johns Hopkins University Press, 1992.

Rubenstein, Richard L., and John K. Roth. *Approaches to Auschwitz: The Holocaust and Its Legacy.* Rev. edn. Louisville, KY: Westminster John Knox Press, 2003.

Rubenstein, Richard L. *Jihad and Genocide.* Lanham, MD: Rowman & Littlefield, 2010.

Rubin, Agi, and Henry Greenspan. *Reflections: Auschwitz, Memory, and a Life Recreated.* St. Paul, MN: Paragon House, 2006.

Rudin, James A. *Cushing, Spellman, O'Conner: The Surprising Story of How Three American Cardinals Transformed Catholic-Jewish Relations.* Grand Rapids, MI: William B. Eerdmans, 2012.

Rummel, R. J. *Death by Government.* New Brunswick, NJ: Transaction Publishers, 1997.

Ryan, Kay. *The Niagara River.* New York: Grove Press, 2005.

Sacks, Jonathan. "Europe's Alarming New Anti-Semitism." *Wall Street Journal,* October 3, 2014.

Sajjad, Tazreena. "Rape on Trial: Promises of International Jurisprudence, Perils of Retributive Justice, and the Realities of Impunity." In *Rape: Weapon of War and Genocide,* edited by Carol Rittner and John K. Roth, 61–81. St. Paul, MN: Paragon House, 2012.

Sands, Tommy. *The Songman: A Journey in Irish Music.* Dublin: Lilliput Press, 2005.

Santilli, Paul C. "Philosophy's Obligation to the Human Being in the Aftermath of Genocide." In *Genocide and Human Rights: A Philosophical Guide,* edited by John K. Roth, 220–32. New York: Palgrave Macmillan, 2005.

Schabas, William. *Unimaginable Atrocities: Justice, Politics, and Rights at the War Crimes Tribunals.* Oxford: Oxford University Press, 2012.

Schleunes, Karl A. *The Twisted Road to Auschwitz: Nazi Policy toward German Jews, 1933–1939.* Urbana, IL: University of Illinois Press, 1990.

Schleusser, Jennifer. "Heidegger's Notebooks Renew Focus on Anti-Semitism." *New York Times*, March 31, 2014, C1.

Seidman, Naomi. "Elie Wiesel and the Scandal of Jewish Rage." *Jewish Social Studies* 3, no. 1 (1996): 1–19.

Seidman, Naomi. *Faithful Renderings: Jewish-Christian Difference and the Politics of Translation*. Chicago, IL: University of Chicago Press, 2006.

Sereny, Gitta. *Into That Darkness: An Examination of Conscience*. New York: Vintage Books, 1983.

Shaw, Martin. *What Is Genocide?* Cambridge, UK: Polity Press, 2007.

Shelton, Dinah L., ed. *The Encyclopedia of Genocide and Crimes against Humanity*. Detroit, MI: Macmillan Reference, 2004.

Sheratt, Yvonne. *Hitler's Philosophers*. New Haven, CT: Yale University Press, 2013.

Shuster, Martin. "Philosophy and Genocide." In *The Oxford Handbook of Genocide Studies*, edited by Donald Bloxham and A. Dirk Moses, 217–35. Oxford: Oxford University Press, 2010.

Siebert, D. T. *Mortality's Muse: The Fine Art of Dying*. Newark, DE: University of Delaware Press, 2013.

Skloot, Robert. *The Darkness We Carry: The Drama of the Holocaust*. Madison, WI: University of Wisconsin Press, 1988.

Skloot, Robert, ed. *The Theatre of Genocide: Four Plays about Mass Murder in Rwanda, Bosnia, Cambodia, and Armenia*. Madison, WI: University of Wisconsin Press, 2008.

Skloot, Robert, ed. *The Theatre of the Holocaust*. 2 vols. Madison, WI: University of Wisconsin Press, 1982–99.

Sluga, Hans. *Heidegger's Crisis: Philosophy and Politics in Nazi Germany*. Cambridge, MA: Harvard University Press, 1993.

Smith, David Livingston. *Less Than Human: Why We Demean, Enslave, and Exterminate Others*. New York: St. Martin's Press, 2011.

Snyder, Timothy. *Bloodlands: Europe between Hitler and Stalin*. New York: Basic Books, 2010.

Stafford, William. *The Way It Is: New & Selected Poems*. St. Paul, MN: Graywolf Press, 1998.

Stangneth, Bettina. *Eichmann before Jerusalem: The Unexamined Life of a Mass Murderer*. Translated by Ruth Martin. New York: Alfred A. Knopf, 2014.

Staub, Ervin. *The Roots of Goodness and Resistance to Evil: Inclusive Caring, Moral Courage, Altruism Born of Suffering, Active Bystanding, and Heroism*. Oxford: Oxford University Press, 2015.

Steiner, George. *Language and Silence: Essays on Language, Literature, and the Inhuman*. New York: Atheneum, 1967.

Steinweis, Alan E. *Studying the Jew: Scholarly Antisemitism in Nazi Germany*. Cambridge, MA: Harvard University Press, 2006.

Straus, Scott. "Contested Meanings and Conflicting Imperatives: A Conceptual Analysis of Genocide." *Journal of Genocide Research* 3, no. 3 (2001): 349–75.

Tessman, Lisa. *Moral Failure: On the Impossible Demands of Morality.* Oxford: Oxford University Press, 2014.

Theriault, Henry C. "Rethinking Dehumanization in Genocide." In *The Armenian Genocide: Cultural and Ethical Legacies*, edited by Richard Hovannisian, 27–40. New Brunswick, NJ: Transaction Publishers, 2007.

Totten, Samuel, and William S. Parsons, eds. *Centuries of Genocide: Critical Essays and Eyewitness Accounts.* 4th edn. New York: Routledge, 2013.

Uekoetter, Frank. *The Green and the Brown: A History of Conservation in Nazi Germany.* Cambridge, UK: Cambridge University Press, 2006.

Valentino, Benjamin A. *Final Solutions: Mass Killing and Genocide in the Twentieth Century.* Ithaca, NY: Cornell University Press, 2004.

Valls, Andrew, ed. *Race and Racism in Modern Philosophy.* Ithaca, NY: Cornell University Press, 2005.

Van Harn, Roger E., ed. *The Ten Commandments for Jews, Christians, and Others.* Grand Rapids, MI: William B. Eerdmans Publishing Company, 2007.

Verdeja, Ernesto. "Moral Bystanders and Mass Violence." In *New Directions in Genocide Research*, edited by Adam Jones, 153–68. New York: Routledge, 2012.

Wade, Nicholas. *Before the Dawn: Recovering the Lost History of Our Ancestors.* New York: Penguin Books, 2006.

Warnock, G. J. *Contemporary Moral Philosophy.* London: Macmillan, 1967.

Weikart, Richard. *Hitler's Ethic: The Nazi Pursuit of Evolutionary Progress.* New York: Palgrave Macmillan, 2009.

Weisman, Alan. *The World Without Us.* New York: St. Martin's Press, 2007.

Weiss, Thomas G. "R2P after 9/11 and the World Summit." *Wisconsin International Law Journal* 24, no. 3 (2006): 741–60.

Weiss, Thomas G. *Humanitarian Intervention: Ideas in Action*, 2nd edn. Cambridge, UK: Polity Press, 2012.

Weitzman, Lenore J. "Women." In *The Oxford Handbook of Holocaust Studies*, edited by Peter Hayes and John K. Roth, 203–17. Oxford: Oxford University Press, 2010.

Wiesel, Elie. *Legends of Our Time.* New York: Holt, Rinehart, and Winston, 1968.

Wiesel, Elie. *One Generation After.* Translated by Lily Edelman and the author. New York: Random House, 1970.

Wiesel, Elie. *Messengers of God: Biblical Portraits and Legends.* Translated by Marion Wiesel. New York: Random House, 1973.

Wiesel, Elie. *A Jew Today.* Translated by Marion Wiesel. New York: Random House, 1978.

Wiesel, Elie. *Five Biblical Portraits*. Notre Dame, IN: University of Notre Dame Press, 1981.

Wiesel, Elie. *The Fifth Son*. Translated by Marion Wiesel. New York: Summit Books, 1985.

Wiesel, Elie. *Sages and Dreamers: Biblical, Talmudic, and Hasidic Portraits and Legends*. New York: Summit Books, 1991.

Wiesel, Elie. *All Rivers Run to the Sea: Memoirs*. New York: Alfred A. Knopf, 1995.

Wiesel, Elie. *Wise Men and Their Tales: Portraits of Biblical, Talmudic, and Hasidic Masters*. New York: Schocken Books, 2003.

Wiesel, Elie. *Night*. Translated by Marion Wiesel. New York: Hill and Wang, 2006.

Wiesel, Elie. *Open Heart*. Translated by Marion Wiesel. New York: Alfred A. Knopf, 2012.

Wyatt, Edward. "The Translation of Wiesel's 'Night' Is New, but Old Questions Are Raised." *New York Times*, January 19, 2006.

Young, James E. *The Texture of Memory: Holocaust Memorials and Meaning*. New Haven, CN: Yale University Press, 1993.

Zimmerer, Jürgen, ed. "Climate Change, Environmental Violence and Genocide." Special issue, *The International Journal of Human Rights* 18, no. 3 (2014).

Index